Modern Moonshine

Modern Moonshine

The Revival of White Whiskey in the Twenty-First Century

Edited by Cameron D. Lippard and Bruce E. Stewart

West Virginia University Press
Morgantown 2019

ISBN
Cloth 978-1-946684-81-3
Paper 978-1-946684-82-0
Ebook 978-1-946684-83-7

Library of Congress Cataloging-in-Publication Data
Names: Lippard, Cameron D., editor. | Stewart, Bruce E., editor.
Title: Modern moonshine : the revival of white whiskey in the 21st century / edited by Cameron
        D. Lippard and Bruce E. Stewart.
Description: First edition. | Morgantown : West Virginia University Press, 2019 | Includes
        bibliographical references and index. | Identifiers: LCCN 2018040069 (print) | LCCN
        2018041325 (ebook) | ISBN 9781946684813 (cloth : alk. paper) | ISBN
        9781946684820 (pbk. : alk. paper) | ISBN 9781946684837 (ebook)
Subjects: LCSH: Whiskey industry--Appalachian Region. | Whiskey industry--Appalachian
        Region--History. | Distilling industries--Appalachian Region. | Appalachian
        Region--Social life and customs--21st century.
Classification: LCC HD9395.A62 (ebook) | LCC HD9395.A62 M63 2019 (print) | DDC
        338.4/7663520974--dc23
LC record available at https://lccn.loc.gov/2018040069

Cover design by Than Saffel / WVU Press

CONTENTS

Illustrations

FIGURES

TABLES

Introduction

The Revival of Moonshine in Southern Appalachia and the United States

BRUCE E. STEWART AND CAMERON D. LIPPARD

"Considered a mountain craft as much as a crime, the art of moonshining is vanishing now as fast and surely as a man with sugar sacks on his shoulders can drop and run through the shadowed woods at twilight." So wrote *Chicago Tribune* reporter Timothy McNulty in 1979, insisting that the manufacturing and drinking of illegal unaged corn white whiskey (popularly known as moonshine) was on the verge of extinction.[1] McNulty's observation was in large part accurate. By the 1970s the production of moonshine had plummeted in Appalachia and other rural parts of the nation, where many residents—struggling to make ends meet—had long distilled alcohol without paying the federal liquor tax. This trend continued into the 1980s and 1990s. According to McNulty and other journalists and scholars, improved enforcement methods, the rising availability of cheap legal alcohol, and increased job opportunities in rural areas had caused an irreversible decline in moonshining, turning the craft of making unaged corn whiskey into a dying art.[2]

Over the past decade, however, a revived consumer interest in white whiskey has caught the attention of legal alcohol manufacturers throughout the United States. By 2017 at least 137 craft distilleries have begun to produce unaged liquor, marketed to the public as moonshine.[3] In particular, legal whiskey makers in southern Appalachia—capitalizing on relaxed state regulations and the region's national reputation as the center of illicit distilling—have embraced the burgeoning moonshine industry. Mountain distilleries, such as Ole Smoky Distillery in Sevier County, Tennessee, and Copper Barrel Distillery in Wilkes County, North Carolina, have sold millions of cases of "white lightning" since 2010. Corporate liquor companies have followed suit. In 2013 Jack Daniel's unveiled its own moonshine product, unaged Tennessee rye, and Jim Beam released Jacob's Ghost white whiskey. American distillers have even begun to sell "mountain dew" in Canada and the United Kingdom. Far from a dying art, as journalists and scholars believed the craft to be in the 1980s and 1990s, the manufacturing of legal moonshine has become a multimillion-dollar industry.[4]

While journalists and nonfiction travel writers have bestowed a growing amount of attention on the so-called modern moonshine revival, academic scholarship on this cultural and economic phenomenon remains nonexistent, a gap that *Modern Moonshine: The Revival of White Whiskey in the Twenty-First Century* fills.[5] Focusing on southern Appalachia, the book's eleven chapters explore the varied reasons for the reemergence of the moonshine industry and its impact on society. What role have state laws played in the moonshine revival? How has the revival contributed to the image of Appalachia? Why has consumer demand for unaged whiskey increased, and what does this tell us about American culture? What role has the national media played in this movement? By answering these and other questions, *Modern Moonshine* ultimately provides a more contemporary and holistic understanding of both the production and consumption of moonshine in southern Appalachia and beyond in the twenty-first century.

Whiskey Manufacturing in the United States before the Twenty-First Century

The distillation of corn and other crops into whiskey has a long and rich history in America. As early as 1620, Virginia colonists had begun to manufacture corn liquor, which they believed was healthier than water and milk.[6] By the eighteenth century, whiskey distilling had become an important cottage industry throughout colonial America, especially in the backcountry and other regions that lacked adequate transportation arteries. There, farmers found it easier and more profitable to convert some of their crops—often corn—into liquor before carrying them to market. Using small copper stills, they typically produced between one hundred and one thousand gallons a year and seldom aged their whiskey, eager to make money as soon as possible.[7] These farmer-distillers regarded liquor distilling as an economic necessity and vehemently opposed the federal government's first and short-lived attempt to tax domestically manufactured alcohol in the 1790s.[8]

During the antebellum period, the whiskey industry underwent several changes, most notably the decline of the farmer-distiller and the rise of large-scale commercial distilleries. By the 1830s improvements in transportation allowed many farmers to quickly and cheaply ship their crops to market and thus no longer rely on whiskey manufacturing to supplement their incomes.[9] Consequently, the number of distilleries declined from 20,000 in 1830 to 10,000 in 1840.[10] Farmers also found themselves unable to compete with a growing handful of commercial operators who utilized the column still, a new and expensive apparatus that could distill 3,000 gallons of corn mash in a single hour. Located mostly in Ohio River Valley, these large-scale manufacturers also began to age their product in charred barrels, creating a red-colored whiskey with rich vanilla and caramel flavors (popularly known as bourbon) that consumers increasingly preferred over unaged corn liquor.[11]

Federal policies further transformed the nineteenth-century whiskey industry. In 1862 the U.S. Congress reinstituted the federal liquor tax. Regardless of the amount of alcohol manufactured, all distillers now had to purchase licenses and pay a duty on each gallon. This excise ultimately benefited commercial distillers by forcing many small producers—who were unable to afford the tax—out of business. It also created a new breed of outlaw: the illicit distiller or moonshiner, who continued the tradition of making white whiskey (without paying a tax).[12] Meanwhile, large-scale operators, emboldened by the federal government's pro-business stance, scrambled to consolidate their control over the legal liquor industry. In 1887 Joseph B. Greenhut, a wealthy distiller from Peoria, Illinois, organized the so-called Whiskey Trust, which included "sixty-five distilleries and some eighty industrial alcohol plants spread throughout the country."[13] By the end of the nineteenth century, such cartels produced the bulk of the nation's whiskey.[14]

During the early twentieth century, many Americans embraced the temperance movement, and the liquor industry was under attack. A number of local and state laws banned the sale of alcohol, and the crusade culminated with the ratification of the Eighteenth Amendment in 1919, which prohibited the sale, transportation, and manufacturing of alcohol throughout the entire country.[15] For the next thirteen years, the whiskey industry teetered on the verge of collapse. Many distilleries went bankrupt or sold out to a handful of liquor producers who had secured federal licenses to make medicinal and industrial alcohol.[16] Though devastating to legal whiskey distillers, national Prohibition proved a blessing for moonshiners, who saw the demand for and price of their unaged corn liquor skyrocket during the 1920s.[17]

After the repeal of the Eighteenth Amendment in 1933, the whiskey industry continued to struggle.[18] The Great Depression, high federal license fees, and strict local and state regulatory policies made it difficult for most legal distilleries to reopen their doors. The federal government's ban on alcohol manufacturing during World War II only made the situation worse. Unable to turn a profit, the few remaining smaller distilleries began to sell their whiskey stocks and brand rights to one of the so-called Big Four: National Distillers, Schenley, Seagram, and Hiram Walker. By 1958 these four corporations controlled more than three-quarters of the market.[19] Consequently, as journalist Clay Risen noted, "the dominance of the [Big Four] and the disappearance of smaller, distinctive brands meant that the once-diverse world of American whiskeys was being slowly replaced by a bland, standardized style."[20]

These companies enjoyed a decade of relative prosperity. However, the whiskey industry again found itself in crisis during the 1960s. By then, a growing number of consumers—particularly women and young people—had turned away from high-proof intoxicants to wine and beer. Perhaps even more alarming, vodka also emerged as the drink of choice for cocktail enthusiasts. Whiskey distillers responded by developing lighter flavored brands, to little avail. Between 1970 and 1985, whiskey sales declined 50 percent, forcing many operators to close their doors or cut back on production.[21] By 1980 the number of legal distilleries in the country had dropped to fewer than one hundred.[22] Though the introduction of single-barrel and small-batch brands helped to increase whiskey sales in the 1990s, the industry faced an uncertain future on the eve of the twenty-first century.[23]

Meanwhile, moonshine manufacturing also took a turn for the worse. Following World War II, economic hardship, high federal and state liquor taxes, and the continuation of local prohibition laws had sparked a dramatic increase in illicit distilling. This was true especially in Appalachia and other parts of the rural South, where federal agents seized over one hundred thousand unregistered stills between 1963 and 1973.[24] During the late 1970s, however, moonshining in those regions plummeted as higher production costs and improving job opportunities caused many illicit distillers to quit the business. By the 1990s, the number of stills captured had dropped to twenty per year, leading many people to bemoan the apparent passing of an American icon: unaged white whiskey.[25] It was in this context that the craft distilling movement—and along with it, the moonshine revival—emerged at the turn of the twenty-first century.

The Rise of Craft Distilling

In recent decades, American consumer attitudes and behaviors concerning what they eat and drink have changed. Before 1960 corporate giants such as ConAgra, Kraft Foods, Anheuser-Busch, Ernest Gallo, and Jim Beam dominated consumer markets, as most Americans seemed content with mass-produced food and alcohol. Since then, however, consumer demand for products that are fresh, handmade, and unique has grown considerably. According to Michael Kinstlick, CEO of Coppersea Heritage Distilling, "Knowledgeable and adventurous consumers . . . began seeking unusual and strongly-flavored products, in contrast with those designed for the mass-market, and those [new consumer] taste-makers broadened the appeal of once unique and hard-to-find items."[26] Increasing middle-class incomes also accounted for this shift away from cheap food and drink during the late twentieth century.[27] Moreover, these new tastes reflected middle-class Americans' desire to distance themselves from low-income, mass-produced consumption patterns.

Changing consumer tastes have ultimately caused three significant shifts in the American alcohol industry. The first shift came in the 1960s with the production of quality wines. Before that decade, more than 95 percent of U.S. wine consumption was "jug wine," an inexpensive gallon-size bottle of sweet table wine that had little flavor or distinction.[28] Manufacturers often used California-grown grapes to make their wine and sometimes enhanced their product with other flavors to make it an "adult soda pop" of sorts.[29] These jug wines were mislabeled as "Chablis" and "Burgundy" wines by Paul Masson, Almaden, Gallo, and other mass producers. In short, wine began as blends that were sweet and generic with no clear distinctions in flavor or style.

Due to wine's generic start, fewer than 440 wineries existed in the nation in 1980. However, by the early 2000s, more than 7,000 wineries operated in the United States, selling unique vintages and blends of white and red wines that rivaled European brands.[30] In addition, wineries were established in all fifty states (although California continued to produce the vast majority of American wines).[31] As of 2016 the American wine industry estimated retail value was around $60 billion in the United States, with another $1.62 billion in exports.[32] This industry has also surpassed the production rates of European wine makers, and Americans now consume more wine than their French and Italian counterparts.[33]

Two important factors account for the wine industry's growth since the 1960s. First, significant local and foreign investment in California wineries helped to revive the struggling U.S. wine industry.[34] Beginning in the 1970s, investors from France and various American-based businesses such as Coca-Cola expanded vineyards from hundreds to thousands of acres and invested millions of dollars into producing better and more specific varieties of wines as well as into marketing campaigns. In addition, local and state governments supported the wine industry as an "agricultural economic advantage," passing laws that liberalized production and sales of wine both locally and globally.[35] Second, small- and medium-sized boutique wineries opened throughout the nation, providing tourists with unique tasting experiences that included wines made from local varieties of grapes and other fruits (i.e., blackberries, muscadines, and cherries).[36] These local wineries also hosted wine festivals and built extravagant wine-tasting venues to draw consumers in for a "weekend picnic" or "date-night."[37] With the intensification of mass marketing and boutique winery options, American consumption of wine surpassed that of beer for the first time ever in 2005.[38] As of 2016, however, wine sales have plateaued in the United States as craft beer and liquor makers have begun to offer consumers new choices and flavors.[39]

A second significant shift in the U.S. alcohol industry was the growth of craft beer. Between the 1940s and 1990s, Anheuser-Busch, Coors, and Miller brewing companies (i.e., the "Big Three") cornered almost 100 percent of the American beer market. Much of this beer was a pilsner or lager style that was light, sweet, and low in alcoholic content (less than 6 percent alcohol by volume).[40] As of 2015, with the merger of Anheuser-Busch InBev and SABMiller, these three companies, owned by the same beverage conglomerate, accounted for 88 percent of all beer sales in the nation.[41]

Throughout the 1960s and 1970s, craft beer struggled to compete with the Big Three, which controlled more than 99 percent of the market during those decades. This was in part because craft beers were only produced in small batches and sold locally. For example, underground home brewing clubs such as the Maltose Falcons and pioneer brewing entrepreneurs like Fritz Maytag of Anchor Brewing offered handmade, traditional, and flavorful ales to parties and local restaurants around San Francisco, California, but seldom sold their products outside of that town or state.[42] Moreover, the craft beer industry continued to lag because it remained illegal to make beers at home, thereby discouraging many people from creating new recipes that could lead to their participating in the industry.[43]

This would change in 1978, when President Jimmy Carter signed the Home Brew Act. This legislation ushered in a new era of craft brewing, allowing homebrewers to legally practice their craft and open craft breweries. Within two years, ninety-two craft breweries, mostly located in California and Washington, were operating in the United States.[44] By 1999 more than 1,500 craft breweries had opened, many finding new homes in small rural towns and revitalized industrial sites of cities.[45] By 2015 more than 4,000 craft breweries and more than 1.5 million self-identified homebrewers across the nation were making beer.[46] This number represented the most breweries operating in the United States since 1873, a year that boasted around 2,000 breweries.[47]

By 2013 craft beer was booming. The profits from the sale of kegs, cans, and bottles of craft beer reached $14.3 billion, 14 percent of the $100 billion beer market. Craft breweries have also opened in all fifty states, but as with wine the bulk of these new breweries are located in the American West, with California and Washington having the most breweries as of 2015. The rise of the craft beer industry has chipped away at the profits of the Big Three, causing them to increasingly purchase craft breweries and develop a line of their own craft beers to compete against brewing upstarts.[48] However, craft breweries continue to weather this onslaught by selling their beer as fresh with local ingredients and exotic flavors.[49]

Several factors encouraged the rise of the craft beer industry, most notably a shift in consumer demand for quality beers. By the 1990s light beer no longer satisfied a growing number of middle-class Americans who now wanted to drink beers related to traditional brews of Western Europe (i.e., ales, porters, and stouts).[50] Consumers also increasingly wanted local pubs and venues to serve great-tasting and fresh beer. More important, smaller craft breweries— aided by new local and state laws that allowed them to sell their products in taprooms, local bars, and other retail establishments—succeeded in meeting consumer demands faster than commercial breweries did.[51]

The infusion of new economic and human capital further promoted the growth of craft brewing. Although expensive to open and maintain, craft breweries represent a solid investment since brewing equipment is moderately priced and resalable.[52] Moreover, beer can be quickly produced for consumption, thereby making it easier for breweries to earn a profit in their first year of operation. In addition, craft brewers often have peers or outside investors who provide them with the necessary capital to finance their upstart businesses.[53] As Sam Calagione of Dogfish Head Craft Brewery observes, many craft breweries began with grassroots fundraising campaigns and private investors to raise around $1 million to start these businesses.[54] As of 2016 the craft beer industry's share of the beer market has reached 18 percent, although some experts suggest that the industry has begun to plateau due to brewery saturation in several states.[55]

The recent rise of craft distilling constitutes the final shift in the American alcohol industry. Throughout the twentieth century, craft distilling—largely due to high liquor taxes and prohibition laws—was almost nonexistent. According to Michael Kinstlick, between 1960 and 2001, there were fewer than twenty-five craft distilleries in the United States. Over the past decade, however, the popularity of craft distilling has skyrocketed. By 2011 there were 234 in-production craft distilleries.[56] Five years later, that number had increased to 1,315.[57] The industry has also become more profitable. In 2015 the U.S. craft spirits market had reached 4.9 million cases and $2.4 billion in retail sales, growing at a compound annual rate of 27.4 percent in volume and 27.9 percent in value between 2010 and 2015. Craft distilleries also had significant exports of around 523,000 cases sent worldwide, taking over about 4.1 percent of the national liquor market. Consequently, craft distilling has emerged as a formidable competitor to Jim Beam and other "Big Whiskey" manufacturers as well as distilling companies such as Proximo Spirits.[58]

The American Craft Spirits Association (ACSA) defines craft distillers as licensed manufacturers who produce "no more than 750,000 proof gallons (or 394,317 9 liter cases) from bond, market themselves as craft, are not controlled by a large supplier, and have no proven violation of the ACSA Code of Ethics."[59] Most of the craft distilleries are concentrated in Washington, California, New York, Colorado, and Texas (see fig. i.1). As of 2015 these five states represented about 35.6 percent of the craft distilling market share.[60] However, since 2011 craft distilleries have opened in all fifty states.[61] Recently, there has also been a significant growth in craft distilling in more conservative and historically dry regions such as the American South, which is now home to about 28 percent of all craft distillers in the nation.[62]

In addition to its rapid growth, craft distilling provides a variety of distillates. In figure i.2, craft distilleries have been categorized by types of distillates and the year in which craft distilleries started to produce each distillate. This figure reveals that an assortment of products exists, including but not limited to vodka, gin, whiskey, and rum. Almost 50 percent of craft distillers began with vodka or whiskey as their initial distillates and other liquors such as brandy or grappa (made primarily by vineyards associated with the California wine industry).[63] More important to the discussion of modern moonshine, several craft distillers opted to first manufacture unaged white whiskey in order to turn a quick profit as they waited for their other whiskeys and bourbons to age in barrels.[64]

Several factors account for the rise of craft distilling. For one, the industry appealed to wine and craft beer enthusiasts who, wanting to try something new, decided to manufacture craft liquor.[65] "I was a brewer who was in love with single malts," California native Lance Winter explained in 2007 when asked why he became interested in craft distilling. "As soon as I realized I was halfway to making single malts, I wanted to learn the other half. . . . There's a whole other level, a creative freedom you can engage through distilling."[66] By the late 1990s, a growing number of West Coast craft breweries, including Anchor, Rogue, New Holland, and Ranger Creek, had begun to make vodka, whiskey, gin, and other liquors. Moreover, aspiring craft distillers, especially in California and Washington, benefited from legislative changes that permitted them to open shop and sell their products. By the early 2010s, several southern states—scrambling to increase revenue following the economic recession of 2008—also began to loosen alcohol and distribution laws to accommodate craft distillers. There, legitimate liquor sales now seemed appropriate in light of the significant amount of tax and tourism revenues being generated by craft breweries.[67]

Moreover, craft distilling benefited from American consumers' desire to experience something "new" and "adventurous."[68] "People are tired of the same old choices, the same Jack and Jim," Jim Blansit, founder of Copper Run Distillery in Missouri, observed in 2015. "They're attracted to the hands on and the homemade and the attention to quality."[69] By making small, creative batches of whiskey, vodka, rum, and other liquors, craft distillers ultimately provide an artisan product different from that of corporate distilleries. Craft distilleries have also profited from the burgeoning "foodie" movement, which encouraged many Americans, especially millennials, to consume products made from local ingredients. Not surprisingly, craft distillers target this demographic, marketing their liquors as "home-grown" and partnering with local farmers to provide them with corn and other grains. "I believe the craft distilling industry couldn't exist without . . . all the local and farm-to-table movements in food," Tom Burkleaux of New Deal Distillery in Oregon concluded. "Without them, our customers wouldn't exist."[70]

Finally, the craft distilling industry has capitalized on the public's nostalgia for symbols and tastes of the American past.[71] Claiming to use recipes and methods of early American distillers, many craft liquor producers offer consumers the opportunity to go "back to a storied yesteryear, when whiskey makers . . . crafted their liquor with care and pride."[72] "We use traditional methods of distilling with a 140 gallon, direct fire, copper pot still," Jim Blansit boasts; "in keeping with time honored techniques, we blend the feints from our last batch with new wash in the stripping run."[73] The distillery itself has also emerged as a popular attraction, providing visitors with an opportunity to see firsthand how small distillers from "yesteryear" made their liquor and to participate in a tasting of the products. As the Thistle Finch Distillery in Pennsylvania posts on its webpage: "We invite you to experience a hidden world where nostalgia and liberation rule. . . . Step back in time with a classic rye whiskey cocktail . . . or enjoy free samples of our distinctive, small-batch spirits. There are many ways to experience Thistle Finch—whether you are looking to learn about the history and process . . . or you just want to relax with a drink and some quiet conversation—we've got what you're looking for."[74] Responding to increased consumer demand for homemade products associated with the nation's past, craft distillers have also resurrected a liquor that many believed was on the verge of extinction: moonshine.

The National Moonshine Revival: A Brief Overview

In the late 1990s, Payton Fireman, a lawyer from Morgantown, West Virginia, was driving home from New York, when he was struck with an idea. Thinking about possible ways to improve his home state's economy, Fireman realized

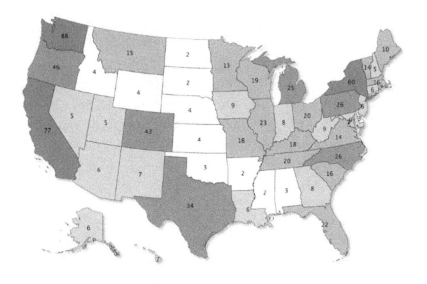

Figure i.1. Identified Craft Producers by State, 2015. Source: Michael Kinstlick, "The U.S. Craft Distilling Market: 2015 Update," Coppersea Distilling, 2015.

that there might exist a market for legal moonshine and decided to open a distillery. "I had a jar or two of moonshine over the years," he later recalled. "I knew I could be the first at this." Unable to find any "old-timers" to teach him the craft, Fireman ultimately had to learn it on his own by "studying distillery textbooks and consulting the half-dozen other legal micro-distillers who [had] cropped up . . . in other parts of the country." Eventually, he purchased a distilling license, invested forty thousand dollars in a still and other equipment, and began to make, bottle, and market his own eighty-proof, unaged corn whiskey, which he called Mountain Moonshine, to liquor stores in West Virginia and nearby Ohio. By 2001 Fireman's West Virginia Distilling Company (founded in 1999) had "managed a profit of at least $1 on a bottle sold for $9."[75] The key to his distillery's success, Fireman said in 2005, was that "the 'shine you're likely to get from an illegal moonshiner is almost ALL sugar-likker. There's no corn or grain of any kind in it, not even flavor. That's not the kind of spirit I want to make."[76]

Though one of the first craft distilleries to legally make unaged white whiskey and market it to the public as moonshine, West Virginia Distilling Company would not be the last.[77] Over the past decade, hundreds of craft distilleries have begun to produce "white lightning," often packaging it in mason jars and flavoring it with apples and other fruits. "Of the 155 people I know making whiskey," Bill Owens, founder of the American Distilling Institute, observed in 2011, "a full third of them are now making white whiskey."[78] Nationally, moonshine sales grew from $5 million in 2011 to $46 million in 2015, solidifying white whiskey's status as one of America's newest favorite liquors.[79]

The recent growth in the production of legal moonshine is partially because craft distillers can quickly market it to consumers. While waiting for their handcrafted bourbons and whiskeys to age in barrels, these distilleries have to manufacture a product that can support them during their first years of business. As distiller Phil Prichard explains, starting a distillery "is a very capital-intensive operation, especially if you maintain an aged product. . . . The problem is that most whiskeys need to be aged at least a few years before they are sold. This makes it a challenge to persuade banks and investors to help fund a business that is not even going to have a product to sell for a few years."[80] As such, many fledgling distilleries initially rely on unaged whiskey to keep them afloat. Legal moonshine is "obviously a boon to small distilleries," Max Watman observed in 2010. "If you're making whiskey, you've got to keep the lights on and wait. It helps to be able to sell something right away."[81]

More important, increased public fascination with illegal moonshine has encouraged craft distillers to make white whiskey. In recent years, Discovery Channel's reality show *Moonshiners*, popular documentaries on "Popcorn" Sutton and other illicit distillers, and movies such as *Lawless* (2012) have led many Americans to rediscover moonshine and its history. Especially among millennials, white whiskey has become a symbol of Americana, a product that is "authentic." "When you think about it, there is not a lot of authentic spirits: there's bourbon and there's moonshine," craft distiller Adam von Gootkin remarked in 2012. "Moonshine is such a big part of American history. Why not cultivate it and turn it into something everyone can enjoy—legally."[82] In particular, young "hipster" professionals in New York and other cities have developed a fascination with and taste for white whiskey, believing that it is "cool" and "edgy."[83] Legal moonshine "ties into American traditions in ways

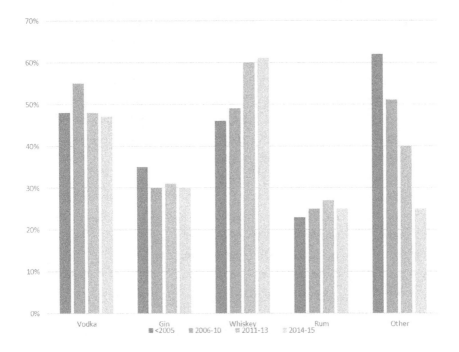

Figure i.2. Craft Distillery Products by Category and Year of Entry. Source: Michael Kinstlick, "The U.S. Craft Distilling Market: 2015 Update," Coppersea Distilling, 2015.

that resonate with people," Watman pointed out. "You can have a little frisson, a brush with the wild life, without doing anything you can't tell your in-laws about."[84] White lightning has also become a favorite among many high-end chefs and bartenders, as Los Angeles restaurant owner Joshua Kopel explained in 2015: "It's a beautiful ingredient to work with. It mixes cleanly like vodka but, because of its corn base, adds a little something extra. It provides a unique kick that other types of alcohol don't provide."[85]

Like their clientele, most distillers who make legal moonshine are not "hillbillies," a derogatory term often used to describe those who produced (and continue to produce) illicit liquor in southern Appalachia.[86] In many cases, they are urban, middle-class professionals or "hipsters" who brewed or distilled alcohol as a hobby and decided to leave their jobs to open distilleries.[87] In 2005, for instance, Joe Michalek, a New York native and marketing executive at R.J. Reynolds Tobacco Company, founded Piedmont Distillers in his adopted state of North Carolina. "For my work at RJR, I went to a lot of concert festivals and a lot of stock car races, and . . . somebody would always pull the moonshine out . . . and it always got everyone's attention," Michalek remembered why he went into the distilling business. "For marketing, it's so rare to see a product that has the kind of mystique that gets a reaction out of 100 percent of people. I wondered why wasn't anyone selling this legally."[88] Several former illicit distillers have managed to profit from the moonshine revival, most notably Tim Smith, the star of Discovery's *Moonshiners*, who released his own Climax Moonshine brand in 2013.[89] However, ex-moonshiners like Smith remain the exception to the rule. "Now the moonshiners are urban moonshiners," Colin Spoelman, a Yale University alum and owner of Kings County Distillery in New York City, concluded in 2013. "They're people who are chefs; people who are home brewers; and people who are interested in it not for profit. I think the moonshiner in the woods really does not exist in the way that it exists in the public's imagination."[90]

Despite its commercial success, the legal moonshine industry faces an uncertain future. For one, many consumers continue to view white whiskey as inauthentic, believing that "if it's legal, it ain't moonshine," and refuse to purchase it. "What this stuff being passed off as moonshine at liquor stores nowadays really is, mostly, is unaged corn whiskey," Dan Dunn wrote in 2011. "Calling it moonshine is as much an affront to the memory of this country's outlaw rutgutters as labeling Blink 182 'punk' is a kick in the balls to Iggy Pop."[91] Some consumers and distillers alike further insist that white whiskey's illegal counterpart remains far superior in quality. As former moonshiner Tim Smith complained:

> What I've learned over say the last 20 years . . . is that those legal distilleries out there have never made legal moonshine before, have no experience at all. They only know the process. They go to an institute where they learn the process of it from a chemical engineer. Anyone can learn the basic process. You can learn it in elementary school. It's chemistry. But actually doing it and tasting it and understanding what you're doing, nobody's done that.[92]

The production of legal moonshine has also begun to wane, as many craft distilleries have now survived long enough to sell their aged liquors and thus no longer rely on white whiskey to stay in business. Moreover, the recent glut of legal moonshine in the marketplace has caused a growing number of distilleries that specialize in making white lightning to diversify their operations by manufacturing vodka and other mainstream liquors. "Right now, it's really on the decline," Carl Petzold, owner of Carl's Carolina Spirits in Marshall, North Carolina, admitted in 2015. "If you look at the state's numbers, yes, moonshine is selling. But if you look at the total revenue it produces and divide that by the number of distillers, it's getting harder and harder for us to sell."[93] Whatever its fate, the moonshine revival has at least kept the memory of a vanishing craft alive for the foreseeable future.

The Moonshine Revival in Appalachia and Organization of the Book

Although a national phenomenon, the moonshine revival has taken on great importance in the American South and particularly southern Appalachia, a region where many residents and communities have struggled economically. Since the early 2010s, the number of distilleries there—especially in western North Carolina, eastern Tennessee, northwestern South Carolina, and southwestern Virginia—has steadily grown. One of the earliest of these distilleries is Ole Smoky in Gatlinburg, Tennessee, which saw sales of its legal moonshine skyrocket from fifty thousand cases in 2010 to 280,000 in 2013. Like Ole Smoky, most of the distilleries attempt to capitalize on the region's moonshine heritage, marketing themselves and their products as traditional and authentic. Meanwhile, the moonshine revival has helped to boost tourism in many parts of Appalachia, as visitors increasingly come to not only enjoy the mountain landscape but also to tour local distilleries, drink unaged whiskey, and participate in so-called moonshine festivals.

Modern Moonshine: The Revival of White Whiskey in the Twenty-First Century provides one of the first interdisciplinary examinations of the legal moonshine industry in southern Appalachia. The coeditors organized the eleven chapters into three thematic parts—part I, "Socially Constructing the Origins of the Modern Moonshine Revival," part II, "The Legalization and Marketing of Modern Moonshine," and part III, "Historic Preservation and

Tourism in the Name of Moonshine." Each of these parts uses unique and thought-provoking approaches to deconstruct the resurgence of public and private interest in moonshine, explain how this illicit liquor has become legitimate, and explores the causes and impacts of the moonshine revival in southern Appalachia. Each also challenges various caricatures and stereotypes of Appalachian culture as represented by moonshine, moonshiners, and the new entrepreneurial rise of craft distilling. Taken together, the following chapters reveal that the moonshine revival in Appalachia is not exceptional. Indeed, the forces shaping the movement—most notably the Great Recession of 2008 and the public's nostalgia for symbols of the American past—were the same in both Appalachia and other parts of the nation.

In part I, "Socially Constructing the Origins of the Modern Moonshine Revival," authors examine the various ways in which moonshine has historically existed and how past and present representations have shaped modern interpretations. In chapter 1, historian and coeditor Bruce E. Stewart sets the stage to understanding the origins of modern moonshine by providing a historical overview of alcohol manufacturing in Appalachia from the eighteenth century to the late twentieth century. In chapter 2, historian Daniel S. Pierce explores southern Appalachian moonshine culture by highlighting how two moonshiners, Jim Tom Hedrick and Popcorn Sutton, have played major roles in shaping today's views of moonshining and its cultural heritage. Media studies professor Emily D. Edwards's chapter 3 critiques the portrayal of Appalachian moonshiners in reality shows and movies. One reason, she argues, why the image of the illicit distiller continues to fascinate Americans is due to popular media promotion of the moonshiner's Trickster personality. Sociologist Robert T. Perdue's chapter 4 rounds out this section by exploring the social construction of deviance as it applies to the illicit and legal production of moonshine in Franklin County, Virginia.

In part II, "The Legalization and Marketing of Modern Moonshine," contributors focus on the rise of craft distilling and the production of modern moonshine by distillers to sell as a unique and legal Appalachian product. In chapter 5, criminologist Kenneth J. Sanchagrin discusses how state laws have changed in the last two decades to encourage craft distilleries in Appalachia and other parts of the nation to open and produce unaged white whiskey. He also argues that the legalization of craft distillation is a result of several U.S. states' realizing the economic potential of allowing the distilling industry to flourish.

In chapter 6 sociologists Kaitland M. Byrd, J. Slade Lellock, and Nathaniel G. Chapman examine how recent southern Appalachian craft distilleries have used cultural and historical concepts to give modern moonshine a distinctive and marketable southern foodway identity for consumers eager to experience something unique and "authentic." In chapter 7 sociologist Jason Ezell carries on the discussion of marketability by chronicling how some craft distillers in Appalachia have actually challenged moonshine stereotypes that often are heteronormative, family-oriented, masculine, and white. He suggests that while these craft distillers bend the stereotypes of moonshining, they often must do so in nuanced ways in southern states that do not support their alternative lifestyles. Chapter 8 completes this section with sociologist and coeditor Cameron D. Lippard's presentation of a case study of how one illicit moonshining family in Appalachian North Carolina became legitimate craft distillers by using its specific family heritage to create a moonshine-focused brand.

Finally, in part III, "Historic Preservation and Tourism in the Name of Moonshine," authors discuss how places and spaces impact modern moonshine in southern Appalachia and attract tourists to learn about moonshine's local and historical roots. In chapter 9, geographer Helen M. Rosko describes how place matters in selling moonshine. Particularly, she argues that moonshine has become a unique element in shaping what it means to live, work, and visit East Tennessee and Appalachia. Public historian Kristen Baldwin Deathridge's chapter 10 examines how craft distillers in Appalachia use historic preservation and cultural tourism to sell their products but also keep history alive in their communities. Finally, in chapter 11, historic preservationist Barry L. Stiefel chronicles how modern-day heritage and moonshine festivals throughout Appalachia attempt to keep the legacy of moonshine adventures alive through craft moonshine tastings and hot rod "bootlegger" car shows.

NOTES

1. *Chicago Tribune*, March 25, 1979.
2. See chapter 1 herein.
3. In 2017 ninety-six other craft distilleries were planning to make unaged corn whiskey. See Sku's Recent Eats, "The Complete List of American Whiskey Distilleries and Brands," accessed March 14, 2016, http://recenteats.blogspot.com/p/the-complete-list-of-american-whiskey.html. When compiling this list,

we included distilleries that marketed their brands as moonshine, 'shine, unaged (corn) whiskey/bourbon, white dog, white whiskey, or white lightning. We excluded those distilleries making unaged rye or wheat whiskey.

4. In 2015 moonshine sales in the United States reached $41 million. See *Advertising Age*, July 20, 2015.

5. For examples, see Jaime Joyce, *Moonshine: A Cultural History of America's Infamous Liquor* (Minneapolis: Zenith Press, 2014); James Rodewald, *American Spirit: An Exploration of the Craft Distilling Revolution* (New York: Sterling Epicure, 2014); David Haskell and Colin Spoelman, *The Kings County Distillery Guide to Urban Moonshining: How to Make and Drink Whiskey* (New York: Abrams Image, 2013); Max Watman, *Chasing the White Dog: An Amateur Outlaw's Adventures in Moonshine* (New York: Simon and Schuster, 2010); and Matthew B. Rawley, *Moonshine: Recipes, Tall Tales, Drinking Songs, Historical Stuff, Knee Slappers, How to Make It, How to Drink It, Pleasin' the Law, Recoverin' the Next Day* (New York: Lark Books, 2007).

6. For a discussion on whiskey distilling in early colonial America, see Reid Mitenbuler, *Bourbon Empire: The Past and Present Future of America's Whiskey* (New York: Viking Press, 2015), 13–24; Clay Risen, *American Whiskey, Bourbon, and Rye: A Guide to the Nation's Favorite Spirit* (New York: Sterling Epicure, 2013), 21–24; and Sarah Hand Meacham, *Every Home a Distillery: Alcohol, Gender, and Technology in the Colonial Chesapeake* (Baltimore: Johns Hopkins University Press, 2009).

7. Michael R. Veach, *Kentucky Bourbon Whiskey: An American Heritage* (Lexington: University Press of Kentucky, 2013), 3–19; Bruce E. Stewart, *Moonshiners and Prohibitionists: The Battle over Alcohol in Southern Appalachia* (Lexington: University Press of Kentucky, 2011), 9–30; Henry G. Crowgey, *Kentucky Bourbon: The Early Years of Whiskeymaking* (Lexington: University Press of Kentucky, 2008), 52, 62–82.

8. For more on the so-called Whiskey Rebellion, see William Hogeland, *The Whiskey Rebellion: George Washington, Alexander Hamilton, and the Frontier Rebels Who Challenged America's Newfound Sovereignty* (New York: Simon and Schuster, 2006); and Thomas P. Slaughter, *The Whiskey Rebellion: Frontier Epilogue to the American Revolution* (New York: Oxford University Press, 1986).

9. Veach, *Kentucky Bourbon Whiskey*, 31–37; and Risen, *American Whiskey*, 27.

10. W. J. Rorabaugh, *The Alcoholic Republic: An American Tradition* (New York: Oxford University Press, 1981), 87.

11. Dane Huckelbridge, *Bourbon: A History of the American Spirit* (New York: William Morrow, 2014), 118–22; Veach, *Kentucky Bourbon Whiskey*, 19–29, 31–44; Risen, *American Whiskey*, 27–32; and Mitenbuler, *Bourbon Empire*, 57–62, 87–88.

12. For more on federal liquor taxation and moonshining during the late nineteenth century, see Wilbur R. Miller, *Revenuers and Moonshiners: Enforcing Federal Liquor Law in the Mountain South, 1865–1900* (Chapel Hill: University of North Carolina Press, 1991); and Stewart, *Moonshiners and Prohibitionists*.

13. Mitenbuler, *Bourbon Empire*, 124.

14. Veach, *Kentucky Bourbon Whiskey*, 63–76; Risen, *American Whiskey*, 33–42; Mitenbuler, *Bourbon Empire*, 111–27.

15. For more on the temperance movement and national Prohibition, see Lisa McGirr, *The War on Alcohol: Prohibition and the Rise of the American State* (New York: W. W. Norton, 2016); and Daniel Okrent, *Last Call: The Rise and Fall of Prohibition* (New York: Scribner, 2010).

16. Veach, *Kentucky Bourbon Whiskey*, 77–90; Huckelbridge, *Bourbon*, 184–209; Mitenbuler, *Bourbon Empire*, 183–94.

17. Daniel S. Pierce, *Corn from a Jar: Moonshining in the Great Smoky Mountains* (Gatlinburg, TN: Great Smoky Mountains Association), 56–72; Joseph Earl Dabney, *Mountain Spirits: A Chronicle of Corn Whiskey from King James' Ulster Plantation to America's Appalachians and the Moonshine Life* (New York: Charles Scribner's Sons, 1974), 102–16; Jess Carr, *The Second Oldest Profession: An Informal History of Moonshining in America* (Englewood Cliffs, NJ: Prentice-Hall, 1972).

18. For more on how the repeal of federal Prohibition merely returned the issue of prohibition to the state legislatures, see Anthony Stanonis, *Faith in Bikinis* (Athens: University of Georgia Press, 2014); and Michael Lewis, *The Coming of Southern Prohibition* (Baton Rouge: Louisiana State University Press, 2016).

19. Fred Minnick, *Bourbon: The Rise, Fall, and Rebirth of an American Whiskey* (Minneapolis: Voyageur Press, 2016), 118–59; Mitenbuler, *Bourbon Empire*, 198–224; Veach, *Kentucky Bourbon Whiskey*, 91–104; and Risen, *American Whiskey*, 46–49.

20. Risen, *American Whiskey*, 49.

21. Kevin R. Kosar, *Whiskey: A Global History* (London: Reaktion Books, 2010), 109–110; Risen, *American Whiskey*, 49–52; Minnick, *Bourbon*, 176–87, 191; Mitenbuler, *Bourbon Empire*, 237–44; and Huckelbridge, *Bourbon*, 227–28, 240–42.

22. Michael Kinstlick, "The U.S. Craft Distilling Market: 2011 and Beyond," Coppersea, April 2012, https://www.coppersea.com/wp-content /uploads/2012/04/Craft_Distilling_2011_White_Paper_Final.pdf.

23. Veach, *Kentucky Bourbon Whiskey*, 113–19; Minnick, *Bourbon*, 188–210; Huckelbridge, *Bourbon*, 242–53; and Mitenbuler, *Bourbon Empire*, 244–51.

24. Betty Boles Ellison, *Illegal Odyssey: 200 Years of Kentucky Moonshine* (Bloomington: First Books Library, 2003), 133.

25. It is important to note that the decline in stills seized also reflected changing law enforcement practices. By the 1980s federal and state authorities began to focus most of their attention on apprehending local residents engaged in the production or transportation of marijuana, cocaine, and prescription drugs. Pierce, *Corn From a Jar*, 88. See also chapter 1 herein.

26. Michael Kinstlick, "The U.S. Craft Distilling Market: 2015 Update," accessed September 21, 2017, http://axisofwhisky.com/wp-content/uploads/2016/04 /Craft_Distilling_2015_white_paper_update.pdf.

27. Pierre Bourdieu, *Distinction: A Social Critique of the Judgment of Taste* (Cambridge: Harvard University Press, 1984).

28. Dorothy J. Gaiter and John Brecher, "The Joy of 'Jug' Wines," *Wall Street Journal*, accessed September 15, 2017, https://www.wsj.com/articles/SB100014240529702 04621904574244103180757152.

29. Janice Robinson and Linda Murphy, *American Wine: The Ultimate Companion to the Wines and Wineries of the United States* (Berkeley: University of California Press, 2013), 4.

30. Kinstlick, "The U.S. Craft Distilling Market: 2015." Wine America reports that 8 percent of the world's wine production comes from the United States as of 2014; only two decades ago that number was less than 5 percent. See Wine America, "About the United States Wine and Grape Industry," accessed September 15, 2017, http://wineamerica.org/policy/by-the-numbers. See also Kollen Goy, *When Champagne Became French* (Baltimore: Johns Hopkins University Press) for a discussion on how champagne became authentically French.

31. Wine America, "About the United States Wine and Grape Industry." Ninety percent of American wines are produced in California.

32. Wine Institute, "Wine Sales in the U.S.," accessed September 15, 2017, www .wineinstitute.org/resources/pressroom/05012017.

33. Lydia Zuraw, "Wine Revolution: As Drinkers and Growers,

U.S. Declares Independence," *NPR*, accessed September 15, 2017, www.npr.org/sections/thesalt/2013/03/16/174431437/wine-revolution-as -drinkers-and-growers-u-s-declares-independence.

34. Thomas Pinney, *A History of Wine in America: From Prohibition to the Present* (Berkeley: University of California Press, 2005), 224–31.
35. Ibid.
36. Robinson and Murphy, *American Wine*, 12–16.
37. Ibid.
38. Thomas Pellechia, "The American Wine Industry Has Been Going Great, but the Party May Be Winding Down," *Forbes*, accessed September 15, 2017, https://www.forbes.com/sites/thomaspellechia/2017/03/21/the-american-wine -industry-has-been-doing-great-but-the-party-may-be-winding-down /#7d709c476594.
39. Pellechia, "American Wine Industry."
40. Nathaniel G. Chapman, J. Slade Lellock, and Cameron D. Lippard, *Untapped: Exploring the Cultural Dimensions of Craft Beer* (Morgantown: West Virginia University Press, 2017), 4–6.
41. Ibid.
42. Ibid.
43. Ibid.
44. Brewers Association, "Historical U.S. Brewery Count," accessed September 15, 2017, https://www.brewersassociation.org/statistics/number-of-breweries/.
45. Chapman, Lellock, and Lippard, *Untapped*, 2.
46. Ibid., 6.
47. Ibid., 1–3.
48. Alastair Bland, "Craft Beer, Brought to You by Big Beer," *NPR*, accessed September 18, 2017, www.npr.org/sections/thesalt/2017/07/28/539760477 /craft-beer-brought-to-you-by-big-beer.
49. Ibid.
50. Ibid.
51. Local and state governments became more accepting of craft brewing. Following the passage of the Home Brew Act of 1978—which legalized home brewing throughout the nation—several local municipalities and state assemblies began to revise prohibition and zoning laws to allow the sale of brewing ingredients, permit breweries to operate within town limits, and sell in taprooms and local bars. For example, in North Carolina, which now boasts more than 150 craft

breweries, state laws had to be rewritten to allow breweries to exist and have taprooms for customers to sample products, as well as for breweries to sell their products through regional distribution hubs.

52. Krista E. Paulsen and Hayley E. Tuller, "Crafting a Place," in Chapman, Lellock, and Lippard, *Untapped*, 115–19.

53. Cameron D. Lippard and Seth Cohen, "More to It than Just Beer: The Pedagogy of Fermentation Sciences," *MBAA Technical Quarterly* 53, no. 3 (2016), 177.

54. Sam Calagione, *Brewing Up a Business: Adventures in Beer from the Founder of Dogfish Head Craft Brewery* (Hoboken, NJ: Wiley, 2011), 89–119.

55. Brewers Association, "Selling Your Beer," , accessed September 18, 2017, https://www.brewersassociation.org/statistics/national-beer-sales-production-data/; John Kell, "How Craft Beer's Popularity is Hurting Craft Beer," *Fortune*, accessed September 18, 2017, http://fortune.com/2017/03/28/craft-beer-sales-fall/.

56. Kinstlick, "The U.S. Craft Distilling Market."

57. Chris Lozier, "The Craft Spirits Data Project," accessed September 12, 2017, www.parkstreet.com/wp-content/uploads/ArtisanSpirit_Issue017_CSDP.pdf.

58. Ibid.

59. Ibid.

60. Ibid.

61. Kinstlick, "The U.S. Craft Distilling Market."

62. Lozier, "The Craft Spirits Data Project," 69.

63. Kinstlick, "The U.S. Craft Distilling Market."

64. Risen, *American Whiskey*, 59; Rodewald, *American Spirit*, xvi–xix.

65. Risen, *American Whiskey*, 58.

66. "Craft Brewers Turn to Whiskey Chasers," *New York Times*, February 28, 2007.

67. Spoelman and Haskell, *Kings County Distillery Guide*, 90–91; Katy Steinmetz, "A Booze of One's Own: The Micro Distillery Boom," *TIME*, accessed May 4, 2017, http://business.time.com/2012/04/06/craft-distillers/; and John F. Trump, *Still and Barrel: Craft Spirits in the Old North State* (Winston-Salem, NC: John F. Blair, 2017), 132–33.

68. "Rise of Microdistilleries," *The Futures Laboratory*, October 2010, accessed October 2, 2017, http://deathsdoorspirits.com/images/sitefiles/press/company/Alcohol_Luxe_2010.pdf.

69. "Craft Distilling Is on an Upswing in Missouri," *Feast Magazine*, December 23, 2015, accessed October 3, 2017, www.feastmagazine.com/drink/features/article_85a19532-a4d5-11e5-9c31-17ff0d9d4afc.html.

70. New Deal Distillery, "Our Story," accessed September 30, 2017, www.newdeal distillery.com/philosophy/.

71. Risen, *American Whiskey*, 58.

72. "North Carolina Moonshine Gets a Modern Twist," *Our State: Celebrating North Carolina*, July 9, 2014, accessed October 2, 2017, www.ourstate.com /modern-moonshine/.

73. "American Craft Sprits Interview [with Jim Blasit]," Copper Run Distillery, accessed October 2, 2017, www.copperrundistillery.com/american-craft -spirits-interview/.

74. Thistle Finch Distillery, accessed October 2, 2017, www.thistlefinch .com/#visit-us.

75. "Yuppie Moonshine with the Old Kick, and It's Legal Too," *New York Times*, May 13, 2002.

76. "West Virginia Distilling Company," American Whiskey, accessed on September 20, 2017, www.ellenjaye.com/wh_mountainmoon.htm.

77. The first craft distillery to make unaged whiskey and market it to the public as moonshine was likely Belmont Farm Distillery in Culpepper, Virginia, which was founded in 1988.

78. "Glasses High for the Rise of Moonshine," *Philadelphia Inquirer*, August 14, 2011.

79. "Old Smoky Moonshine Sheds Its Hillbilly Roots," *Advertising Age*, July 20, 2015.

80. "Tennessee Distillers Enjoy Sip of Success," *Knoxville News Sentinel*, February 12, 2016.

81. "White Dog: A Whiskey Having Its Day," *New York Times*, May 5, 2010.

82. "Moonshine Moves out of the Mason Jar," *New York Times*, July 20, 2012.

83. Recently, moonshine has showed up in "Hick Hop," made famous on YouTube. This includes songs and music videos of Big Smo's "Kickin' It in Tennessee" and Moonshine Bandits' "We All Country," to a name a few.

84. "Moonshine Moves Out of the Mason Jar," *New York Times*, July 20, 2012.

85. "Thoroughly Modern Moonshine," *Chilled Magazine*, June 5, 2015, accessed September 22, 2017, http://chilledmagazine.com/thoroughly-modern -moonshine.

86. For more on the construction of the hillbilly stereotype, see Anthony Harkins, *Hillbilly: A Cultural History of an American Icon* (New York: Oxford University Press, 2004).

87. As journalist Jesse Ellison reported in 2010, "Modern moonshiners are

among the artisanal, locavore, do-it-yourself foodies who made home-brewed beer, rooftop chickens, and at-home pickling part of the modern lexicon." See "Moonshine's Not Just for Hillbillies Anymore," *Newsweek*, December 22, 2010, accessed September 20, 2017, www.newsweek.com/moonshines-not-just -hillbillies-anymore-69027.

88. "Make Mine Virginia Shine: Backwoods Brew Becomes Big (and Now Legal) Business," *The Hook*, January 3, 2008, accessed September 27, 2017, www. readthehook.com/81613/cover-make-mine-virginia-shine-backwoods-brew -becomes-big-and-now-legal-business.

89. "Moonshine Moves out of the Hills and on to the Shelves," *New York Daily News*, July 19, 2013.

90. Quoted in Joyce, *Moonshine*, 140–41.

91. "The Conundrum of Legal Moonshine," *Food Republic*, March 31, 2011, accessed September 22, 2017, www.foodrepublic.com/2011/03/31/the-conundrum-of -legal-moonshine/.

92. "Moonshine Moves out of the Mason Jar."

93. "Bottle Lightning: Appalachian Moonshining in the 21st Century," *Mountain Xpress*, June 23, 2015, accessed September 22, 2017, https://mountainx.com /news/bottled-lightning-appalachian-moonshining-in-the-21st-century/.

PART I

Socially Constructing the Origins of the Modern Moonshine Revival

CHAPTER 1

Fire Up the Stills: A Brief History of Moonshining in Southern Appalachia before the Twenty-First Century

BRUCE E. STEWART

The illicit mountain distiller first gained national attention in the late nineteenth century when journalists, novelists, and missionaries—hoping to promote the benefits of industrialization and "progress"—began to portray Appalachia as a "strange land" whose inhabitants were culturally and economically at odds with modern America. For these outsiders, the moonshiner epitomized what was wrong with the region. Like other mountain whites, they insisted, illicit distillers were holdovers from a backward and isolated culture resistant to change and modernization. During the early 1900s, temperance advocates, middle-class townspeople, and other reformers continued to cast moonshiners in a negative light. The illicit distillers, they lamented, were violent criminals on the fringes of society who, unwilling to abandon their primitive way of life, refused to embrace commercial agriculture, wage labor, and other "civilized" pursuits. By the end of the twentieth century, however, journalists, movie producers, and musicians had recast the image of mountain distillers, idealizing them as the remnants of a vanishing pioneer culture that many Americans had begun to look upon with nostalgia. In this new light, the moonshiner was not a barbaric outlaw but rather a harmless, overall-wearing, bearded good old boy who simply sought to exercise his natural right to make "a little licker."

Far from presenting a completely accurate representation of moonshining, however, these varied depictions of illicit distillers—whether sympathetic or not—mostly served to reinforce Americans' belief that Appalachia was a "strange land" and that the profession was the product of a traditional mountain culture that remained isolated from the outside world. This is misguided, as Appalachia was neither a static nor closed society.[1] After the Civil War and largely due to the advent of industrialization, the region experienced a tremendous amount of change, most notably the decline of subsistence farming and the rise of poverty. Consequently, many mountain farmers began to rely on a variety of alternative "revenue-earning opportunities" to supplement their declining incomes, including the manufacturing of moonshine.[2] Meanwhile, other factors—the passage of prohibition laws, increases in the federal liquor tax, and the expansion of markets due to urbanization—increased the profitability of illicit distilling and encouraged some highlanders to produce alcohol, even if that meant breaking the law. More so than tradition, economic hardship, government policies, and market forces played an integral role in the rise and persistence of moonshining in southern Appalachia during the late nineteenth and twentieth centuries.

Appalachia's First Industry

By 1800 thousands of Anglo-Americans had migrated to southern Appalachia, which at that time constituted part of the western frontier. Most were of English, Scots Irish, and German ancestry and had moved to the region from Pennsylvania in search of cheap and fertile land. Traveling down the Great Wagon Road, a transportation artery linking Pennsylvania to the southern backcountry, some of them settled in the Valley of Virginia and the foothills of North Carolina. Others pushed westward, crossing over the Blue Ridge Mountains and establishing farms throughout eastern Tennessee and Kentucky.[3] All the while, these immigrants survived by borrowing traditions from one another and the Native Americans they encountered, creating a hybrid frontier culture.[4] They adopted the Cherokees' slash-and-burn technique of clearing farmland and constructed log cabins based on German carpentry methods.[5] Many settlers also embraced the distilling of alcohol, a practice likely introduced to the region by the Scots Irish.[6]

One of Appalachia's first industries, liquor manufacturing quickly became popular because it gave frontiersmen access to cash, a scare commodity in the region. Recent scholarship has demonstrated that most mountain residents did not live in completely self-sufficient households but needed money to buy land, pay taxes, and purchase goods that they were unable to make at home.[7]

As such, they frequently devoted a portion of their crops—often corn—to sell on the market. Due to the region's rugged terrain and relatively poor roads, however, trips to market proved time consuming, with crops often spoiling en route. Given the difficulties of travel, many farmers opted to convert some of their corn into whiskey, and for good reason: liquor did not spoil and was more profitable than corn alone. As historian W. J. Rorabaugh observed, "A farmer could realize handsome profits from processing his grain into spirits, since a bushel of corn worth 25 cents yielded 2 ½ gallons of spirits worth $1.25 or more."[8] By the late eighteenth century, thousands of market-oriented and profit-driven farmers had begun to operate stills throughout the Appalachian countryside.[9]

High consumer demand for intoxicants encouraged these men and women to continue to manufacture whiskey during the antebellum period. Indeed, between 1790 and 1840, Americans drank more alcohol than at any other time in the nation's history. They imbibed distilled spirits as medicine, downed them in large quantities at social events, and frequently used them as a substitute for milk and water (which were often not safe to consume). By 1830 the average American drank nearly five gallons of liquor per year.[10]

Eager to participate in the market economy, mountain residents scrambled to capitalize on the public's thirst for whiskey. In eastern Tennessee and eastern Kentucky, a handful of ambitious entrepreneurs began to establish commercial distilleries and ship thousands of gallons of corn whiskey (often aged in barrels) to New Orleans and other cities in the West.[11] Most distillers, however, were small farmers who made liquor for local markets, selling it to neighbors and nearby stores. On the eve of the Civil War, alcohol manufacturing had solidified itself as an important commercial and cottage industry in Appalachia.[12] By then, residents there—responding to the demands of the marketplace—were producing more than 88 million gallons of whiskey annually.[13] But these distillers would soon receive unwelcome news.

Federal Liquor Taxation and the Beginning of Moonshining

In 1862 the U.S. Congress, hoping to raise revenue for the Union war effort, levied a duty on liquor and established the Bureau of Internal Revenue to collect it.[14] This was not the first time that the federal government had enacted such a tax. In 1791 Secretary of Treasury Alexander Hamilton had persuaded Congress to place an excise on alcohol and other luxuries to help pay off the national debt. Widespread resistance to the duty soon erupted throughout the Appalachian frontier, forcing Congress to repeal it in 1802.[15] The liquor tax of 1862 was met with similar opposition. In the Midwest and North, where the duty was first enforced, residents rallied against it, arguing that it was "unfair" to small farmers who relied on alcohol distilling to earn extra money, and refused to abide by the law. "Great numbers of small stills . . . [are] secreted in garrets and cellars," Commissioner of Internal Revenue Joseph Lewis complained, "while many of the recognized and licensed distillers [are] run by night, their proprietors keeping fraudulent accounts of their consumption of grain and other vegetable substances."[16]

Following the Civil War, bureau agents (often called revenuers) began to enforce liquor taxation in the former Confederate states. There, opposition also quickly emerged, especially in the Mountain South, where distillers complained that the duty challenged local control over alcohol manufacturing and reduced their profit margin. Some of them, mostly small farmers, soon became moonshiners, a term popularized by the national media to describe individuals who made liquor without paying the excise.

These men and women would not resist the Bureau of Internal Revenue alone, at least during Reconstruction. Many highlanders and other southerners who did not distill alcohol regarded moonshiners as the victims of an "oppressive" federal government that impinged upon the natural rights of its citizens to earn a living. As one revenuer complained in 1881, supporters of illicit distillers "claimed that inasmuch as this is a free government—a Republic—every [person] should be allowed to make a living for himself and family as best he can; and if he does not steal, or trample upon the rights of his neighbors, the Government should not interfere with him."[17] Former Confederates, including prominent Democratic politicians, also sympathized with the moonshiners, believing that liquor taxation was a tool used by the federal government to prevent them from restoring "home rule."[18]

Meanwhile, revenuers and moonshiners engaged in a game of cat-and-mouse, with most illicit distillers preferring to use their wits rather than a Winchester rifle to evade capture.[19] Instead of fighting, they sought to avoid fines and imprisonment by placing their stills "in unfrequented districts, sometimes in the midst of an impenetrable jungle or laurel brake, and carefully concealed when not in operation."[20] Others hid their stills in caves and stored their illegal cargo in ponds.[21] Moonshiners also circumvented violence by posting pickets to give warning of a revenue posse's approach. When searching for illegal stills in western North Carolina during the 1870s, bureau agent William Ball complained that he often heard "the blowing of horns and the peculiar hoots employed as signals of coming danger." "Throughout the sections where these violations of the law take place," he continued, "the whole country is patrolled and picketed. So complete is the system of signals that no stranger can be seen without instantaneous alarm being given all through the neighborhood."[22]

These tactics proved effective. By 1876 an estimated three thousand illicit stills remained in operation throughout southern Appalachia, costing the federal government $2.5 million annually.[23] That August President Ulysses S. Grant responded by appointing Green B. Raum as commissioner of the Bureau of Internal Revenue and instructing him to suppress moonshining. Raum promptly increased the number of revenuers and launched the first of several seasonal sweeps in the Mountain South.[24] Over the next four years, federal agents seized 3,011 illegal stills and arrested 6,096 moonshiners.[25] Despite these successes, many illicit distillers continued to resist government regulation. Though most of them opted to hide themselves and their stills, some resorted to violence. Between 1876 and 1880, twenty-five agents were killed in southern Appalachia, an average of about six per year.[26]

Although this violence was an exception to the rule, it brought unwanted national attention to the region. By then, novelists and journalists had already popularized Appalachia as a "strange land" whose residents—supposedly due to geographical isolation—remained uncivilized.[27] When the conflict between moonshiners and revenuers came to a head in the late 1870s, these writers increasingly began to include illicit distillers as central characters in their stories and use them as a symbol of what was wrong with Appalachia. Like other mountain whites, they argued, moonshiners were rugged individualists who relied on violence to preserve their "primitive" way of life. Illicit distillers "despise . . . towns and cities, and think the inhabitants of such places much inferior to themselves in wisdom, character, and happiness," one journalist claimed in 1882. "The continued manufacture of whisky in violation of the laws [is] partly a feature of [this] old warfare of the mountaineers against the civilization and the people of the towns."[28] Such depictions not only reinforced middle-class Americans' belief that the region was a land of lawlessness but also made moonshining synonymous with Appalachia.[29]

Meanwhile, the Bureau of Internal Revenue continued to make headway in its campaign against the moonshiners. In 1878, confident that increased enforcement had convinced illicit distillers that the federal agency was determined to crack down on lawbreakers, Raum initiated a new course of action: offering amnesty to moonshiners who pled guilty in court and vowed to cease manufacturing alcohol illegally.[30] Highlanders and other southerners who had sympathized with illicit distillers quickly approved of Raum's amnesty order. "This is a right step of the government, both as a corrective and preventative," a newspaper from upcountry South Carolina read that August. "It will accomplish more, and promptly, in securing obedience to the law than all the marshals and commissioners in the State could effect in a year of turmoil . . . and confusion."[31] To Raum's delight, thousands of moonshiners in Appalachia began to turn themselves in to authorities and admit their guilt in court. Overall, the number of convictions for evading federal liquor taxation in the mountain region rose from 1,114 in 1877 to 2,648 in 1879, an increase of 138 percent.[32] By 1882 it appeared that moonshiners were on the verge of defeat. "The business of 'blockading', so called, that is the sale of illicit whisky . . . has almost been suppressed," Raum reported that year. "Bands of illicit distillers combined together in defiance of law have been broken up, and forcible resistance to the officers of the government . . . is of much less frequent occurrence than heretofore."[33]

The Resurrection of Moonshining, 1880–1920

Such optimism proved short lived. By 1900 a growing number of mountain residents, mostly small farmers, had returned to moonshining. Again, this turn of events was neither the result of geographical isolation nor the product of ethnic origins, as early-twentieth-century writers claimed. Rather, it was a response to economic and social forces that had begun to transform Appalachia and other rural parts of the nation. During the 1880s, the slash-and-burn technique of forest farming that many highlanders had long used to cultivate crops became ineffective as soil exhaustion and deforestation increased in the region. Population growth and inheritance practices "exacerbated the situation by decreasing farm acreage, and large amounts of land had to be left fallow to restore the fertility of the soil."[34] To make matters worse, a nationwide depression caused farm prices to plummet throughout the 1890s, making it more difficult for farmers to acquire enough money to sustain their households and pay property taxes. "Under such circumstances," historian Daniel Pierce has explained, "making a little whiskey to help them hold on to their farms did not seem like such a bad thing."[35]

Moonshining also appealed to some mountain residents because it was becoming more profitable than legally manufacturing alcohol. In 1894 the U.S. Congress, hoping to create additional revenue without raising the tariff, increased the federal liquor tax to $1.10 per gallon.[36] This new tax significantly reduced the profit margin of small legal producers, who could now only earn "50 cents of profit by distilling two bushels of corn." Meanwhile, a moonshiner "could make $7.50 off the same amount."[37] Some formerly legal distillers began to evade the federal excise, causing moonshining operations to spread quickly throughout Appalachia. "There is more illicit distilling and trading in 'blockade' whisky . . . than ever before since the internal revenue laws were enacted," the *New York Times* reported in 1895. "Consequently, the revenue officers were never more active than at present."[38] Indeed, between 1894 and 1897, stills seized by revenue agents in the region rose from 1,016 to 2,273.[39]

A growing regional market for illicit alcohol further enticed distillers to break the law. By 1900 industrial development had begun to transform the Appalachian countryside.[40] Coal mining and logging companies, eager to capitalize on the region's natural resources and cheap labor, arrived in force, establishing camps for their employees, most of whom were young, single, and male. The advent of industrialization also brought about dramatic increases in urbanization. As historian Wilbur Miller observed, "Some regions in the mountains witnessed the sudden growth of . . . new cities like Middlesborough, Kentucky, which increased from sixty valley farmers to five thousand people between 1883 and 1889. Older communities also expanded, like Asheville, North Carolina, a tourist center and rail hub that grew from two thousand residents in 1880 to ten thousand in 1890."[41] These demographic changes opened a new market for moonshiners, who quickly sold their product to thirsty miners, lumberjacks, townspeople, and travelers.

This market continued to expand with the passage of prohibition laws in the South at the turn of the twentieth century. By then, many southerners had embraced the temperance movement, believing that alcohol impeded the region's economic and moral prosperity. In Appalachia as elsewhere, these reformers began to enact local-option laws that banned the sale of intoxicants in their communities. By 1907 825 of the 996 counties in the South had passed such legislation. That same year, Georgia voters, determined to eliminate alcohol consumption once and for all, approved of statewide prohibition. North Carolina, Tennessee, and Mississippi soon followed suit. By 1916 five other southern states had become "dry," solidifying Dixie's status as the leading champion for alcohol reform in the nation.[42]

These statutes ultimately encouraged illicit distilling by providing a wider market for moonshiners, who, without legal competition, could now raise the price of alcohol and increase their profit margin. "The fact is that blockading as a business conducted in armed defiance of the law is increasing by leaps and bounds since the mountain region went 'dry,'" Horace Kephart observed in 1913. "The profits today are much greater than before, because liquor is harder to get, in country districts, and consumers will pay higher prices without question."[43] Indeed, due to local and state prohibition, the price of illicit whiskey rose from $1.50 to $4.50 per gallon.[44] The lure of high profits enticed some mountain distillers to expand production by running multiple stills or using commercial stills that could manufacture hundreds of gallons of whiskey a day. However, these so-called "kingpins" were the exception to the rule, at least for the time being. Most moonshiners continued to be farmers who seldom made more alcohol than was needed to sustain their households and pay taxes.[45]

Unlike earlier periods, local support for the moonshiners began to plummet in the early twentieth century. Despite prohibition laws, alcohol continued to flow into "dry" communities, causing many mountain residents to turn against illicit distillers. These highlanders no longer viewed moonshiners as heroes who defied an "oppressive" federal government but embraced the popular opinion that they were purveyors of violence, crime, and intemperance.[46] "More and more is the blockader becoming a social pariah, where formerly he would hold up his head with—if not above—the best of them," a western North Carolina newspaper observed in 1913. "Then 'moonshining' used to be a money-making business—it may still be but money is to be made just as easy in more honorable and less hazardous pursuits."[47] Understaffed local and state authorities proved unable to crack down on the illicit liquor trade, much to the dismay of prohibitionists.[48] But the worst was yet to come.

National Prohibition and Its Consequences

"The reign of tears is over. The slums will soon be only a memory. We will turn our prisons into factories and our jails into storehouses and corncribs. Men will walk upright now, women will smile and children will laugh."[49] So proclaimed the famous evangelist Billy Sunday on January 17, 1920, celebrating the first of day of national Prohibition. The previous year, the states had ratified the Eighteenth Amendment, which prohibited the sale, transportation, and manufacturing of alcohol throughout the nation, and the U.S. Congress passed the Volstead Act, creating the Prohibition Unit—renamed the Bureau of Prohibition in 1927—to enforce the new law. Like Sunday, reformers across America believed that national Prohibition would at last bring an end to "King Alcohol" and usher in a new chapter in the country's history.[50] "Nation-wide prohibition means more joy, wealth, prosperity, and betterment for our nation," one mountain newspaper declared. "It means that the drink will be less a factor in the future and that the happiness of many homes will be increased."[51]

Although Prohibition succeeded in reducing the annual per capita consumption of alcohol, it created a national market for illicit spirits and caused the price of whiskey to increase significantly.[52] Moonshining subsequently skyrocketed throughout the nation, including southern Appalachia, where distillers could now sell their product for ten to fifteen dollars a gallon.[53] By 1922 an estimated ten thousand illicit stills operated in the mountain region, producing three hundred thousand gallons of whiskey each week. "Conditions are steadily growing worse instead of better," a Prohibition agent from West Virginia complained that year. Illicit distilling "was never more open, never more flagrant, and were it not for the fact that business in the coal fields and lumber mills is depressed and that those who would patronize the moonshiners liberally are now without funds conditions would be appalling."[54]

Meanwhile, as moonshiners scrambled to meet demand and make profits, the distilling process changed dramatically. By the 1920s most distillers began to use refined sugar—instead of cornmeal alone—to make their mash, reducing the fermentation period by three-quarters.[55] "There's as much difference in the stuff they make today and the liquor they made 15 years ago as there is in daylight and dark," an "old-time" moonshiner, complaining about the rise of sugar-based whiskey, remarked in 1930. "When I was in the heyday of my stilling career, moonshiners didn't put anything in their liquor but the heart of the corn."[56] Three new inventions—the thumper keg, the steamer, and the groundhog—further revolutionized the distilling process, allowing moonshiners to expand their volume of production.[57] As historian Daniel Pierce observed, moonshining was now becoming "more mechanized and shaped by modern industrial processes and technology rather than traditional knowledge."[58]

With an increased emphasis on quantity, the quality of moonshine also rapidly declined during national Prohibition. The lure of profits encouraged many illicit distillers to begin to water down their whiskey (typically from hundred proof to fifty proof) and include adulterants such as lye, buckeyes, and glycerin to make their product "bead" like high-proof liquor.[59] Others attempted to give their moonshine more "bite" by adding tobacco, pepper, rubbing alcohol, and even embalming fluid to it.[60] "Such decoctions are known in the mountains by the expressive terms 'pop-skull,' 'bust head,' 'bumbling' ('they make a bumbly noise in a feller's head')," Horace Kephart wrote in 1921. "Some of them are so toxic that their continued use might be fatal to the drinker. A few drams may turn a normally good-hearted fellow into a raging fiend who will shoot or stab without provocation."[61] Indeed, as historian Charles Thompson has argued, "Prohibition was not making the liquor business go away, it was just making it bad."[62]

The growing profitability of moonshining also led to political corruption and the proliferation of kingpins. In Franklin County, Virginia, for instance, commonwealth attorney Carter Lee (the grandnephew of Confederate Gen. Robert E. Lee) and other local authorities became wealthy by extorting protection money from moonshiners and bootleggers.[63] These officials often worked with kingpins, who began to control the bulk of whiskey being produced in southern Appalachia and profited the most from the moonshine trade during national Prohibition. These well-financed lawbreakers seldom distilled liquor themselves, opting to hire local residents to make and transport alcohol. "Men with money are setting up illicit stills and paying moonshiners regular wages to operate them," the *New York Times* reported in 1922. "When the operators are caught . . . they either escape jail sentences as first time offenders or receive $3 a day from their employers while in prison to protect their backers."[64]

Meanwhile, as federal officials scrambled to crack down on moonshining, violence escalated in Appalachia and other parts of the nation. "Arrests have rapidly increased since prohibition, and so have mortal combats between officers and outlaws," Horace Kephart observed. "The war between enforcement agents and blockaders is more widespread and deadly than ever before in our history."[65] Despite the increase in violence, most mountain distillers continued to rely on their wits rather than their guns to evade capture. In 1923, for instance, a moonshiner from Walker County, Georgia, eluded Prohibition agents by running "a pipe line from his still to his store, about a mile away," where he "served his patrons without a moment's delay with the fruit of corn."[66] A Letcher County, Kentucky, blockader proved just as creative, installing a pipe "to carry the smoke from his still to a hollow tree some distance away."[67] Moonshiners also increasingly used a modern invention—the telephone—to warn each other of danger.[68]

Though the repeal of the Eighteenth Amendment in 1933 significantly reduced the national market for and price of moonshine, political and economic forces continued to encourage some Appalachian residents to manufacture alcohol illegally in the 1930s and 1940s.[69] During those years, many mountain counties continued to enforce state and local prohibition laws, which caused local demand for moonshine to increase. The federal government did not help the situation, raising the liquor tax to a then-record-high nine dollars per gallon in 1944.[70] Economic hardship, however, remained the leading culprit responsible for the persistence of moonshining in the mountain region. Declining farm prices, combined with the collapse of the timber and coal industries, compelled many residents to break the law.[71] As one western North Carolinian recalled: "Everybody was needy; half of them didn't have shoes. I finally got to where I just didn't care. Young and stout and couldn't get jobs. . . . And I started making liquor. I had to have some money."[72]

The Rise of Thunder Road: Moonshining in the 1950s

By the 1950s moonshining had reemerged as big business throughout the nation. Largely due to rising federal and state liquor taxes, the price of legal whiskey increased to $2.80 a pint, enticing many consumers to begin to purchase moonshine, which sold for as low as $0.75 a pint on the black market. In Appalachia as elsewhere, the growing demand for cheap liquor soon caused moonshining to skyrocket again.[73] Throughout "the Appalachian range . . . the still fires are burning perhaps as briskly as they did twenty years ago when prohibition came to an end," one mountain newspaper reported in 1953. "Hidden in the hills there is an army of moonshiners who . . . are dodging federal agents and tending their stills."[74] More so than tradition, market forces continued to encourage some mountain residents to make moonshine.

Like those during national Prohibition, many mountain moonshiners in the 1950s placed emphasis on quantity instead of quality when manufacturing their whiskey. Scrambling to meet consumer demand and earn a profit, they continued to use refined sugar to ferment mash. "A hundred pounds of sugar will make about 12 gallons of 100 proof," a former revenuer from eastern Kentucky observed in 1959. "That's a lot more than corn will make. That's why they use it—more profitable and quicker action."[75] Some moonshiners also continued to cut the proof of their liquor and add such harmful substances as bleach to give it more "kick."[76] The use of car or truck radiators—instead of copper "worms"—as condensers to cool alcohol vapors further eroded the quality of moonshine, introducing a new hazard to consumers: lead poisoning.[77] "We find that the product now being sold as moonshine whiskey is far below the standards heretofore observed," bemoaned a federal official in 1954. "Much of it contains chemicals that could be very dangerous to a person's health—causing blindness or even death."[78]

The 1950s also witnessed the peak of the moonshine industry's so-called Thunder Road era in southern Appalachia. During the 1920s, mountain distillers had begun to hire "trippers" to transport their illegal product to more distant markets. Mostly young men, these haulers proved up to the task, capitalizing on a new invention—the automobile—to evade Prohibition agents and earn a living. After World War II, trippers—who could make as much as $450 on a single run—became the primary transporters of moonshine in the region. Their engine of choice was the flathead, V-8 Ford, which—after being modified with additional carburetors and superchargers—could outrun most law enforcement vehicles.[79] As one revenuer in Cocke County, Tennessee, remembered: "The moonshiners built some good, high performance cars. . . . What they had was far superior to what we had."[80] Ever resourceful, trippers also disguised their heavy cargos by mounting extra springs onto their cars' axles and even installed smokers and other gadgets to thwart pursuers.[81] All the while, they developed into highly skilled drivers, mastering such moves as the "bootleg turn," which "involved slowing the car down, dropping the gear into second, punching the brake, and spinning the car around in the opposite direction of those who were giving chase."[82]

News of daredevil moonshiners with souped-up cars evading revenuers captured the fascination of Americans in the 1950s and 1960s. Hollywood was eager to capitalize on this interest, and several films and television shows began to focus on the topic of illicit distilling. Unlike previous imagery in popular culture, the moonshiner was portrayed not as an ignorant criminal but as the defender of a traditional culture doomed to fall victim to capitalism. In particular, Arthur Ripley and Robert Mitchum's 1958 cult classic *Thunder Road* helped to change the public's perception of illicit distillers. Subsequent films and shows often sympathized with moonshiners and characterized them as lovable good old boys who—like their ancestors—manufactured and transported illicit whiskey to make ends meet. Bluegrass and country musicians also increasingly cast moonshining in a positive light, celebrating it as a holdover from the nation's pioneer past and a symbol of resistance to modernity.[83]

The Decline of Moonshining

While Americans romanticized the moonshiner as a harmless good old boy, illicit distilling was quickly dying out throughout southern Appalachia. By the 1960s the U.S. Treasury Department's Alcohol and Tobacco Tax Division (ATTD)—renamed the Bureau of Alcohol, Tobacco, and Firearms in 1968—had begun to make headway against the moonshiners, most notably with its Operation Dry Up program. Initiated in South Carolina in 1962, Operation Dry Up employed a two-phase approach to combating illicit distilling. Enlisting the services of Andy Griffith and other celebrities, it first sought to reduce the demand for moonshine by launching a massive public information campaign about the dangers of drinking illegal alcohol.[84] The next phase involved doubling the number of ATTD agents in South Carolina.[85] "We wanted to see what would happen if we applied enough pressure, if we saturated an area with enforcement," a federal official later recalled. "What happened was that illicit production of whiskey in [South Carolina] was reduced by 80 percent."[86] Hailing it as an unqualified success, the ATTD then implemented Operation Dry Up in Georgia and Alabama with similar results.[87] Elsewhere in Appalachia, moonshiners also found themselves in retreat as revenuers increasingly used spotter planes and heat detectors to locate illegal stills.[88]

Meanwhile, the profitability of moonshining plummeted in the mountain region. By the 1970s the federal government's embargo on Cuba and enactment of a higher tariff on imported sugar had caused the price of sugar to more than double, making it impossible for most illicit distillers to turn a profit. Rising inflation did not help the situation, as the price of corn, copper, and other materials used to manufacture alcohol increased dramatically in the 1970s.[89] As one West Virginia moonshiner complained in 1976, "Sugar's better than $23 a hundred [pounds] right now. And corn, corn's gone plumb out of sight. It costs you more to make liquor now than you can sell it for."[90] Higher production costs ultimately forced illicit distillers to raise the price of moonshine to that of legal whiskey, which was becoming more accessible due to the relaxation of local prohibition laws.[91] Consequently, consumers began to purchase bonded liquor, driving many moonshiners out of business.[92] "Add moonshine whiskey to your list of nostalgic items from the past," a journalist concluded in 1975. "Place it right below cheap sugar, because when the latter faded into history, the former was doomed to follow."[93]

Improving economic conditions further discouraged a growing number of mountain residents from manufacturing moonshine. By the 1970s the arrival of new industries "and the expansion of previous ones" in the region "created job opportunities that paid enough to make folks reconsider the hard work and stress that came with the blockade liquor business."[94] "Why should you turn down a job with good, steady money to make or run whiskey?" a former moonshiner from Franklin County, Virginia, remarked. "People can buy whiskey at the stores everywhere now. And if you got caught you'd lose your car and your still—a bunch of money's tied up in that. It's too expensive."[95] No longer dependent on moonshining to supplement their incomes or earn a living, most mountain distillers began to quit the business. As Daniel Pierce noted, "In 1967, federal agents destroyed over 6,000 stills in the Southeast U.S., most of them in the southern Appalachian region. By 1977 the number had dropped to less than 500, and by 1997, only about 20 per year."[96]

By the end of the twentieth century, journalists, scholars, and mountain residents alike had concluded that moonshining as well as the knowledge of making unaged corn whiskey were on the verge of extinction.[97] "You had some of what I call 'the old mountain people' who made whiskey. I think they got old and I don't think any of the younger people followed in their footsteps," Bill Lewis, a former sheriff from Swain County, North Carolina, explained in 1996. "People talk to me all the time about dying arts, and this really is one. It's something that very few people are carrying on."[98] But nothing could have been further from the truth. As the following essays reveal, recent economic, cultural, and political forces have opened a new chapter in the history of moonshine, one that promises to reestablish "outlaw hooch" as an American icon.

NOTES

1. For a sample of scholarship that has debunked the long-standing assumption that Appalachia is geographically, economically, and culturally at odds with the nation, see Richard A. Straw and H. Tyler Blethen, eds., *High Mountains Rising: Appalachia in Time and Place* (Urbana: University of Illinois Press, 2004); Ken Fones-Wolf and Ronald L. Lewis, eds., *Transnational West Virginia: Ethnic Communities and Economic Change, 1840–1940* (Morgantown: West Virginia Press University, 2002); John C. Inscoe, ed., *Appalachians and Race: The Mountain South from Slavery to Segregation* (Lexington: University Press of Kentucky, 2001); Dwight B. Billings and Kathleen M. Blee, *Road to Poverty: The Making of Wealth and Hardship in Appalachia* (Cambridge: Cambridge University Press, 2000); Ronald L. Lewis, *Transforming the Appalachian Countryside: Railroads, Deforestation, and Social Change in West Virginia, 1880–1920* (Chapel Hill: University of North Carolina Press, 1998); Mary Beth Pudup, Dwight B. Billings and Altina L. Waller, eds., *Appalachia in the Making: The Mountain South in the Nineteenth Century* (Chapel Hill: University of North Carolina Press, 1995); Allen W. Batteau, *The Invention of Appalachia* (Tucson: University of Arizona Press, 1990); Henry S. Shapiro, *Appalachia on Our Mind: The Southern Mountains and Mountaineers in the American Consciousness, 1870–1920* (Chapel Hill: University of North Carolina Press, 1978); and Helen Lewis, Linda Johnson, and Donald Askins, eds., *Colonialism in Modern America: The Appalachian Case* (Boone, NC: Appalachian Consortium Press, 1978).

2. Daniel S. Pierce, *Real NASCAR: White Lightning, Red Clay, and Big Bill France* (Chapel Hill: University of North Carolina Press, 2010), 15 (quotation).

3. For more on eighteenth-century Appalachia, see John Alexander Williams, *Appalachia: A History* (Chapel Hill: University of North Carolina Press, 2003); Wilma A. Dunaway, *The First American Frontier: Transition to Capitalism in Southern Appalachia, 1700–1860* (Chapel Hill: University of North Carolina Press, 1996); and John Anthony Caruso, *The Appalachian Frontier: America's First Surge Westward* (1959; reprint, Knoxville: University of Tennessee Press, 2003).

4. Most historians no longer view the frontier as a dividing line between uncivilized and civilized society. Instead, they insist that the frontier was a place where different cultures, environments, experiences, economies, motives, and perspective came into contact. On this frontier, people exchanged ideas, cultural traits, values, and sometimes lifestyles, thereby creating a new culture. See Caruso, *Appalachian Frontier*, xv; Gregory H. Nobles, "Breaking into the Backcountry: New Approaches to the Early American Frontier, 1750–1800," *William and Mary Quarterly* 46 (October 1989): 641–70; Robert D. Mitchell, ed., *Appalachian Frontiers: Settlement, Society, and Development in the Preindustrial Era* (Lexington: University Press of Kentucky, 1991); and H. Tyler Blethen and Curtis W. Wood, Jr., *From Ulster to Carolina: The Migration of the Scotch-Irish to Southwestern North Carolina* (Raleigh: Division of Archives and History, North Carolina Department of Cultural Resources, 1998).

5. Donald Edward Davis, *Where There Are Mountains: An Environmental History of the Southern Appalachians* (Athens: University of Georgia Press, 2000), 97–107.

6. For more on the Scots Irish, see Joseph Earl Dabney, *Mountain Spirits: A Chronicle of Corn Whiskey from King James' Ulster Plantation to America's Appalachians and the Moonshine Life* (New York: Charles Scribner's Sons, 1974), 31–41.

7. For a sample of this scholarship, see Straw and Blethen, *High Mountains Rising*; Dunaway, *First American Frontier*; Pudup, Billings, and Waller, *Appalachia in the Making*; and Mitchell, *Appalachian Frontiers*.

8. W. J. Rorabaugh, *The Alcoholic Republic: An American Tradition* (New York: Oxford University Press, 1979), 74.

9. Dabney, *Mountain Spirits*, 42–73.

10. Jack S. Blocker, Jr., *American Temperance Movements: Cycles of Reform* (Boston: Twayne Publishers, 1989), 3–11; and Rorabaugh, *Alcoholic Republic*, 95–100, 232.

11. For more on commercial distilling in eastern Tennessee and eastern Kentucky before the Civil War, see Michael R. Veach, *Kentucky Bourbon Whiskey: An American Heritage* (Lexington: University Press of Kentucky, 2013); Henry G. Crowgey, *Kentucky Bourbon: The Early Years of Whiskeymaking* (Lexington: University Press of Kentucky, 2008); and Rorabaugh, *Alcoholic Republic*.

12. For more scholarship on alcohol distilling in Appalachia before the Civil War, see Cratis Williams, "Moonshining in the Mountains," *North Carolina Folklore* 15 (May 1967): 11–17; Esther Kellner, *Moonshine: Its History and Folklore*

(Indianapolis: Bobbs-Merrill, 1971); Jess Carr, *The Second Oldest Profession: An Informal History of Moonshining in America* (Englewood Cliffs, NJ: Prentice-Hall, 1972); David W. Maurer, *Kentucky Moonshine* (Lexington: University Press of Kentucky, 1974); Dabney, *Mountain Spirits*; Rorabaugh, *Alcoholic Republic*; Wilbur R. Miller, *Revenuers and Moonshiners: Enforcing Federal Liquor Law in the Mountain South, 1865–1900* (Chapel Hill: University of North Carolina Press, 1991); and Bruce E. Stewart, *Moonshiners and Prohibitionists: The Battle over Alcohol in Southern Appalachia* (Lexington: University Press of Kentucky, 2011).

13. Carr, *Second Oldest Profession*, 23.

14. Initially $0.20 a gallon, the federal liquor tax had gone up to $2.00 a gallon by 1865. In 1868 the U.S. Congress reduced the tax to $0.50 a gallon. See Kellner, *Moonshine*, 68; and Stewart, *Moonshiners and Prohibitionists*, 94. For more on the administrative structure of the Bureau of Internal Revenue, see Miller, *Revenuers and Moonshiners*, 61–67.

15. For more on the so-called Whiskey Rebellion of the 1790s, see William Hogeland, *The Whiskey Rebellion: George Washington, Alexander Hamilton, and the Frontier Rebels Who Challenged America's Newfound Sovereignty* (New York: Simon and Schuster, 2006); Kevin T. Barksdale, "Our Rebellious Neighbors: Virginia's Border Counties during Pennsylvania's Whiskey Rebellion," *Virginia Magazine of History and Biography* 111 (January 2003): 5–32; Jeffrey J. Crow, "The Whiskey Rebellion in North Carolina," *North Carolina Historical Review* 66 (January 1989); 1–28; Thomas P. Slaughter, *The Whiskey Rebellion: Frontier Epilogue to the American Revolution* (New York: Oxford University Press, 1986); and Mary K. Bonsteel Tachau, "The Whiskey Rebellion in Kentucky: A Forgotten Episode of Civil Disobedience," *Journal of the Early Republic* 2 (Fall 1982): 239–59.

16. *Annual Report of the Commissioner of Internal Revenue*, 1866, House Executive Document 55, 39th Cong., 2nd Sess., xiv. See also Stewart, *Moonshiners and Prohibitionists*, 77–78.

17. George Wesley Atkinson, *After the Moonshiners, by One of the Raiders* (Wheeling: Frew and Campbell, 1881), 13–14.

18. "Home rule" meant Democratic control of state governments in the South. For more on moonshiner support and the anti-liquor tax argument in the South during Reconstruction, see Miller, *Revenuers and Moonshiners*, 40–81; Stewart, *Moonshiners and Prohibitionists*, 79–114.

19. Miller, *Revenuers and Moonshiners*, 45.

20. A. H. Guernsey, "Illicit Distilling of Liquors—Southern Mode of Making Whiskey," *Harper's Weekly* 11 (December 7, 1867): 733.

21. Stewart, *Moonshiners and Prohibitionists*, 98.

22. William S. Ball to C. Devens, February 23, 1878 (microfilm, reel 2, M1345), Letters Received from the State of North Carolina, 1871–1884, Records of the Attorney General, General Records of the Department of Justice, Record Group 60, National Archives, College Park, Maryland.

23. *Annual Report of the Commissioner of Internal Revenue*, 1877, House Executive Document 20, 44th Cong., 2nd sess., xxx.

24. Miller, *Revenuers and Moonshiners*, 100–126.

25. "Enforcement of Internal Revenue Laws: . . . Report of the Commissioner of Internal Revenue . . . to Explain the Necessity for Employment of Armed Men . . . ," House Executive Document 62, 46th Cong., 2nd sess. (1880), 210.

26. Ibid.

27. For more on the creation of the Myth of Appalachia during the late nineteenth century, see Shapiro, *Appalachia on Our Mind*.

28. Jonathan Baxter Harrison, "Studies in the South," *Atlantic Monthly* 49 (January 1882), 90.

29. For more on the role that the so-called Moonshine Wars played in the creation of the Myth of Violent Appalachia, see Bruce E. Stewart, "'These Big-Boned, Semi-Barbarian People': Moonshining and the Myth of Violent Appalachia, 1870–1900," in *Blood in the Hills: A History of Violence in Appalachia*, ed. Bruce E. Stewart (Lexington: University Press of Kentucky, 2012): 180–206.

30. Miller, *Revenuers and Moonshiners*, 137–44.

31. *Keowee (SC) Courier*, August 15, 1878.

32. *Annual Report of the Attorney-General*, 1877, House Executive Document 20, 44th Cong., 2nd sess., 18; *Annual Report of the Attorney-General*, 1879, House Executive Document 8, 46th Cong., 2nd sess., 24–25.

33. *Annual Report of the Commissioner of Internal Revenue*, 1882, House Executive Document 4, 47th Cong., 2nd sess., vii.

34. Stewart, *Moonshiners and Prohibitionists*, 182.

35. Daniel S. Pierce, *Corn from a Jar: Moonshining in the Great Smoky Mountains* (Gatlinburg, TN: Great Smoky Mountains Association), 40.

36. The federal liquor tax had previously been ninety cents a gallon. Miller, *Revenuers and Moonshiners*, 166.

37. Pierce, *Corn from a Jar*, 40.

38. *New York Times*, April 14, 1895.

39. Miller, *Revenuers and Moonshiners*, 167.

40. For more on the impact of industrialization on Appalachia, see Williams, *Appalachia*; Lewis, *Transforming the Appalachian Countryside*; Paul Salstrom, *Appalachia's Path to Dependency: Rethinking a Region's Economic History, 1730–1940* (Lexington: University Press of Kentucky, 1994); and Ronald Eller, *Miners, Millhands, and Mountaineers: Industrialization of the Appalachian South, 1880–1930* (Knoxville: University of Tennessee Press, 1982).

41. Miller, *Revenuers and Moonshiners*, 30.

42. Those five other southern states were Alabama, West Virginia, Virginia, South Carolina, and Arkansas. For more on the rise of temperance and prohibition in the South following the Civil War, see Michael Lewis, *The Coming of Southern Prohibition: The Dispensary System and the Battle Over Liquor in South Carolina, 1907–1915* (Baton Rouge: Louisiana State University Press, 2016); Stewart, *Moonshiners and Prohibitionists*; Lee L. Willis, *Southern Prohibition: Race, Reform, and Public Life in Middle Florida, 1821–1920* (Athens: University of Georgia Press, 2011); Joe L. Coker, *Liquor in the Land of the Lost Cause: Southern White Evangelicals and the Prohibition Movement* (Lexington: University Press of Kentucky, 2007); William A. Link, *The Paradox of Southern Progressivism, 1880–1930* (Chapel Hill: University of North Carolina Press, 1992); Ted Ownby, *Subduing Satan: Religion, Recreation, and Manhood in the Rural South, 1865–1920* (Chapel Hill: University of North Carolina Press, 1990); Paul E. Isaac, *Prohibition and Politics: Turbulent Decades in Tennessee, 1885–1920* (Knoxville: University of Tennessee Press, 1965); James Benson Sellers, *The Prohibition Movement in Alabama, 1702–1943* (Chapel Hill: University of North Carolina Press, 1943); Daniel Jay Whitener, *Prohibition in North Carolina, 1715–1945* (Chapel Hill: University of North Carolina Press, 1946); and Leonard S. Blakey, *The Sale of Liquor in the South: The History of a Normal Social Restraint in Southern Commonwealths* (New York: Columbia University Press, 1912).

43. Horace Kephart, *Our Southern Highlanders* (New York: Macmillan, 1921), 189.

44. Kellner, *Moonshine*, 90.

45. Kephart, *Our Southern Highlanders*, 126–27; and Pierce, *Corn from a Jar*, 47.

46. For more on this backlash against moonshiners in Appalachia, see Miller, *Revenuers and Moonshiners*; Stewart, *Moonshiners and Prohibitionists*; and Bruce

E. Stewart, ed., *King of the Moonshiners: Lewis R. Redmond in Fact and Fiction* (Knoxville: University of Tennessee Press, 2008).

47. *Asheville (NC) Gazette-News*, November 4, 1913.

48. For more on enforcing local and state prohibition, see Miller, *Revenuers and Moonshiners*; and Stewart, *Moonshiners and Prohibitionists*.

49. Quoted in Dabney, *Mountain Spirits*, 103.

50. Believing that the passage of the Eighteenth Amendment would cause the price of and demand for their product to skyrocket, many moonshiners also supported—and sometimes provided financial assistance to—the national Prohibition movement.

51. *Rutherfordton (NC) Sun*, January 23, 1919. For more on national Prohibition, see Lisa McGirr, *The War on Alcohol: Prohibition and the Rise of the American State* (New York: W. W. Norton, 2016); and Daniel Okrent, *Last Call: The Rise and Fall of Prohibition* (New York: Scribner, 2010).

52. McGirr, *War on Alcohol*, 50–51.

53. Maurer, *Kentucky Moonshine*, 27.

54. *Washington Post*, April 2, 1922.

55. Dabney, *Mountain Spirits*, 110.

56. *Kingsport (TN) Times-News*, June 6, 1954.

57. The thumper keg eliminated the time-consuming second distilling. The thumper, usually fifty gallons in size, is placed between the cooking pot and condenser, and filled with beer. Hot vapors sent bubbling up from the pot through the thumper beer produce a second distillation in the keg along with a rhythmic thumping sound. The resulting whiskey is thus double distilled on only one run. Next, a new type of still was put into operation—a steamer, which enabled the illicit distillers to boost production tremendously. The steamer sends hot vapors through one or a series of pots of fresh beer, providing very efficient distillations. Many of the early steamers were "stack steamers"—two or three metal drums welded together. In some isolated areas, the groundhog still came onto the scene—giant metal cylinders that enabled a man to produce two or three hundred gallons of whiskey a day and to ferment and distill in the same giant pot (Dabney, *Mountain Spirits*, 110).

58. Pierce, *Corn from a Jar*, 60.

59. The bead is "little bubbles that form along the meniscus of liquor when shaken in a bottle, allowing an experienced moonshiner to judge the proof and quality of the liquor with great accuracy" (Maurer, *Kentucky Moonshine*, 113).

60. Pierce, *Corn from a Jar*, 57–58; Dabney, *Mountain Spirits*, 108, 111; Alec Wilkinson, *Moonshine: A Life in Pursuit of White Liquor* (New York: Alfred A. Knopf, 1985), 25–27; and Betty Boles Ellison, *Illegal Odyssey: 200 Years of Kentucky Moonshine* (Bloomington: First Books Library, 2003), 87–88.

61. Kephart, *Our Southern Highlanders*, 137–38.

62. Charles D. Thompson, Jr., *Spirits of Just Men: Mountaineers, Liquor Bosses, and Lawmen in the Moonshine Capital of the World* (Urbana: University of Illinois Press, 2011), 170.

63. Ibid.

64. *New York Times*, May 21, 1922.

65. Quoted in Pierce, *Corn from a Jar*, 63–64.

66. *Wall Street Journal*, May 18, 1923.

67. Ellison, *Illegal Odyssey*, 86.

68. Pierce, *Corn from a Jar*, 64.

69. Due to the end of national Prohibition, the price of whiskey "dropped from as high as $20 to as low as $2 per gallon." Ibid., 73.

70. "After prohibition was repealed, a federal levy of $2 a gallon was imposed in 1934. It was raised to $2.25 in 1938, to $3 in 1940, to $4 in 1941, [and] to $6 in 1942" (*Wall Street Journal*, August 30, 1951).

71. For more on economic decline in Appalachia during and after the Great Depression, see Salstrom, *Appalachia's Path to Dependency*; Billings and Bee, *Road to Poverty*; and Ronald Eller, *Uneven Ground: Appalachia Since 1945* (Lexington: University Press of Kentucky, 2008).

72. Michael Ann Williams, *Great Smoky Mountains Folklife* (Oxford: University Press of Mississippi, 1995), 104–5.

73. In 1951 the federal liquor tax was raised to $10.50. *New York Times*, April 19, 1954; *Danville (KY) Advocate-Messenger*, December 7, 1953, April 19, 1954; *Los Angeles Times*, November 10, 1954; and *Wall Street Journal*, September 21, 1956.

74. *Danville (KY) Advocate-Messenger*, December 7, 1953.

75. *Hartford Courant*, March 15, 1959.

76. *Beckley (WV) Post-Herald*, December 20, 1956; *Danville (KY) Advocate-Messenger*, December 7, 1953.

77. *Atlanta Daily World*, December 18, 1953. The worm is "the coiled tubing that is commonly seen connected to the top of the still where the alcohol vapors condense" (W. D. Washburn, *Secrets on the Mountain* [Hickory, NC: Tarheel Press, 2002], 9).

78. *Atlanta Daily World*, December 24, 1954.

79. Pierce, *Real NASCAR*, 17, 26–28.

80. Pierce, *Corn from a Jar*, 80.

81. Dabney, *Mountain Spirits*, 154, 157.

82. Jaime Joyce, *Moonshine: A Cultural History of America's Infamous Liquor* (Osceola: Zenith Press, 2014), 101.

83. J. W. Williamson, *Hillbillyland: What the Movies Did to the Mountains and What the Mountains Did to the Movies* (Chapel Hill: University of North Carolina Press, 1995), 123–47; and Pierce, *Corn from a Jar*, 89–92. For more on the construction of the hillbilly stereotype in films and television, see Anthony Harkins, *Hillbilly: A Cultural History of an American Icon* (New York: Oxford University Press, 2004).

84. *Kingsport (TN) Times-News*, January 23, 1966, May 17, 1967; *Greenville (SC) News*, July 28, 1965, January 23, 1966.

85. *Asheville (NC) Citizen-Times*, July 17, 1968; *Kingsport (TN) Times-News*, January 23, 1966.

86. *Aiken (SC) Standard*, June 6, 1973.

87. *Asheville Citizen-Times*, July 17, 1968; *Anniston (AL) Star*, December 17, 1967, January 30, 1975; *Greenville (SC) News*, January 23, 1966, October 10, 1971; *Kingsport (TN) Times-News*, January 23, 1966; *Kingsport (TN) Times*, May 17, 1967.

88. *The Tennessean*, December 3, 1970, November 5, 1971; *Danville (KY) Advocate-Messenger*, December 15, 1970; *Greenville (SC) News*, October 10, 1971.

89. According to one Virginia newspaper, the price sugar increased from between $12 and $15 per 100 pounds to between $25 and $40. *The (VA) Bee*, August 19, 1974. See also *Anniston (AL) Star*, January 30, 1975; *Kingsport (TN) News*, August 14, 1975; *Charleston (WV) Gazette-Mail*, March 14, 1976; and *Louisville (KY) Courier-Journal*, February 18, 1976.

90. *Charleston (WV) Gazette-Mail*, March 14, 1976.

91. According to one Tennessee paper, the price of moonshine increased from six to fifteen dollars a gallon during the 1970s. See *Kingsport (TN) News*, August 14, 1975.

92. In addition to becoming more accessible, legal whiskey was also becoming less expensive "because the federal excise tax did not increase between the mid-1950s and the mid-1980s" (Pierce, *Corn from a Jar*, 88).

93. *Anniston (AL) Star*, January 30, 1975.
94. Pierce, *Corn from a Jar*, 87. See also Maurer, *Kentucky Moonshine*, 102; *Statesville (NC) Record and Landmark*, September 10, 1976, January 14, 1977; *The Tennessean*, December 3, 1970, November 5, 1971, January 26, 1978; *Kingsport (TN) Times*, January 3, 1978; *Greenville (SC) News and Piedmont*, September 30, 1979; and *Chicago Tribune*, April 6, 1986.
95. *The Progress-Index*, January 13, 1963.
96. Pierce, *Corn from a Jar*, 88. It is important to note that the decline in stills seized also reflected changing law enforcement practices. By the 1980s federal and state authorities began to focus most of their attention to apprehending local residents engaged in the production or transportation of marijuana, cocaine, and prescription drugs.
97. For examples, see Kellner, *Moonshine*; Maurer, *Kentucky Moonshine*; Ellison, *Illegal Odyssey*; Jack Allen Powell, *A Dying Art* (Catskill, NY: Press Tige, 1996); and Jerry L. Alexander, *Where Have All Our Moonshiners Gone?* (Seneca, SC: Jerry L. Alexander, 2006).
98. *Asheville (NC) Citizen-Times*, August 18, 1996.

Chapter 2

Jim Tom Hedrick, Popcorn Sutton, and the Rise of the Postmodern Moonshiner

DANIEL S. PIERCE

The report of my death was an exaggeration.
—Mark Twain, *New York Journal*, June 2, 1897

Reports in the 1980s and 1990s of the demise of moonshine were akin to the reports of Mark Twain's death in 1897, "an exaggeration." Indeed, Twain would live for almost thirteen more years, and moonshine in the twenty-first century is looking downright immortal. To be sure, the moonshine business seemed in the 1990s to be on its last legs, an anachronism, a cultural and economic appendix with no obvious purpose or future. That is, until an amazing revival began around the turn of the century that made moonshine both culturally and economically relevant for the first time in decades. A number of factors contributed to this moonshine renaissance, but one of the key factors was the appearance on first the regional, then the national and even international media scene of two iconic characters who played to traditional moonshiner stereotypes, who updated the moonshiner image in a very postmodern manner, and who became the trademark faces of this revival: Jim Tom Hedrick and Popcorn Sutton.

Moonshiners and Stereotypes

The popular image of the moonshiner has deep roots in American cultural history beginning soon after the passage of the federal excise tax on spirits in 1862, but it is an image that has been changed and updated repeatedly.

Surprisingly, the earliest stereotypes were positive ones, particularly in the South. Politicians, reporters, dime novelists, and ordinary citizens in the region during the 1870s and 1880s often characterized famous moonshiners—or blockaders as they were commonly called during the period—such as Lewis Redmond, Amos Owens, and Quill Rose as heroic symbols of defiance of federal authority. Major politicians such as South Carolina governor and later U.S. senator Wade Hampton and North Carolina governor and later U.S. senator Zebulon Baird Vance regularly praised such individuals. Redmond, in particular, was widely depicted in the region as a sympathetic victim and a living symbol "of the Yankee oppression resulting from the late war."[1] By the later years of the nineteenth century and with the rapid growth of the Prohibition movement and the rise of the Local Color literary movement, descriptions of the moonshiner became much less positive, and many of the longest lasting popular images of moonshiners—of laziness, ignorance, lack of hygiene and teeth, violent behavior, and overall shiftlessness—became common tropes. These images were reinforced during the silent movie era, when, in the words of historian Anthony Harkins, filmmakers made hundreds of "feud and moonshine" movies highlighting the backwardness and violent nature of mountain people.[2]

Late in the silent film era, the moonshiner image began to change as comedians such as Buster Keaton began to play illegal distillers for laughs. This image of the moonshiner as a character more to be laughed at than to be feared was reinforced by Billy DeBeck's *Snuffy Smith* and Al Capp's *Lil' Abner*, popular cartoon strips of the mid-twentieth century. Movies and later television picked up on this cartoonish moonshiner image, which culminated in the 1960s with the myriad comedic appearances of moonshiners and moonshine played in such hit TV series as *The Andy Griffith Show* and *The Beverly Hillbillies*. Even before these shows appeared, however, a shift began to take place in the aftermath of the release of Robert Mitchum's B-movie classic, *Thunder Road*. Mitchum built on the image popularized by James Dean in *Rebel without a Cause* and Marlon Brando in the *Wild Bunch* and placed the moonshiner (himself in this case) in the role of misunderstood rebel. This image dominated a burgeoning number of movies made in the South for the drive-in movie market in the 1960s and saw its climax in the 1970s with the wildly popular *Smokey and the Bandit* movies and *The Dukes of Hazzard* television show.[3]

While scholars have generally condemned such stereotyping, some have looked into the ways that stereotyped individuals have played on and taken advantage of their popular image and sold it back to unsuspecting individuals, generally tourists. In *Creating the Land of the Sky*, historian Richard Starnes briefly looked into the phenomenon of "chiefing" among the Eastern Band of Cherokee Indians. These "chiefs" adopt the dress and dances of western Indians for their own personal profit and for the benefit of the tourists who believed all Indians dress alike and who were looking for an "authentic" experience. Starnes quotes "chief" Henry Lambert as saying, "If you're going into show business, dress for it."[4] Wayne Caldwell has explored the practice of mountain people playing the hillbilly for tourists in western North Carolina in his fictional work *Requiem by Fire*. In the chapter entitled "Real Mountaineers," Caldwell tells the story of folks who move to a nearby resort community from the Great Smoky Mountains and, as a joke, dress as hillbillies in the souvenir store they open. When a customer asserts she bought merchandise in the store because "you're real mountaineers," one of the proprietors exclaims, "I think we've struck oil. If they want real mountaineers, we'll give it to them."[5] Perhaps the best and most thorough exploration of this practice, particularly as it pertains to the hillbilly image, is in Brooks Blevins's work *Arkansas/Arkansaw*. Blevins writes of Arkansans who take advantage of the "dual nature" of the stereotypical "Arkansaw" image, "local yarn spinners, the folklorists, hillbilly hustlers, and champions of anachronism" who "sought to profit" off the image and myth of "the unshaven Arkie, the moonshiner, . . . shoelessness, illiteracy, poverty . . . windy politicians and hillbillies."[6] Turning the stereotypical image of the moonshiner back on the stereotype and using outsiders' own ignorance of reality for both fun and profit is an important part of the story of twenty-first century moonshiners, particularly Jim Tom Hedrick and Marvin "Popcorn" Sutton.

Like the moonshiner himself (though there were plenty of women moonshiners, just not in popular culture), moonshiner images largely disappeared from the popular consciousness by the late twentieth century. However, by the turn of the twenty-first century, moonshine experienced a resurgence, and the image was due for an updating. Jim Tom Hedrick and Popcorn Sutton were up to the task of creating a modern moonshiner. While boosting the popularity of moonshine, Hedrick and Sutton tapped into moonshiner stereotypes of the past but put a decidedly postmodern spin on the moonshine business. In the early years of the century, they transformed from real, authentic, and modern moonshiners into moonshiners artfully and profitably playing the role of stereotypical moonshiners to an international media audience.

Two Moonshining "Characters"

Hedrick and Sutton have similar roots: both were born and raised in rural mountainous areas of western North Carolina, Hedrick near the Snowbird Community in Graham County (one of the most remote areas in the eastern United States) and Sutton in the Hemphill Bald area of Haywood County. Jim Tom was born around 1940 while Popcorn came into the world in 1946. Jim Tom claims to have started out as a moonshiner at the age of fifteen, when "one of the best whisky makers that ever come along learned me how."[7] He later revealed that his teacher was "an old guy by the name of Clyde Barker" who was breaking at least two federal laws by making moonshine and making it on federal land in the Great Smoky Mountains National Park in the early 1960s. Jim Tom hauled in sacks of sugar for Barker and performed other physical labor in exchange for a quart of moonshine a day and the knowledge of how to make liquor. His sister Pat Williams later recalled, "Mom and dad sure didn't approve of that."[8]

Sutton was at least a third-generation illegal liquor maker. He spoke fondly of his grandfather "Little" Mitch Sutton and his lasting influence: "My Grand Daddy made, drank and sold likker most of his life. People worry about likker killing them: I don't. Because my Grand Daddy is proof it won't. He smoked Camel cigarettes [unfiltered] just like I do, one after another. He also drunk all the likker he could get and chased all the women he could. He lived to be about 90 years old." While his father, Vader Sutton, also "knew the moonshine trade," Popcorn learned the craft over in Cocke County, Tennessee, working with some of that county's legendary distillers. After a few years, he went back over the Smokies to Maggie Valley and made liquor with his father "in one place for 20 years, never was caught at that location because we was careful as hell."[9]

Sutton did get busted three times—for tax evasion, possession and sale of untaxed alcohol, and assault with a deadly weapon—before he became a celebrity around 2000, but he received probation on each occasion. For him, it was part of the deal: "If you're worried about the law you shouldn't be doing this. They gonna catch you sooner or later."[10] Jim Tom, surprisingly, seems to have never been busted for making moonshine. "The law tried to catch me," he told an *Asheville Citizen-Times* reporter in 1984. "Never have yet. But they've been pretty close."[11] He has, however, had numerous arrests for drunken driving and claimed in the 1999 documentary *Moonshine* to hold the record in North Carolina for DUI arrests at age twenty-one.[12]

By the 1980s both were well known in their communities as moonshiners and as local characters. In addition to his DUIs, Hedrick was known in Graham County as the survivor of a head-on collision with a station wagon while driving his Harley-Davidson motorcycle more than one hundred miles per hour on Halloween night 1962.[13] He lived simply, making his living distilling moonshine, dumpster diving, and crafting miniature copper stills which he sold to tourists. As his sister Pat Williams observed, "He don't care what kind of shack he lives in. He says as long as he has a loaf of bread, and a pound of bologna, and a pound of cheese, he's fine. He don't care which way the wind blows. He's happy. He's happy the way he is."[14] Hedrick was also known as a big talker and storyteller who often regaled spectators who came to watch his demonstrations of corn liquor making at special heritage events and at local businesses. Hedrick would set up his copper still at events like the Great Smoky Mountains Heritage Festival in Robbinsville. "All this is to show people how it's done and how our folks here in the mountains have made 'cork [probably corn—the reporter most likely misunderstood given Jim Tom's thick mountain accent] liquor' as long as anybody can remember, and even beyond that."[15]

Sutton developed a similar reputation in Maggie Valley and looked and acted the part of the moonshiner for the tourists who came to the area. He generally sported overalls, a flannel shirt, and a well-worn felt fedora and drove around in a Model A truck with a still in the back. Sutton was also known for his salty language and his series of marriages (supposedly he married four times and never divorced) and love affairs that produced an estimated twelve children, only one of whom he acknowledged. There are varying stories involving the source of his name, but all the stories involve an uncooperative popcorn machine that took Sutton's money but produced no treat. Whether he then shot the machine with a pistol or hammered it with a pool cue has never been determined, but whatever happened lived on in the nickname Popcorn embraced. Like Hedrick, Sutton also did demonstrations of moonshine making, most notably at Mountain Heritage Days at nearby Western Carolina University.[16]

Both moonshiners were also surprisingly religious. The *Moonshine* documentary shows Hedrick, definitely no stranger to the lyrics, singing along to the hymns at a Wednesday night prayer meeting in a small Baptist church; features "ordained Bible minister" Gilford Williams helping him make liquor; and ends with Hedrick playing "What a Friend We Have in Jesus" on a lap organ he found in a dumpster dive.[17] Sutton was a religious person as well. He shared that his grandfather used the proceeds of a liquor run to help build the Baptist church on Hemphill.[18] When photographer Don Dudenbostel asked him if he could come by on a Sunday for a photo shoot, Sutton responded, "Hell no, goddammit. If it's Sunday I'll be in church."[19]

Moonshiners in the Postmodern Era

Until 1999 Hedrick's and Sutton's reputations were strictly local. That began to change around the turn of the century, and within the next fifteen years, both developed an international reputation, as did their mountain moonshine. The road to fame for Hedrick came when Kelly L. Riley, a student at the Rhode Island School of Design, discovered the moonshiner and came to Graham County in 1999 to film a short documentary. The resulting film, simply entitled *Moonshine*, soon became a cult classic after Riley screened it at several film festivals and as bootleg copies spread rapidly throughout the region. The film features Hedrick hauling the pieces of a moonshine still out of the woods, assembling it, and making a run of illegal corn liquor. The highlight of the film, however, is Hedrick's ongoing commentary and his observations on moonshine, life, religion, motorcycle crashes, and his many DUI convictions. It also shows him blowing into a breathalyzer in order to start his car and belting out snatches of "The Ballad of Thunder Road" and "Cigarettes and Whiskey and Wild, Wild Women" while he makes his moonshine.[20]

About the same time as Riley discovered Jim Tom Hedrick, Popcorn Sutton decided that he ought to write a book about his life. In collaboration with his live-in girlfriend Ernestine Upchurch, who wrote down Sutton's words and translated some of them into comprehensible English, he self-published a book entitled *Me and My Likker*. The book—in a sort of postmodern, stream-of-consciousness manner—tells his life story with frequent asides into whatever caught his attention at the time. He does give a warning up front that "this book is not going to be wrote in chapters or uniform in any way," and he does not lie. In the book Sutton began to refine the image that he would carefully craft over the next nine years as the last of the old-time moonshiners, the practitioner of a dying craft. "I am one of the last true moonshiners left that knows how to make likker the way the old moonshiners did." He also explained why he kept making liquor: "Making likker is the hardest work you have ever done. But once you get in to it, it gets in your blood. You won't quit."[21]

Sutton followed up on his book with a decidedly amateur video with the same title instructing viewers, using as much profanity as he could possibly squeeze into each sentence, on the nuances and dangers of producing moonshine in a huge three-hundred-gallon stainless steel gas-fired still. He also instructed viewers on the three varieties of moonshine—"fightin'," "lovin'," and "banjer pickin'"—on how to judge the proof of liquor, and if they didn't already know, how to get drunk on it. All of this came with a banjo accompaniment provided by Sutton's buddy Leon Wells.[22] Sutton marketed his book and video—and later souvenir clocks and T-shirts reading "Jesus turned the water into wine. I turned it into liquor. —Popcorn Sutton"—at his Maggie Valley junk shop and in area restaurants, gas stations, and barber shops. As had the *Moonshine* documentary, Sutton's book and video soon became underground hits in the region, and his reputation began to spread beyond Haywood County.[23]

In 2002 another documentarian, Neal Hutcheson, discovered Hedrick and Sutton and gave both significant air time in a film entitled *Mountain Talk*. The film was a production of the North Carolina Language and Life Project, an ongoing endeavor started by North Carolina State English professor Walt Wolfram to document the unique dialects of North Carolina and the United States at large. While the focus of the film was on mountain dialect and Hedrick's and Sutton's speech provided the film with fascinating footage, both talked a bit about their experience in the moonshine business. In addition, footage of Hedrick cruising around Graham County on his moped (he had evidently lost his driver's license once again after the filming of *Moonshine*) and Sutton driving Hutcheson around in his Model A Ford pickup further heightened their images as genuine mountain characters.[24] However, the most important byproduct of the film was the long-term collaboration between Hutcheson and Sutton, a collaboration that would take the Maggie Valley moonshiner to a national audience.

That collaboration began when, not long after the filming of *Mountain Speech*, Hutcheson did extensive filming of Sutton driving around on dirt mountain roads in his Model A Ford pickup to find an appropriate still site, setting up a small copper wood-fired still, and making what Sutton repeatedly told the camera was "the last damn run of likker I'll ever make." It is apparent that between the filming of *Me and My Likker* and his work with Hutcheson that Sutton had refined his image a good deal to better fit his narrative that he was the "last true old-time moonshiner" making 'shine the "way the old moonshiners did." His still in his first video was decidedly modern, made of stainless steel and fired by propane gas, rather industrial and not very romantic, and was operated in a cinder-block outbuilding on his Maggie Valley property. By the time Hutcheson did his filming, Sutton depicted himself as an old-time, copper-pot craftsman, making liquor the old-fashioned way up in a remote holler in the Smokies and hauling it in his antique truck, the last of a dying breed. Of course, the prime feature of the footage was Sutton's ongoing, profane commentary on making and drinking likker, on his relationships with women, and on the raccoon penis bone he stuck through his trademark porkpie hat and used to ensure the condensed moonshine flowed smoothly into a collection container.[25] Like many other natives of the southern Appalachian region, Sutton was artful in figuring out what image of mountain people the world wanted and then happily selling it back to them. As Sutton's biographer Tom Jester put it, "Yes, Popcorn was the embodiment of a colorful stereotype, and he knew how to work it."[26] Doug O'Neil of the *Newport Plain Talk*, a longtime friend of Sutton, asserted, "He gave the world what they expected of a moonshiner. He dressed the part and he talked the talk."[27]

Hutcheson made a rough cut of the footage he shot, titled it *This Is the Last Dam Run of Likker I'll Ever Make*, and turned it over to Sutton, who began selling VHS copies of the film at his junk store. When the film became a "bootleg sensation," Hutcheson was shocked: "It just went everywhere so fast," particularly in the Southeast.[28] Footage from *Last Dam Run* soon took on a long and profitable life for both Sutton and Hutcheson. Cable television company CMT used footage from the project for a 2004 program entitled "Moonshine Madness," part of its *Most Shocking* series, which gave Sutton a national audience for the first time.[29]

As Sutton's fame spread, regional and national media as well as ordinary people who read about him or saw one of his videos began to beat a path to the doorstep of his junk shop. He told a reporter from the *Asheville Citizen-Times* in 2005, "Likker put me in the spotlight. My likker has been in every state and to England, Scotland, France, places like that. People bought it here and took it back with them." Carver's Maggie Valley Restaurant even put up a sign reading, "Maggie Valley, Home of Popcorn Sutton." Owner James Carver commented, "Popcorn is a good ambassador for the valley and promotes tourism. He has friends all over. He talks to people, encourages them to come to Maggie."[30] In 2007 producers from Moore-Huntley Productions found Sutton's doorstep and made him a key part of their documentary, *Hillbilly: The Real Story*, which aired for several years on the History Channel. While the film ostensibly starred Billy Ray Cyrus as narrator, Sutton really stole the show.[31]

By this time, Neal Hutcheson realized what a gold mine he had and recut the footage he had shot back in 2002 into an hour-long documentary entitled *The Last One*. He hit the festival circuit with the film, which quickly gained significant notoriety. He also was able to have the film aired on PBS stations across the nation and later on the Documentary Channel. The film won a 2009 Southeast Emmy Award for Best Cultural Documentary.[32]

While Jim Tom Hedrick did not develop the same fame and notoriety as Sutton had during the 2000s, he did have his turn at playing the stereotypical moonshiner for a national audience when he starred in rising country music artist Matt Stillwell's "Shine" music video in 2008. The video, using footage cut from Kelly Riley's *Moonshine* film, begins with Hedrick standing in front of some mash barrels and instructing folks on the recipe for moonshine: "You fill your still on up with water. Put sixty pound a sugar in it and a gallon of sprouted malt corn, that's just sprouted corn to make it work and cover it up like this. . . . Wednesday, Thursday, Friday, Saturday, about Monday, it'll be ready to pour back in the still . . . and get this right 'chere. Hundred forty proof! Let me smell of it!" The video ends with Hedrick taking a big swig of 'shine from a gallon jug and chasing it with orange juice while commenting, "I don't have to have that chaser, but I love to take one because this is high-proof alcohol." Except for the Tweety Bird hat he wore in the closing scene, Hedrick played the stereotypical moonshiner to a T with his mountain accent, folksy ways, and his grizzled look.[33]

The thing that probably gave moonshine its greatest public relations boost, however, came ironically with Popcorn Sutton's death in 2009. Just as Sutton reached the height of celebrity, like many a tragic character, hubris brought it all crashing to an end. While tourists bought the occasional Popcorn Sutton T-shirt or clock, what everyone really wanted was genuine Popcorn-made moonshine. It turned out that the moonshine that Sutton had made for Neal

Hutcheson back in 2002 was not "the last damn run of moonshine" he'd "ever make," and Sutton returned to cranking out the sugar liquor with a thousand-gallon still on his Parrottsville, Tennessee, farm to supply the demand. He also needed the money to cover his growing medical expenses due to multiple ailments, including a recent diagnosis of cancer. His friends tried to warn him he was flying too close to the sun by trying to be a major media figure while making lots of moonshine, but he ignored their warnings. Mark Ramsey told him, "Old man, you can't be a movie star and make liquor too." Sutton replied, "You can't sell it if nobody knows you got it."[34]

However, federal authorities grew tired of Sutton's open defiance of the law and launched an undercover operation to catch him. Their investigation was aided when a fire broke out in an outbuilding on Sutton's Parrottsville farm in April 2007. When the fire department and local law enforcement arrived, they discovered the remains of a large still and 650 gallons of "untaxed alcohol" in another outbuilding. Sutton was brought up on local charges of "possession of untaxed liquor in excess of three gallons" and in July 2007 was once again sentenced to two years' probation.[35]

The probation sentence seemed to embolden Sutton, and he resumed his moonshining even as federal authorities began closing in. In February and March 2008, federal undercover agents bought "large amounts of moonshine" from Sutton. Sutton recalled selling the liquor to men who turned out to be agents: "Undercover guy got me, see. He'd made buys off of me before and he got me to where he's wantin' to buy me out, everything I had. I thought that was all right, you know. He's supposed to be a backer, said he'd knowed me for five years. Hell, I've sold likker to everybody in the world. I can't remember who I've sold it to and who I didn't. So he just kept on till he got the goods on me and they come down on me, all in one day."[36]

That day was March 13, when twenty-two agents from the Bureau of Alcohol, Tobacco, and Firearms raided Sutton's farm and a storage building in Maggie Valley. They found three thousand-gallon stills, 850 gallons of moonshine, and "hundreds of gallons of mash and other ingredients used to make liquor." They also discovered firearms and ammunition, which added charges of possession of firearms by a convicted felon to the illegal liquor charges. Sutton faced up to twenty-five years in federal penitentiary and some serious fines if convicted on all charges, essentially a life sentence for a sixty-one-year-old chain smoker already in poor health. Special Agent Jim Cavanaugh—a principle figure in the infamous raid of the Branch Davidian compound in Waco, Texas, in 1993—defended Sutton's arrest: "Moonshine is romanticized in folklore and the movies. The truth, though, is that moonshine is a dangerous health issue and breeds other crime. The illegal moonshine business is fraud on taxpayers in Tennessee and across the country."[37]

Sutton pleaded guilty to the charges and—despite his request for leniency, a number of petitions calling for his release, and a Facebook campaign entitled "Leave Popcorn Sutton Alone"—the judge sentenced him to eighteen months in a federal penitentiary. At this point, Sutton paid the ultimate penalty for his celebrity. He had sworn publicly that he would not go back to prison, and on March 16, 2009, he committed suicide. He sent his wife Pam to the grocery store, ran PVC pipe from the tailpipe into the trunk of his favorite car—a green 1960s Ford Fairlane that he had paid for with three jugs of moonshine—and cranked the car up. A public funeral held in October brought out a crowd of more than 350 people—including country music star Hank Williams Jr.—featured an antique hearse pulled by two black Percheron horses, a procession through Parrottsville, and private interment on the family property. His death was reported nationally, including an obituary in the *Wall Street Journal*.[38]

Sutton's death did not end his fame but if anything heightened it. The story of his death especially benefited Neal Hutcheson, the producers of *Hillbilly: The Real Story*, and Sutton's last wife, Pam, to whom Sutton had left two thousand autographed copies of *Me and My Likker,* which she sold for fifty dollars a copy. Hutcheson recut some old footage and added footage taken between 2002 and the moonshiner's death, even scenes of Sutton meeting "Dancing Outlaw" and YouTube star Jesco White, and produced a new film entitled *Popcorn Sutton: A Hell of a Life*.[39] Most notably, in 2011 Hutcheson's footage of Sutton became the star of the first season of a new reality show on the Discovery Channel entitled *Moonshiners*. The show's first season featured the exploits of two Climax, Virginia, moonshiners, Tim Smith and his comedic-relief sidekick Steven Ray Tickle (known simply as Tickle). Clips of Sutton were interspersed with the "reality" pieces featuring Tim and Tickle. The Sutton segments fit perfectly with the show's premise of depicting "real-life" moonshiners at work. And it all fit perfectly with Sutton's postmodern spin on the real-life moonshiner—playing one in popular media while emphasizing the stereotypes of moonshiners still prevalent in American society. In fact,

Tim and Tickle are almost as adept as Sutton at selling the stereotype back to the American people. The show quickly became a hit, one of the top-rated cable shows on the air.[40]

Sutton's death and the rise of the *Moonshiners* show also greatly boosted Jim Tom Hedrick's career as a postmodern moonshiner. He became a regular on the show in its second season, ostensibly replacing Sutton in the role of the authentic, old-time moonshiner. In seasons 3 and 4, Discovery even aired special episodes of *Moonshiners* featuring Hedrick trying to make it in the country music business and singing such favorites as the classic "Rye Whiskey" and his original tune "Golly That's Good/Moonshine Man" which he made into a popular music video.[41]

Although it would be impossible to quantify the impact of Hedrick and Sutton on the rising popularity of moonshine and the moonshiner in the twenty-first century, there was definitely a symbiotic relationship between the two men's popularity and the popularity of moonshine, and before them the illegal liquor business had not seen this level of activity and demand in probably fifty years. As Sutton discovered, people did not just want to be around him and hear his stories; they wanted to taste his moonshine. Indeed, the increasing media presence of moonshiners made people intensely curious about actually drinking some moonshine and meeting other moonshiners, and many new to the business came out of the woodwork to quench their curiosity, if not their thirst. The rise of the internet, social media, and a plethora of how-to books aided and abetted new producers and curious individuals who wanted to try their hand at the craft on their own stove tops. What many people found was that much of the moonshine out there was pretty vile stuff, produced to get folks drunk quickly, not for sipping pleasure. Many also discovered the truth of the old moonshiner's adage that "anyone can make liquor, but it takes talent to make good liquor" when they tried to make it themselves with some contraption they bought on Craigslist and ended up with something totally undrinkable. However, there are those who make what distiller Troy Ball calls "keeper liquor" and who developed a steady business. To some extent but not recommended, as long as a novice keeps production relatively low, sells only to known customers, and, unlike Hedrick and Sutton, keeps a low profile, they can generally evade law enforcement. Given the nature of the business, it is hard to know how many moonshiners like this exist, but it seems as if many people know someone like this. Of course, there is always uncertainty in consuming a product that has not been subject to any sort of health or safety standards, and the principle of *caveat emptor* applies to anyone who chooses to buy illicit moonshine.

Perhaps the greatest benefit that the rising popularity of moonshine and the moonshiner produced for both Hedrick and Sutton, or at least his heirs, was their connection in the early 2010s with another postmodern manifestation of the moonshine business, the rise of so-called legal moonshine. Of course, as many observers have noted, "If it's legal, it ain't moonshine." Reporter Clay Risen even wrote an article in *The Atlantic* in 2011 entitled "The World's Silliest Liquor: Fake Moonshine."[42] Be that as it may, the legal moonshine business was a byproduct of changes in the liquor laws of many states, including North Carolina and Tennessee, in the 2000s, which allowed small-batch distillers to operate legally and profitably. For many consumers legal moonshine offers the opportunity to satisfy their curiosity about the taste of moonshine as well as the safety of consuming a product subject to state and federal regulation. In addition, producers soon realized that most folks do not have palates that appreciate even good corn liquor so they began dropping the proof and adding flavorings such as apple, peach, lemon, strawberry, and dozens of other varieties to their lists. Ole Smoky Moonshine in Gatlinburg now offers more than thirty varieties. Legal moonshine gives consumers a little bit of the thrill of doing something naughty without fearing they might go blind, and for tourists in places like Gatlinburg and Pigeon Forge, a quart of moonshine makes a nice souvenir.[43]

By the late 2000s, the microdistilling business was exploding in both North Carolina and Tennessee, and distillers were looking for ways to distinguish their products from those of their competitors. The oldest craft distillery in North Carolina, Piedmont Distillers in Madison, hit on a successful formula in 2007 when it partnered with former moonshiner and NASCAR legend Junior Johnson to produce Junior Johnson's Midnight Moon. The product, supposedly following an "old Johnson family recipe," exploded in popularity and as of July 2018 is available in all fifty states.[44]

Even before Popcorn Sutton's death, Californian and former professional motocross racer Jamey Grosser believed that Sutton's recipe and craggy visage would make a Popcorn-branded product a winner in the marketplace. Grosser approached the legendary moonshiner and soon before his death made a deal for the use of Sutton's recipe, his name, and his image on a product. In

November 2010 Popcorn Sutton's Tennessee White Whiskey was launched in front of a crowd of country music royalty in Nashville. One of Grosser's partners in the business was, appropriately, Hank Williams Jr. The company—which now produces its liquor in Cocke County—advertises that it "use[s] a 100 year old family recipe passed down through generations" with "the same ... rebel attitude as our namesake." In 2018 Popcorn Sutton–branded liquors are now available in much of the nation in liquor stores from Philadelphia to Denver.[45]

Hedrick's turn to grace a mason jar full of legal moonshine came in 2014, when he partnered with Sugarlands Distillery of the new "legal moonshine capital of the world," Gatlinburg, Tennessee. Hedrick's Unaged Rye was the first of the Sugarlands Legends Series which also features branded products fronted by Sutton's buddy Mark Ramsey and *Moonshiners* stars Steven Tickle and Mark Rogers. When Sugarlands launched its Hedrick product, Brent Thompson, director of strategy for the distiller, asserted, "Jim Tom has such an authentic moonshine story. We're thrilled to partner with him to launch our Legends Series—a product line that celebrates the real craftsmen of the trade in Southern Appalachia."[46] How "authentic" any of this is is questionable, but Hedrick has profited significantly from his skillful role of playing the authentic moonshiner. In 2013, even before his partnership with Sugarlands, the website Celebrity Net Worth estimated his net worth at $200,000, assuredly a sizable increase from 1999, when Kelly Riley discovered him. No press releases have been issued as to whether Hedrick still dumpster dives, but it does appear as if he has had some cosmetic work done on his teeth and face.[47]

Conclusion

To be sure, the now ubiquitous popular media presence of Jim Tom Hedrick, Popcorn Sutton, and myriad postmodern moonshiners they have inspired belies the predictions of the imminent demise of moonshine and the moonshiner made around the turn of the century. However, as is generally the case, what has resulted is not a return to some "authentic" moonshine past but something new and modern or even postmodern. The stories of Hedrick and Sutton represent this development well. Both men's significance lies not in their traditional moonshiner skills or their audaciously and effectively evading law enforcement. No, their greatest legacy lies in their ability to play the public role of authentic moonshiners, to give the American people what they expect, to smile, wink at the camera, and head off to the bank with the proceeds of their "authenticity" on their moped or in their Model A Ford truck.

NOTES

1. Information on Amos Owens can be found in M. L. White, *A History of the Life of Amos Owens: The Noted Blockader of Cherry Mountain, NC* (Shelby, NC: Cleveland Star, 1901). For Quill Rose see Wilbur Ziegler and Ben Grosscup, *The Heart of the Alleghanies: Or Western North Carolina Comprising its Topography, History, Resources, People, Narratives, Incidents, and Pictures of Travel, Adventures in Hunting and Fishing and Legends of Its Wilderness* (Raleigh, NC: A. Williams, 1883); Horace Kephart, *Our Southern Highlanders* (New York: Outing Publishing, 1916). For Lewis Redmond see Bruce Stewart, *King of the Moonshiners: Lewis Redmond in Fact and Fiction* (Knoxville: University of Tennessee Press, 2008).

2. Anthony Harkins, *Hillbilly: A Cultural History of an American Icon* (New York: Oxford University Press, 2004); J. W. Williamson, *Hillbillyland: What the Movies Did to the Mountains and What the Mountains Did to the Movies* (Chapel Hill: University of North Carolina Press, 1995).

3. Ibid.

4. Richard Starnes, *Creating the Land of the Sky: Tourism and Society in Western North Carolina* (Tuscaloosa: University of Alabama Press, 1999), 169.

5. Wayne Caldwell, *Requiem by Fire* (New York: Random House, 2010), 236.

6. Brooks Blevins, *Arkansas/Arkansaw: How Bearhunters, Hillbillies, and Good Ol' Boys Defined a State* (Fayetteville: University of Arkansas Press, 2009), 192–93.

7. John Parris, "Whiskey Maker Displays Ancient Craft at Festival," *Asheville Citizen-Times*, July 1, 1984.

8. Kelly Riley, *Moonshine*, Highproof Films, 1999.

9. Popcorn Sutton, *Me and My Likker: The True Story of a Mountain Moonshiner* (self-published, 2000), 1–5.

10. Tom Wilson Jester, *Popcorn Sutton: The Making and Marketing of a Hillbilly Hero* (self-published, 2011), 41.

11. Parris, "Whiskey Maker."

12. Riley, *Moonshine*.

13. Ibid. You can see Hedrick tell the story on YouTube—"Jim Tom Hedrick

(Moonshiners) Tells about Crashing His Harley Davidson," February 18, 2010, www.youtube.com/watch?v=uyJz7zpWCqA.

14. Ibid.

15. Parris, "Whiskey Maker."

16. Jester, *Popcorn Sutton*, 4–5, 61.

17. Riley, *Moonshine.*

18. Neal Hutcheson, *The Last One*, Sucker Punch Pictures, 2009.

19. Jester, *Popcorn Sutton*, 8.

20. Riley, *Moonshine.*

21. Sutton, *Me and My Likker*, 2, 19.

22. Popcorn Sutton, *Me and My Likker*, self-produced video, 2000.

23. Jester, *Popcorn Sutton*, 38–39.

24. Neal Hutcheson, *Mountain Talk*, The Language and Life Project, 2002, https://languageandlife.org/documentaries/mountain-talk/.

25. Neal Hutcheson, *This Is the Last Dam Run of Likker I'll Ever Make*, Sucker Punch Pictures, 2003.

26. Jester, *Popcorn Sutton*, 65.

27. Campbell Robertson, "Yesterday's Moonshiner, Today's Microdistiller," *New York Times*, February 20, 2012.

28. Glen McDonald, "Documentary Filmmaker Keeps Focus Local with New Projects," *Raleigh News and Observer*, November 20, 2014.

29. Eamon Harrington, *Moonshine Madness*, Planet Grade Pictures, 2004.

30. Edie Burnette, "Mountain Moonshiner's Tales of Runnin' 'Likker' Helps Maggie Valley Tourism," *Asheville Citizen-Times*, October 13, 2005.

31. David Huntley, *Hillbilly: The Real Story*, Moore-Huntley Productions, 2008.

32. Neal Hutcheson, *The Last One*, Sucker Punch Pictures, 2008.

33. Matt Stillwell, "Shine," music video, 2008, https://www.youtube.com/watch?v=LRy8xppsh88.

34. Robertson, "Yesterday's Moonshiner."

35. Bill Jones, "Longtime Moonshiner 'Popcorn' Sutton Faces Charges—Again," *Greenville Sun*, March 15, 2008.

36. Jester, *Popcorn Sutton*, 49.

37. Josh Boatwright, "Feds Bust Moonshiner Again," *Asheville Citizen-Times*, March 18, 2008.

38. Stephen Miller, "Legendary Tennessee Moonshiner Plied His Trade to the End," *Wall Street Journal*, March 21, 2009.

39. Neal Hutcheson, *Popcorn Sutton: A Hell of a Life*, Sucker Punch Pictures, 2009.

40. Discovery Channel, *Moonshiners*, https://www.discovery.com/tv-shows /moonshiners/.

41. Ibid.

42. Clay Risen, "The World's Silliest Liquor: Fake Moonshine," *The Atlantic*, August 23, 2011.

43. Ole Smoky Moonshine, http://olesmoky.com/.

44. Junior Johnson's Midnight Moon, www.juniorsmidnightmoon.com/legacy/.

45. PopcornSutton.com, http://popcornsutton.com/.

46. Sugarlands Distilling, Legends Series, www.sugarlandsdistilling.com/legends/.

47. "Jim Tom Hedrick Net Worth," CelebrityNetWorth.com, https://www .celebritynetworth.com/richest-businessmen/business-executives/jim-tom -hedrick-net-worth/.

CHAPTER 3

Moonshiners and the Media: The Twenty-First-Century Trickster

EMILY D. EDWARDS

The Trickster character has made repeated appearances across cultures from ancient mythologies to modern media, literature, and art. In whatever story the Trickster appears, he mischievously disrupts social life, surviving any challenges he may face with pranks and deceit. The Trickster is amoral but not immoral; nobility and wickedness are tangled within him. He embodies both dark negative energy and light positive strength together in one conflicted being. More frequently depicted as a male character in patriarchal cultures, the Trickster pokes fun at social pretense, good manners, and taboos. Where female Tricksters do exist in patriarchal traditions, their male counterparts tend to culturally overshadow them.[1] Whatever gender, the Trickster's use of cunning, theft, and deception to defy rules and oppressive social structures are among his strongest character traits. In folklore he can be foolish or wise, and in some mythologies he is divine. It is also worth noting that a few Tricksters in myth and folklore were notorious drunkards.

This essay will argue that a prime reason the image of the Appalachian moonshiner has continued to thrive into the twenty-first century is due to popular media promotion of the moonshiner's Trickster personality, appealing to aspects of the American psyche as it fights to sustain traditional, even outmoded ways of thinking in a rapidly shifting and baffling world, an era of profound social tension. Like the mythological Trickster, the moonshining character in moving image media is an outlaw and mischief-maker. He utilizes his clever skills to turn his corn crop (barley, rye, or fruit) into a more valuable high-proof liquor commodity. Using cunning to get away with his illegal entrepreneurship, the Trickster moonshiner dodges taxes, licensing fees, and laws but not the censure of his community's more principled citizens.[2]

Archetypes and Trickster DNA

Carl Jung and Joseph Campbell viewed the Trickster as an archetype of the collective unconscious, a set of primordial patterns that implied a universal human nature.[3] They believed this inherited collective unconscious to be a universally shared aspect of the human psyche that explains similarities in themes, stories, and characters from around the world and across time. Like instinct, the archetypes of the collective unconscious are a universal phenomenon that embodies the psychic life of humanity going back to our earliest ancestors.[4] Archetypes are reoccurring manifestations in art and culture. After an archetype like the Trickster enters an artist's individual consciousness from the collective unconscious, the artist transforms the archetype, giving it expression within his or her own traditions and experience. Archetypes are preconscious mental energies that slip into the media producer's consciousness to activate individual creativity. The influence of the archetype is involuntary. The artist is generally unaware of this process, yet many filmmakers and media producers intentionally hope to tap into the power of archetypes in a deliberate way, giving rise to textbooks such as William Indick's *Psychology for Screenwriters*, which outlines Campbell's mythical hero's journey as a guide for writers and describes the archetypes, including the Trickster, that a protagonist may encounter in the course of his adventures.[5] This intentional manipulation of the archetype is dodgy business and apt to yield weak stereotypes rather than powerful archetypes, yet there seems to be an unconscious and uncontrollable psychic "oozing" between archetypes and media texts.[6] Others believe the Trickster does not necessarily emerge from a shared collective unconscious but argue that the Trickster is embedded in the genetic information that guides human development from the distant past into the future; in other words, the human brain is wired in ways that produce Trickster traits again and again in the stories of wide-ranging cultures.[7]

If the Trickster resides in the human brain or psyche to blatantly scorn and ridicule authority, the moonshining character in American media is clearly one expression of the Trickster, poking fun at manners, taboos, and the laws of government. The moonshiner's very merchandise is designed to free the brain of social pretension and lure it into drunkenness. When characters in movies and television take a drink of moonshine, there is always a notable reaction. Audiences watch as the characters gasp, snort, cough, choke, or wheeze; at the very least, there will be a grimace and a grin. A character might call the moonshine "smooth," but the visual cues say otherwise. Clearly, moonshine is not a sophisticated cocktail, craft beer, or expensive glass of wine. It is harsh, nasty swill whose primary function is intoxication. The moonshiner's creation helps awaken his customers to their own pomposity as they enter that liminal space between the daylight world of sober, respectable consciousness and the darker world of reckless inebriation and oblivion. The moonshiner befuddles his customers, encouraging them to betray their fixation with status, rules, and righteousness. The Trickster moonshiner also invites his customers to remember through that intoxicated cloud that the soul is not pure. Moonshine is the Trickster's best medicine.

Moonshining in Moving Image Media

From the beginning of the American film industry, hundreds of movies and television programs have been made in which moonshining characters emerged to distill plot lines along with their homemade liquors. Moonshiners appeared in movies located in an assortment of settings, but in particular they populated rural areas, often set in the South, from the Appalachian Mountains to the swamps of Georgia and Florida. Some of the earliest appearances of moonshining characters were as shadowy villains, characters who provided the obstacles for a protagonist to overcome. Before the Eighteenth Amendment and during national Prohibition (1920–1933), moonshiners in the movies were often portrayed as bad men with beautiful daughters (or cousins, sisters, or girlfriends). The earliest known fictional film about mountain people, *The Moonshiner* (1904), featured violent moonshining characters and the murder of a revenuer.[8] In movies such as *The Revenue Man and His Girl* (1911), *The Moonshine Maid and the Man* (1914), *The Eyes of Mystery* (1918), *Border River* (1919), and *King of the Pack* (1926), the moonshiner was a villain for the hero to defeat. The protagonist of these early melodramatic films was generally a hapless revenuer or other law officer who sought to uncover the moonshiner's illegal entrepreneurship, bust up the still, and restore law, order, and sobriety to the region. The protagonist often found this mission compromised when he fell in love with the moonshiner's daughter (or cousin, sister, or girlfriend).

By mid-century the rugged still and clear liquid in a mason jar or earthenware jug had been established as the visual cues for moonshine, and the cunning of the mythic Trickster figure had become evident in the moonshining character. Movies like *Private Snuffy Smith* (1942), *Carbine Williams* (1952), and *Stalag 17* (1953) flipped previous roles, making the moonshiner the protagonist rather than the villain and showing how the clever Trickster could triumph over oppression. While some argue that American media depictions have consistently pigeonholed the moonshiner as an ignorant and lazy hillbilly, there is a difference between the media stereotype and the Trickster archetype. The stereotype is that tendency media have to crudely paint all members of a group, such as moonshiners, with the same brush and without regard to individual differences. However, an archetype escapes categorization; the traits surface in media characters regardless of region, ethnicity, race, religion, era, class, or genre.[9]

After television joined movies in the visual entertainment mix, the moonshiner as a humorous and less threatening character began to regularly appear in comedy series such as *The Andy Griffith Show* (1960–68), *The Beverly Hillbillies* (1962–71), and *The Dukes of Hazzard* (1979–85). A few dangerous moonshiners continued to be a part of the media landscape with hapless lawmen still falling for the moonshiner's woman in movies such as *I Walk the Line* (1970) and *White Lightning* (1973). But where the moonshiner as an evil criminal persisted in visual media, lascivious and villainous characters, such as the moonshiners in *Deliverance* (1972), they also served a Trickster role by overturning polite social customs and forcing a protagonist to face his own baser instincts. In movies like *Dixie Dynamite* (1976), *The Moonshine War* (1970), and *Gator* (1976), corrupt law enforcement, sheriffs, and federal agents become part of the moonshining operation or simply demand a cut of the profits. The Trickster moonshiner evolves in these movies from a lawbreaker to a cultural hero, standing on the side of decency even after he has displayed his crudeness and broken the laws of a government he may ultimately defend. The Trickster moonshiner crosses boundaries to protect what the movie portrays as "true justice" from the government's own crooked agents. This ability to cross boundaries is one of the recognized characteristics of the Trickster in myth and folklore; he can change shapes and allegiances, assuming different forms within a story. Media in the second half of the twentieth century generally presented the moonshiner as this Trickster hero, a cunning protagonist with rough edges and a sometimes violent temperament but with a core integrity that is loyal to family and friends. In movies such as *Thunder Road* (1958), *The*

Last American Hero (1973), *Moonrunners* (1975), *Thunder and Lightning* (1977), and *Moonshine Highway* (1996), the Trickster also developed the driving skills and road wisdom that helped to make great car chases a recognized feature of moonshine and bootleg movies.

"Real" Media Moonshiners in the New Millennium

Reality media became increasingly popular in the late 1990s and the status of unscripted entertainment continued to grow into the early 2000s along with scripted entertainment based on actual events and personalities. Even as the "reality" of reality television was questioned, audience apparent fascination with "truthful" entertainment triggered a growing interest in biographical films or biopics as well as documentaries.[10] Though fictional Trickster moonshiners continued into the twenty-first century with movies like *Dixie Times* (2012), *Whiskey Business* (2012), and a movie remake of *The Dukes of Hazzard* (2005), there seemed to be an emerging interest in real moonshiners, so that moonshining personalities would have a robust presence as characters in the reality genres: documentaries, biopics, reality television series, and internet videos.

The historical moonshiner presented in documentaries was often depicted heroically. Lewis Redmond in *The Outlaw Lewis Redmond* (2009) is described as a Robin Hood figure who emerged during the Reconstruction period after the Civil War, when many white southerners distrusted government agents. In this documentary, folklorist Dot Jackson expresses on-screen her disgust for these government representatives, telling us that "the absolute trash of the earth became officials." She suggests that people with criminal backgrounds obtained revenuer jobs, so the moonshiner became a champion for outwitting them, even if the moonshiner's actions involved violence and murder. Similarly, the documentary *Blind Tiger: The Legend of Bell Tree Smith* (2014) describes the moonshiner William Anderson Smith as both a criminal and a humanitarian. However, these historical figures were not the only "reality" moonshiners in the twenty-first century; there were also contemporary personalities. The legacy of the historical moonshiner was important, but the contemporary character seemed to hold audience fascination. The new millennium saw a boom in short documentaries about moonshine produced by both amateur and professional filmmakers. These included many how-to videos introducing viewers to a variety of moonshiners from Tennessee, Georgia, Florida, and Virginia, and even a video about distilling moonshine on a sailboat. These videos helped to promote moonshining celebrities such as North Carolina's Jim Tom Hedrick, who also appears in the short documentary *Moonshine* (2000) and the feature documentary *Still Making Moonshine* (2008).

One of the more visible moonshining celebrities of the new millennium, Marvin "Popcorn" Sutton, appeared in Neal Hutcheson's Emmy award–winning documentary, *This Is the Last Dam Run of Likker I'll Ever Make* (2002). The cult popularity of this documentary encouraged the Discovery Channel's reality television series *Moonshiners* (2011–), and another Hutcheson documentary, released five years after Sutton's suicide in 2009, *Popcorn Sutton: A Hell of a Life* (2014). Sutton also appeared in the History Channel documentary *Hillbilly: The Real Story* (2007), and social media users shared various video clips of the moonshiner. Other footage of Sutton was featured after his death in the first season of the television series *Moonshiners*, which sensationalized the lives of various moonshiners as they produced illegal liquor and evaded the law. The popularity of the *Moonshiners* series additionally inspired a spin-off, *Tickle* (2013–), based on the character of Steven Ray Tickle, who manages a Trickster-like theft of another moonshiner's stash in the first season. These series were among a number of trendy "redneck reality" television series such as *Hollywood Hillbillies* (2014–), *Duck Dynasty* (2012–), *Swamp People* (2010–), and *Hatfield and McCoys: White Lightning* (2013). These series celebrated unfiltered opinions, rude behaviors, and innate ingenuity, presenting a vision of rural, disenfranchised white America and making a joke of anything elite, educated, or cosmopolitan. While moonshine was not always present or an on-screen focus in some redneck reality programming, moonshine was a steady and recognizable prop.

Popcorn Sutton's continued appearances in documentaries, television series, and internet videos after his death provided this moonshiner with the media immortality usually reserved for the Trickster gods of myth. Many things about Popcorn Sutton's continued media presence suggest the Trickster. Sutton posted obscene signs in his house, wore a raccoon penis bone in his hat, and in a YouTube interview with actor Johnny Knoxville bragged that he is "the only man around here that has a two-inch dick and a sixteen-inch tongue and knows how to use both of them." With his suicide, Sutton played the ultimate trick, evading a federal prison term and also cheating cancer out of a slow and painful death. Sutton even had a special gravestone made for himself with the epitaph "Popcorn Says Fuck You."[11]

Jesco White and his extended family also became popular "reality" Tricksters in the new millennium. It is not difficult to see the path of inheritance from the historical moonshiner to his contemporary counterpart and the consumer demand for outlawed substances in addition to moonshine. In many of the documentaries, reality series, and video clips featuring the White family, drugs seem to have supplemented if not usurped moonshine as the preferred route to inebriation, although the iconic moonshine jar is often sitting somewhere nearby. In Julien Nitzberg's documentary *The Wild and Wonderful Whites of West Virginia* (2009) and Dominic Murphy's biopic of Jesco White, *White Lightnin'* (2009), the obvious ambition is to party hard, get high, "pass out, dream, go off." In *The Wild and Wonderful Whites of West Virginia*, Bo White proudly admits to smoking crack, and Derek White asks, "Do you want to hear the Boone County mating call?" as he holds up and shakes a bottle of pills in a lewd gesture of defiant prescription drug abuse. What remains of the moonshine Trickster in these drug-using individuals is the crass behavior, deceit, lawlessness, violence, and guile.

Whether with moonshine, meth, dope, prescription drugs, or lighter fluid, the Trickster has an obvious longing for the high that will set his appetites free from their ever-so-loose tethers. But the high also dampens disappointments and eventually drowns unfulfilled longings so that the aggravations of living can be temporarily forgotten in the stupor. The Trickster's energy seems dedicated to planning for that next excessive binge. Brandon White describes the binge that landed him in prison as "one hell of a night. I went on a rampage pretty much."

Real people are more complicated than an archetype, but popular media depictions of Popcorn Sutton and his fellow moonshiners made these real men into characters. They are portrayed as brazen and ridiculous personalities who persist at their illegal craft in an era when unlawful moonshining would seem a quaint and losing endeavor. Because the illegal production and consumption of moonshine is no longer a priority in national concerns, the contemporary moonshiner seems like an oddity from the dusty pages of a folktale; this is particularly true for a time when interested customers can legally purchase gleaming copper distillation equipment online and lawful moonshine is readily available in liquor stores with sales tax taken at the register. Yet the "reality" moonshiners carry on with their prohibited business. They continue to disturb established perceptions of truth, property, and civilized conduct while their drunken antics are fully documented for public view. The combination of contemporary reality with what seems like the folklore of a bygone era makes the moonshining Trickster an interesting oddity for some viewers and a champion of authentic America for others.

In contemporary media stories about moonshining, the government plays a consistent role as a stern, hypocritical, and dishonest authority. Government laws moralistically forbid the high and complicate the moonshiner's livelihood, but principally the Trickster believes the government objects to the moonshiner's cleverness in evading licensing fees and taxes. The government wants its cut. For his part, the moonshiner cannot see how government taxes and licensing fees benefit him personally with roads, dams, schools, post offices, bridges, clinics, airports, investments in research to advance human potential, or any other service. Such things are not part of his consideration. For the moonshiner, the government is just a giant, greedy, institutional bully that wants to tell him what to do, steal from him, and threaten his freedom. When the Trickster does personally benefit from government services even though he has managed not to pay any taxes, he suffers no guilt. Instead, the Trickster rejoices in his own cleverness in swindling a stupid system.

The perception that a useless government is up to no good becomes reinforced in the media narrative when corrupt agents intimidate or demand a cut of the moonshiner's profits. This may resonate with some contemporary audiences who are suspicious that a dishonest government manipulates and complicates their lives. It also explains a popular internet meme with a photo of Popcorn Sutton that carries the slogan "We honor our outlaws because our leaders are crooks." The Trickster's response to this perceived oppression is a determination to fool the tyrant government and its corrupt representatives in whatever way he can. For example, D. Ray White and his wife Bertie convinced a doctor to report that all thirteen of their kids had psychiatric issues and thereby scammed the government to collect disability checks for each child. Outsmarting the oppressor is a quintessential Trickster move.

The Trickster in folklore is often portrayed as an animal, an instinctual psyche with the potential to turn dangerous. For example, the Trickster in the mythology of several Native American tribes is the anthropomorphic Coyote. The mythological animal Trickster represents that "primitive developmental level common to humanity."[12] The moonshining Trickster in popular media is not literally an animal but represents that instinctual animal psyche. If not precisely comparable to the Coyote Trickster of many Native Americans, the contemporary Trickster moonshiner as he is depicted in popular media might be likened to a mongrel dog—scruffy, unruly, lustful, flea bitten, carpet soiling, garbage scrounging, food stealing, and happily willing to bite the hand that indirectly feeds him. However, on many levels, he is a loyal and likable cur. Let off the leash, the uninhibited drives of the animal psyche can be dangerous, but equally dangerous are drives that are wounded and caged. Suppressed instincts can be overpowering and destructive. As any animal control officer will tell you, a feral dog is at his most dangerous when he is wounded or frightened. Threatened, injured, or imprisoned, the Trickster may turn vicious and attack, which he often does in media depictions. The Trickster Coyote of the Navajos may get pulverized and cut to pieces, but he continuously comes back to life.[13] Similarly, the Trickster moonshiner in popular media is not easily defeated. The Coyote and Dog are both survivors.

The Tricksters of *Lawless*

One big-screen biopic in the new millennium is particularly significant for the portrayal of multiple "real" moonshining Tricksters. Based on Matt Bondurant's historical novel about his grandfather and great uncles who had a moonshining business during the Prohibition era, the movie *Lawless* (2012) portrays the conflict between the Bondurant brothers and a corrupt law that demands a cut of all the area moonshiners' profits, emphasizing the continuing media narrative about ruthless government and its crooked representatives.[14] The biopic is based on historical events, but as Matt Bondurant explains in a video interview with Harry Knowles, the historical records and family stories were vague on the details. This sketchiness meant more interpretive leeway for the archetypal Trickster to emerge in both the novel and in the reinterpretation of that novel into film.

The historical Bondurant brothers owned a gas station and restaurant in rural Franklin County, Virginia, but their primary business was a moonshining operation deep in the Virginia Mountains. In the movie, each of the brothers represents different aspects of the moonshining Trickster: the cunning and unpredictable maliciousness of the oldest brother, Howard (Jason

Clark); the boastful and stubbornly proud middle brother, Forrest (Tom Hardy); and the foolish, lustful, and fun-loving youngest brother, Jack (Shia LaBeouf). In a voice-over at the beginning of the movie, Jack says the brothers believed they were immortal. During World War I, Howard Bondurant was the only survivor from his battalion, and Forrest Bondurant managed to live through the deadly Spanish flu pandemic. Like mythological gods, the brothers do not fear death.

Special Deputy Charley Rakes (Guy Pearce) comes to Franklin County from the city along with the shady Virginia Commonwealth Attorney Mason Wardel (Tim Tolin) to join forces with the local sheriff (Bill Camp) and his deputies in a plan for extortion. These men are not interested in restoring sobriety and order to Franklin County but want to "work it out so everybody gets to do some business." The authorities demand a cut of the profits from each of the substantial number of bootleggers in the area; otherwise, their illegal moonshining operations will be shut down and they will be imprisoned. Rakes tells Forrest, "I'm the one who is going to make your life real difficult from now on if you don't toe the line, country boy." The movie version of this character is no backwoods cop but a villainous urban government official. On the surface, Rakes seems like a fastidious man with fancy clothes, overly finicky about the fine, tight-fitting, almost surgical-looking gloves that he noticeably and persistently wears. However, the movie makes it obvious that Rakes is a sadistic sociopath, a sexual deviant whose cruelty far outshines the violence of the Bondurant brothers. Rakes will protest that he is not a "nance" (as he is called in the movie); however, the movie suggests he is monstrous, far more sinister than the usual corrupt government agent. For some audiences, particularly those who view twenty-first century government protections for LGBT populations and the legalization of gay marriage as repulsive and unchristian, the movie portrayal of Special Deputy Rakes adds another profound reason to hate the federal government.

All the other moonshiners in the area will succumb to Rakes's threats, but Forrest refuses to pay up, warning, "I'm a Bondurant. We don't lay down for nobody." When the local sheriff complains to Rakes that they may have a problem with the Bondurants, Rakes tells the sheriff that these mountain boys have some Indian blood in them, Cherokee. He further insults the Bondurants for being "animalistic" in their nature. When the sheriff implies that Forrest Bondurant is indestructible, Rakes laughs. "You mean immortal?" Not willing to go that far, Rakes tells the sheriff that a Thompson submachine gun can easily handle the "immortal" Bondurant brothers.

The Bondurants' disabled young assistant, Cricket (Dane Dehaan), is "mechanically gifted," building the distillery and putting a souped-up engine in their bootlegging car, but Cricket is too sweet, too innocent, too humble to be a Trickster. When Rakes comes to Cricket's cabin looking for money and a still, the lawman shows his evil nature by severely bludgeoning an unarmed Jack. After Jack is brutalized, Forrest tells his younger brother, "As long as you are my brother, you will never let this happen again. . . . Jack, it is not the violence that sets a man apart; it is the distance he is prepared to go." Forrest reminds Jack that the Bondurants are survivors and that Jack must control his fear in order to go that magical distance. A primary characteristic of the Trickster is his willingness to breach taboos.[15] This willingness sets the Bondurants apart from all the other bootleggers in Franklin County.

The youngest of the three brothers, Jack portrays the Trickster clown, which is most obvious in his courtship of a preacher's daughter, Bertha (Mia Wasikowska). Jack goes to her father's church drunk. During a religious foot-washing ritual, Jack loses a shoe when his inebriated sickness drives him stumbling from the church to vomit. He will suffer further humiliation of having his shoe returned to him in a sack. Jack's humorous courtship contrasts with Forrest's more solemn but sexually charged romance with a former dancer, Maggie, who fled the ruthlessness of the city for a quieter country life.

Jack has a childlike mentality that guides him from one mischievous exploit to another, but he is plucky, unafraid of joining forces with the mobster he admires, Floyd Banner (Gary Oldman). Banner's henchmen capture Jack as he and Cricket are bootlegging moonshine across county lines. When Jack cries out that he is a Bondurant, Banner spares him an execution. Banner appreciates the Bondurant brothers for standing up to Special Deputy Rakes, so he tells Jack the address of the men who had earlier slit Forrest's throat, though the Bondurant, with his legendary indestructibility, managed to survive. These men had been Banner's former employees but betrayed the mobster to work for Rakes. Jack proudly returns to the restaurant with his moonshine profits and Banner's special "gift" for the brothers, the identity and location of the men who attacked Forrest. With this gift in hand, the two oldest Bondurant brothers track down, torture, and kill Rakes's men. They perform a bloody castration on one of the gangsters and have Jack deliver the testicles to Rakes in a jar of moonshine wrapped in pink tissue paper: a particularly gruesome trick, but the Bondurant Tricksters go the distance.

For a time, the Bondurant brothers see nice profits running their moonshine to gangsters, sustaining the urban criminal empire with their backwoods product. However, the world is a precarious one, and when the Trickster thinks he has control over it is when he is at his most vulnerable. Jack sets out to impress Bertha with his newfound riches, his new car, new camera, and nice clothes. He buys Bertha a dress and recklessly shows off the family distillery. Rakes and his men are spying on Jack and follow him. However, the sly Howard is also watching and howls to warn Jack that Rakes and his men are nearby, but too late. Rakes and his posse uncover the brothers' moonshine business and destroy it. Jack and Howard escape and Bertha is let go, but Rakes viciously murders Cricket while his men are busy posing for victory photos at the busted stills. The movie hints that Rakes also did some unspeakable violence to Cricket in addition to murdering him. This encourages further abhorrence for a federal government that would hire and legitimize this urban deviant. Even the local sheriff can no longer stomach the federal government's special deputy.

With Cricket's death and the destroyed distillery, the Bondurant brothers are emotionally wounded, angry, and ready for vengeance. A remorseful sheriff warns the brothers to lay low, explaining that Wardel and Rakes have set up a blockade with agents from the Bureau of Alcohol, Tobacco, and Firearms who have come to wage war on the moonshiners. Even the gentle Maggie cannot tame the wild, wounded animal in Forrest, who is ready for revenge. Forrest learns that on the night he was attacked, he did not miraculously walk to the hospital on his own with a "throat cut from ear to ear" but that Maggie had rescued him. She still refuses to tell him what happened to her at the hands of Rakes's men, but Forrest guesses the truth. All three brothers must have vengeance.

Tricksters may be wily, but they also react emotionally. Determined to get Rakes, Jack races to the blockade without caution or plan. The other bootleggers take up arms to follow, and Jack's older brothers quickly arrive on the scene, where a shootout proceeds. The sheriff turns on Rakes, shooting him in the leg and sparing Jack another bullet. The sheriff desperately tries to calm the situation, but Rakes seems determined to kill the brothers. The brothers are all hit multiple times, but like the Trickster Coyote, all will survive. Though severely wounded, Jack limps after Rakes and shoots him. Howard manages to finish the job with a knife in the special deputy's back.

The movie concludes with the wild animal psyche tamed and the wounded one healed. Jack narrates, explaining that in 1933 Prohibition and the great Franklin County moonshine conspiracy were finished. The brothers recuperate, marry, and become ordinary men with legal occupations like farming and textile mill work. Jack also explains that the brothers were not mythically immortal, even Forrest. "In the end it was dumb luck and pneumonia that got him. It was as simple and indifferent as that." Jack's last observation is that "it sure does get real quiet around here." No longer caged, wounded, or threatened, the wild animal psyche can curl up on the porch and nap.

Myth, Movies, and Moonshine

Like any storyteller, a filmmaker unconsciously transforms story and visual performance into symbols, endowing these with psychological importance for audiences. Displayed in popular media, the moonshining Trickster is not simply an individual flaunting his deviance but a performer on a larger emotional stage. The archetypal Trickster may be most attractive to the adolescent psyche at a time when the young individual is dealing with a changing body, sexual appetites, and powerful emotions in the awkward process of becoming a mature person. The Trickster represents that adolescent celebration of the untamed psyche before it transforms and becomes yoked to adult accountability. The juvenile Trickster may not be juvenile in age but is a character with childish behaviors and immature qualities, yet he will outwit the more powerful adult or responsible characters and defy their grown-up rules.

For the broader culture, the Trickster's appeal arises during times of great social change, so the moonshiner's popularity in American media during the early twenty-first century is not such a complex puzzle. The Trickster represents that volatile creative energy that appears in a society during transitional periods.[16] When contemporary audiences come upon the moonshining Trickster in popular media, they see a character whose actions reflect the proud stubbornness of someone pressured by social situations, economic conditions, and changing American values. The moonshining Trickster becomes the champion for a wounded, twenty-first-century working-class white audience whose lives seems fixed in a hard and seemingly hopeless economic reality that their government has either ignored at best or fueled at worst. This is an audience that will happily subscribe to the unswerving media message that all government agents operate under some degree of corruption. Their perverse government will protect Wall Street gangsters, crooked bankers, dishonest career politicians, illegal immigrants, uppity women, LGBTQ populations, and other minorities but ultimately ignore or cheat the working-class white man. Disadvantaged by globalization and an information economy, white working-class populations can rally their demographic angst around the media moonshiner's illegal business successes and his abilities to deceive a government that has given them both such a raw deal. As Helena Bassil-Morozow noted: "In the sterile post-industrial society, where all the corners are smoothed up and all the grotesqueness is carefully camouflaged, there is no place for strong and raw emotions."[17] It is no accident the moonshining Trickster reflects this anger, transforming him into a sly and arrogant swindler, fighting to maintain an old way of life in a rapidly modernizing and mystifying world.

For others, the present-day stories of the Trickster moonshiner might be viewed as cautionary tales, showing audiences what happens to people who mock progressive values. ("Isn't it sad to be a poor, ignorant redneck?") The toothless antics of the reality Trickster might be amusing for elite audiences, but his behaviors are also offensive to those who find the animal psyche he represents disgusting or frightening. The Trickster poses a danger for polite, urban populations. The media stories reveal that civilized communities cannot force their notions of proper etiquette and political correctness on the outlaw moonshiner; he will stubbornly enjoy the great astonishment of living in his own wicked way.

It is important to understand that the moonshiner is not the only Trickster manifestation in twenty-first century American media. Tricksters can have many incarnations: as fictional characters in various scripted media genres or as personalities in other forms of reality media. He might even appear as the central character in ongoing or reoccurring news stories, perhaps as a politician, sports celebrity, religious leader, or businessman. In patriarchal America the Trickster is most likely a male character: a lustful, promiscuous, foolish, boasting, rebellious, and amusing con man who slips across conventional boundaries to defraud his way to success or simple survival. In mythology the Trickster is "the protagonist of obscene adventures from which he escapes humiliated. . . . He plays abominable tricks for which humans have to pay much of the price."[18] Society may want to control potentially dangerous periods of transition, but whenever the Trickster appears in cultural abundance, humanity may be in for a rocky ride.

When the Trickster takes a leading role in media stories, he is portraying the animal psyche's rebellion but he also symbolizes the primitive cunning and skills necessary for survival. Yet the mythological Trickster does not simply survive; he remakes his world, just as in the mythologies of multiple American Indian nations Coyote sculpts his own feces into human beings, thereby creating the flawed, stinking mess of humankind.[19] According to this myth, it is the animal psyche that made human beings what we are. The Trickster moonshiner celebrates this animal, thumbing his nose at society and rejoicing in the imperfect, scatological human predicament. Whether it is mythical memory or biological inheritance, the reflection of the mythological Trickster in portraits of the media moonshiner helps explain why these characters still fascinate audiences at a particularly volatile juncture of American history.

FILMOGRAPHY

The Andy Griffith Show. Television series. Created by Sheldon Leonard. Prod. Danny Thomas. CBS, 1960–68.

The Beverly Hillbillies. Television series. Created by Paul Henning. CBS, 1962–71.

Blind Tiger: The Legend of Bell Tree Smith. Documentary. Dir. Seth Ingram. Exit Eleven Media, 2014.

Border River. Dir. Edgar Jones. Arrow, 1919.

Carbine Williams. Dir. Richard Thorpe. Metro-Goldwyn-Mayer, 1952.

Deliverance. Dir. John Boorman. Warner Bros., 1972.

Dixie Dynamite. Dir. Lee Frost. Dimension Pictures, 1976.

Dixie Times. Dir. Sherrie Peterson, Ken R. Wheeler, Stacy Turner. Coosa Valley Entertainment, 2012.

Duck Dynasty. Television series. A&E Television Network, 2012–.

The Dukes of Hazzard. Dir. Jay Chandrasekhar. Warner Bros., 2005.

The Dukes of Hazzard. Television series. Created by Gy Waldron and Jerry Rushing. Warner Bros. Television and CBS, 1979–85.

The Eyes of Mystery. Dir. Tod Browning. Metro Pictures Corporation, 1918.

Hatfields and McCoys: White Lightning. Television series. History Channel, 2013.

Hillbilly: The Real Story. Documentary. Dir. David Huntley. History Channel, 2007.

Hollywood Hillbillies. Prod. Mike Pack. ReelzChannels, 2014–.

I Walk the Line. Dir. John Frankenheimer. Columbia Pictures, 1970.

Johnny Knoxville Interviews Popcorn Sutton. YouTube, 2009.

King of the Pack. Dir. Frank Richardson. Gotham, 1926.

The Last American Hero. Dir. Lamont Johnson. Twentieth Century Fox Film Corporation, 1973.

Lawless. Dir. John Hilicoat. The Weinstein Company, 2012.

Lawless Q&A with Harry Knowles and Matt Bondurant. Ain't It Cook News, 2012.

Legendary Moonshiner: Popcorn Sutton (The Day Before He Died). Dir. Andy Armstrong. YouTube, March 15, 2009.

Moonrunners. Dir. Gy Waldron. United Artists, 1975.

Moonshine. Documentary short. Dir. Kelly L. Riley. YouTube, 2000.

The Moonshine Maid and the Man. Dir. Charles Gaskill. Vitagraph, 1914.

The Moonshiner. Biograph Studio, 1904.

Moonshiners. Television series. Discovery Channel, 2011–.

Moonshine Highway. TV movie. Dir. Andy Armstrong. Hallmark Channel, 1996.

The Moonshine War. Dir. Richard Quine. Metro-Goldwyn-Mayer, 1970.

The Outlaw Lewis Redmond. Documentary. Dir. Neal Hutcheson. PBS, 2009.

Popcorn Sutton: A Hell of a Life. Documentary. Dir. Neal Hutcheson. Sucker Punch Pictures, 2014.

Private Snuffy Smith. Dir. Edward F. Cline. Monogram Pictures, 1942.

The Revenue Man and His Girl. Dir. D. W. Griffith. Biograph Company, 1911.

Stalag 17. Dir. Billy Wilder. Paramount Pictures, 1953.

Still Making Moonshine. Documentary. Dir. Kelly Riley. Highproof Films, 2008.

Swamp People. Television series. History Channel, 2010–.

This Is the Last Dam Run of Likker I'll Ever Make. Documentary. Dir. Neal Hutcheson. PBS, 2002.

Thunder Road. Dir. Arthur Ripley. United Artists, 1958.

Tickle. Television series. Prod. Joe Schneider. Discovery Channel, 2013–.

Whiskey Business. Dir. Robert Iscove. Country Music Television, 2012.

White Lightning. Dir. Joseph Sargent. United Artist, 1973.

White Lightnin'. Dir. Dominic Murphy. Filmfreak Distributie, 2009.

The Wild and Wonderful Whites of West Virginia. Documentary. Dir. Julien Nitzberg. Tribeca Film, 2009.

NOTES

1. See William J. Hynes and William Doty, eds., *Mythical Trickster Figures: Contours, Contexts, and Criticisms* (Tuscaloosa: University of Alabama Press, 1993), 335.
2. Jaime Joyce observes that moonshine is the star of many Hollywood films and television productions in *Moonshine: A Cultural History of America's Infamous Liquor* (Minneapolis, MN: Zenith Press, 2014).
3. See Carl Gustav Jung and Joseph Campbell, *The Portable Jung* (New York: Viking Press, 1971), 61–69. For more on the Trickster archetype, see also Joseph Campbell, *The Masks of God: Primitive Mythology* (New York: Penguin, 1976); and Carl Jung, "On the Psychology of the Trickster Figure," in *The Trickster: A Study in America Indian Mythology*, ed. Paul Radin (New York: Philosophical Library, 1956), 195–211.
4. Jung and Campbell, *Portable Jung*, 53.
5. See William Indick, *Psychology for Screenwriters: Building Conflict in Your Script* (Studio City, CA: Michael Wiese Productions, 2004), 126–28.
6. See Terrie Waddell, *Wild/Lives: Trickster, Place and Liminality on Screen* (London: Routledge, 2010), 2.
7. David Williams describes the Trickster character in stories from around the world and attempts to connect these stories to the biological design and function of the human brain in *The Trickster Brain: Neuroscience, Evolution, and Narrative* (Lantham: Lexington Books, 2012).
8. J. W. Williamson examined early movies with hillbilly characters, many of whom were moonshiners. He suggests that the hillbilly character in movies is a monster, alien, free spirit, wild person, occasional hero, and often a comic fool—in other words, a Trickster. See *Hillbillyland: What the Movies Did to the Mountains and What the Mountains Did to the Movies* (Chapel Hill: University of North Carolina Press, 1995). For more about early movie plots, see J. W. Williamson, *Southern Mountaineers in Silent Films: Plot Synopses of Movies about Moonshining and Other Mountain Topics, 1904–1929* (Jefferson, NC: McFarland, 1994).
9. For example, in *Corn from a Jar: Moonshining in the Great Smoky Mountains* (Gatlinburg, TN: Great Smoky Mountains Association, 2013), Daniel S. Pierce argues that media portraits of the moonshiner tend to confirm stereotypes, when

real stories reveal intelligent, hardworking people coping to survive desperate economic circumstances.

10. Lisa K. Lundy, Amanda M. Ruth, and Travis D. Park discuss the rise of reality television in "Simply Irresistible: Reality TV Consumption Patterns," *Communication Quarterly* 56, no. 2 (2008): 208–25. Similarly, Dennis Bingham chronicles the popularity of the biopic in *Whose Lives Are They Anyway?: The Biopic as Contemporary Film Genre* (New Brunswick, N.J.: Rutgers University Press, 2010), 10. Patricia Aufderheide discusses the growing audience interest in documentaries in *Documentary Film: A Very Short Introduction* (New York: Oxford University Press, 2007), 126.

11. Sutton's story is detailed in Tim Murphy, "Tales of the Last Moonshiner," *Mother Jones*, July 11, 2010, accessed November 2, 2016.

12. See Hynes and Doty, *Mythical Trickster Figures*, 15.

13. Williams, *Trickster Brain*, 128. A modern media reflection of the American Indian Coyote Trickster can be found in the character of Wile E. Coyote from the Looney Tunes and Merrie Melodies series of Warner Bros. cartoons. The elaborate tricks of the ever-hungry Coyote always fail, but he survives so he can attempt to deceive successfully in the next episode.

14. See Matt Bondurant's novel *The Wettest County in the World: A Novel Based on a True Story* (New York: Scribner, 2008).

15. Laura Makarius explains in detail how the Trickster must break laws and prohibitions in "The Myth of the Trickster: The Necessary Breaker of Taboos," in *Mythical Trickster Figures*, ed. Hynes and Doty, 67–86.

16. See Helena Bassil-Morozow, *The Trickster in Contemporary Film* (London: New York, 2012), 18.

17. Bassil-Morozow, *Trickster in Contemporary Film*, 109.

18. Makarius, "Myth of the Trickster," 67.

19. Williams, *Trickster Brain*, 35.

CHAPTER 4

Making Criminals, Making Ends Meet: Constructing Criminality in Franklin County, Virginia

ROBERT T. PERDUE

My father is a beer drinker, and I rarely see him drink liquor. He does, however, like to keep some moonshine around. I think the main reason is to share it with those who have never tried the stuff, to be the bad influence in a good-hearted kind of way. The allure of moonshine for my father and many others is that it is illicit. Despite the growing acceptance and enthusiasm surrounding moonshine, it remains illegal in every U.S. state. Does engaging in the illegal action of sipping and sharing untaxed liquor make my father a criminal? Most would probably contend that his is not a serious offense; it may be illegal but not immoral. The lighthearted winking attached to white lightning vanishes, however, when the interest of Alcohol, Tobacco, and Firearms (ATF) or the Alcoholic Beverage Commission (ABC) is piqued. Indeed, construction of the criminal becomes much more complicated when we move from the demand to the supply side of the equation; moonshiners can and do receive harsh penalties for their entrepreneurial activities.

Through an examination of the recent history of moonshining in Franklin County, Virginia, this chapter aims to shed light on criminality and how it is understood in very different ways. How can the moonshiner simultaneously be a criminal and someone simply trying to make ends meet in a challenging world? The processes of construction and normalization of crime is of particular interest to me, as some of my ancestors appear to have been "criminals." As such, maybe my father's attachment to moonshine should be expected; perhaps the criminal element is in his blood, as his forebears arrived in the eventual epicenter of illegal distilling in southwest Virginia as far back as 1783. At this early date, those looking for a nip or some hard currency may well have turned to corn liquor production or trade. My mother's side, replete with French Huguenot exiles, took a more circuitous route but landed in the same region of Virginia generations ago, settling in Floyd, Patrick, and Franklin Counties.

My mother's great-great-uncle Fleming DeHart became a renowned legal distiller in Patrick County, obtaining great wealth through liquor and his farming activities. Fleming went so far as to create his own town, Hartville, installing himself as mayor.[1] His sons followed in his footsteps, with Ike inheriting and expanding his father's distillery, while younger brother, Joseph, established a rival distillery. Ike went on to make his own brand of corn liquor (fig. 4.1), insisting on the purity of his spirits after the implementation of the Pure Food and Drug Act of 1906.

Joseph's distilling proved less lucrative, but he left us a valuable artifact highlighting the social construction of criminality. Foreseeing that he would soon be on the wrong side of the law, he warned his customers to be prepared for the impending constraints of Prohibition, to "make hay while the sun shines," in a newspaper advertisement (see fig. 4.2). As such, we can see how the signing of a piece of legislation, the Commonwealth of Virginia's prohibition of alcohol (which preceded that of the United States by more than three years), created a new population of criminals overnight. Although I have no evidence, my hunch is that on November 1, 1916, Ike and Joseph transitioned from distillers to moonshiners. In neighboring Franklin County, family lore suggests some of my other ancestors may have also become criminals on that date. This would not be surprising, because even at this time, Franklin County was becoming legendary for its liquor production; two decades later it would be labeled the "wettest county in the world."[2]

Moonshiners would be portrayed in very different ways over the next decades, from lovable bumpkins to corrupting forces, from keepers of tradition to peddlers of demon rum, from minor lawbreakers to dangerous gangsters. These differing understandings are intimately linked to one's relationship to these "criminals" and where one is positioned in the community. Attempts to stamp out the production of untaxed liquor in Franklin County have largely fallen to federal and state agencies, with local law enforcement generally disinterested in this task. The redoubled efforts of these agencies in the 1990s

Figure 4.1. Old Ike Rye Whiskey Label. Jack Sullivan, "The DeHarts of Virginia: Moonshine in the Sunshine," *Those Pre-Pro Whiskey Men!*, November 29, 2011.

largely proved successful, resulting, somewhat ironically, in a more pointed celebration of moonshining heritage and the opening of "legal moonshine" distilleries. Before examining these major shifts in Franklin County, we need some context on deviance, and deviance in Appalachia specifically.

Insiders, Outsiders, and Definitions of Crime

"Deviance" is a loaded term. Labeling one a deviant is an act of power, an invitation for discrimination and sanctions. Some have even written the obituary of the sociology of deviance, but the term still holds some utility for its concise definition: a violation of a societal norm.[3] Deviance cannot exist without norms, which begs the question of how individual societies construct

their norms. It is clear that norms are not universal, with different understandings of normalcy abounding across the globe and through time. Ian
Hacking sheds light on the process of creating deviance with his exploration
of categorization in *Making Up People*.[4] What is critical for Hacking, and for
Michel Foucault before him, is the power of discourse and categorization.[5]
Indeed, Hacking traces the "homosexual as a kind of person" back to an academic paper from 1968.[6] That is not to say that "homosexuals" did not exist
before Hacking's writing but that this category is a relatively recent concept
shaped by the label itself, tied to the discourse surrounding the identity, the
behaviors, the attitudes, the *essence* of the homosexual. With this label, the
homosexual could be identified, counted, regulated, and persecuted. This
idea is important for understanding moonshining because just as the law is
imminently tied to sexuality, so too is it tied to other realms labeled as "vice."

Prior to governmental regulation and taxation in the mid-nineteenth century, the distiller was merely someone who happened to make liquor.[7] At this
point, our unlicensed distiller became a moonshiner and hence a criminal.
In turn, the "criminal" label demanded the punishment of our erstwhile
distiller. But as David Maurer explains, the degree of criminality attributed
to the moonshiner is negotiated: "The moonshiner as a criminal is so old
that he has become a part of American tradition. He has become respectable
in a certain sense; his reputation does not suffer in his own community in
proportion to the penalties imposed on him by law. He is a sort of illegal
pet, carefully protected from extermination by both the law and society, but
hunted with just enough diligence to make him constantly aware that he is
a criminal."[8] Indeed, Franklin County residents have generally not deemed
the illegal distiller criminal; that label comes from the outside. As Linda
Stanley of the Franklin County Historical Society succinctly explains, "They
were good people, they just broke the law."[9] As such, for most community
members, the moonshiner was simply trying to take care of his family and
make ends meet.[10]

That the criminal construct is foisted on those in the community from
the outside is critical to this story because it echoes a centuries-long history of discord between insider and outsider perspectives and stereotypes of
Appalachians. The very label "Appalachia" is derived from a mistaken understanding of what the Apalachee tribe of northern Florida meant when they

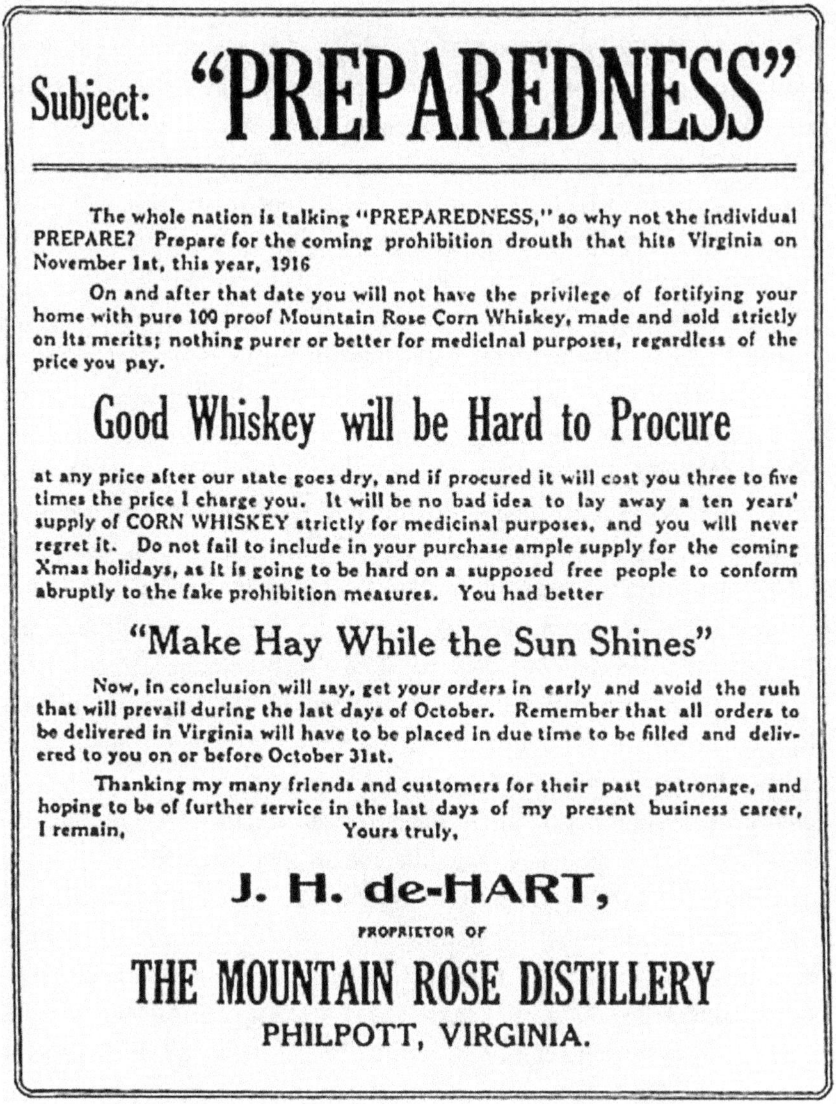

Subject: "PREPAREDNESS"

The whole nation is talking "PREPAREDNESS," so why not the individual PREPARE? Prepare for the coming prohibition drouth that hits Virginia on November 1st, this year, 1916

On and after that date you will not have the privilege of fortifying your home with pure 100 proof Mountain Rose Corn Whiskey, made and sold strictly on its merits; nothing purer or better for medicinal purposes, regardless of the price you pay.

Good Whiskey will be Hard to Procure

at any price after our state goes dry, and if procured it will cost you three to five times the price I charge you. It will be no bad idea to lay away a ten years' supply of CORN WHISKEY strictly for medicinal purposes, and you will never regret it. Do not fail to include in your purchase ample supply for the coming Xmas holidays, as it is going to be hard on a supposed free people to conform abruptly to the fake prohibition measures. You had better

"Make Hay While the Sun Shines"

Now, in conclusion will say, get your orders in early and avoid the rush that will prevail during the last days of October. Remember that all orders to be delivered in Virginia will have to be placed in due time to be filled and delivered to you on or before October 31st.

Thanking my many friends and customers for their past patronage, and hoping to be of further service in the last days of my present business career, I remain, Yours truly,

J. H. de-HART,

PROPRIETOR OF

THE MOUNTAIN ROSE DISTILLERY

PHILPOTT, VIRGINIA.

Figure 4.2. Joseph de-Hart's Warning Ad. Jack Sullivan, "The DeHarts of Virginia: Moonshine in the Sunshine," *Those Pre-Pro Whiskey Men!*, November 29, 2011.

referred to the rolling mountain chain to the north as a "land of gold." This description, and the false belief that this tribe was somehow connected to the gold-possessing tribes of Central America, piqued the interest of gold-seeking conquistadors who had failed to find bounty in southern Florida. Not surprisingly, "gold" held a very different meaning for the Appalachees than the conquistadors; abundant game and fresh water, not ore, represented wealth for the tribe. Nevertheless, European cartographers soon labeled the entire mountain range "Appalachia," and the name has remained ever since.[11]

This anecdote is instructive, for the region's name came from the outside and has ever since been weighted with cultural baggage and negative stereotypes. The post–Civil War period saw the rise of so-called local color writings as publishers of magazines and popular novels welcomed work about all the overlooked "little corners" of the United States. Of these writings, William Wallace Harney's "A Strange Land and a Peculiar People" had a notable impact.[12] Appearing in *Lippincott's Magazine* in 1873, the story relayed a sensational tale of the exploits of Appalachians to urban northeastern readers. Henry Shapiro declared that "in a real sense it was Harney and the editors of Lippincott's who 'discovered' Appalachia, for they were the first to assert an otherness that made the mountainous portions of eight southern states a discrete region, in but not of America."[13] In addition to Harney, authors such as John Fox Jr. and Mary Murfree reinforced many of the Appalachian stereotypes of ignorance, violence, drunkenness, and tribalism presented by Harney, cementing Appalachia as a different, exceptional place.[14] Meanwhile, missionaries had streamed in to this supposedly "unchurched" region to ply their trades, while social scientists sought empirical data to support the otherness of the region.[15] By the mid-twentieth century, regional politicians recognized that the otherness of Appalachia could help alleviate the suffering of the postwar years and embraced "Appalachia exceptionalism" in order to receive federal funds.[16, 17]

Given this history, it is not surprising that those in Franklin County, like many others in Appalachia, would largely dismiss the perspectives of outsiders, especially those trafficking in long-treasured tropes of the hillbilly moonshiner.[18] Coupling this with the contributions made by illicit liquor to the local economy, it is little wonder those in the community have rarely aided those attempting to stifle the industry. But just how did so much attention come to this small, rural corner of the world in the first place?

Making the Moonshine Capital of the World

Sitting on the cusp of the Blue Ridge Mountains, generations of farmers have used Franklin County's fertile agricultural land to grow numerous crops. With little coal, the county has not suffered the boom-and-bust resource roller coaster of its neighbors to the west. Nonetheless, economic development has always been uneven at best, dependent upon tobacco, dairy farming, and fruit trees, as well as the textile mills that would eventually leave in search of cheaper labor. Much like other rural spaces, money has consistently been tight for most Franklin County residents, and a segment of the population has long recognized that corn, alone or combined with damsons, apples, and peaches, could be converted into a nonperishable value-added product that could supplement their income with hard currency.[19] In 1935, however, a trial showed that the small-time moonshiner merely augmenting his income was being pushed aside by more organized networks.

The so-called Great Moonshine Conspiracy Trial of 1935 put Franklin County onto the nation's front page, forever entrenching it as the moonshine capital of the world. The federal investigation resulted in thirty-four people being indicted, including nine government officials, among them a former federal Prohibition agent, a commonwealth's attorney, a county sheriff, and four deputy sheriffs. Sensationalizing the trial to an even higher degree was the gunning down of a key governmental witness, Deputy Jeff Richards (along with the prisoner he was taking to jail), in the lead-up to the trial. In a relatively new strategy, the government sought to prove a widespread conspiracy to commit tax fraud in addition to illegal distilling.[20] Clearly, the primary motivation to stamp out this moonshining operation was economic, for "between 1930 and 1935 local still operators and their business partners sold a volume of whiskey that would have generated $5,500,000 in excise taxes at the old 1920 tax rate."[21] The trial revealed that "Franklin County officials were accepting protection fees from moonshiners, and the Sheriff himself oversaw the complex bribery system. Small-time bootleggers were squeezed out as money and power were consolidated."[22] This longest trial in Virginia's history eventually resulted in thirty-one people being found guilty. Nevertheless, resulting sentences proved light, two years at the maximum, and thirteen conspirators received just probation.[23] These light sentences seem to represent an early disjuncture between the norms of those outside the region from those on the inside.[24]

The sensational events revealed at trial (including the role played by a fast-driving female bootlegger named Willy Carter Sharpe) drew much unwanted attention to the region. A well-known journalist of the day, Sherwood Anderson, covered the trial for *Liberty Magazine* and penned these indelible words: "What is the wettest section in the U.S.A., the place where during prohibition and since, the most illicit liquor has been made? The extreme wet spot, per number of people, isn't in New York or Chicago. By the undisputed evidence given at a recent trial in the United States Court at Roanoke, Virginia, the spot that fairly dripped illicit liquor, and kept right on dripping after prohibition ended is in the mountain country of southwestern Virginia—in Franklin County, Virginia."[25] Moreover, the trial produced many amazing statistics about moonshining in Franklin County. For instance, a yeast company representative testified to selling 70,448 pounds of yeast in the county during a four-year period, to a population of just 24,000. In comparison, the 189,000 citizens of the state capital Richmond purchased merely 2,000 pounds during the same period.[26] Some Franklin County families consumed 5,000 pounds of sugar per month, while almost 34 million pounds of sugar were purchased during the four-year surveillance period.[27] The total amount of moonshine coming out of the county during the period will never be known, but if liquor filled just the 600,000 specially made five-gallon "non-gurgling" tin cans bought in the county during those four years, at least 3 million gallons of white lightning left the county.[28] Perhaps most striking of all is the statement by the National Commission on Law Observance and Enforcement that "in one county (Franklin) it is claimed 99 people out of 100 are making, or have some connection with, illicit liquor."[29] Since this time, for good or ill, Franklin County has become synonymous with white lightning, and its famed moniker has adorned everything from T-Shirts to racetracks.

Regulating Moonshine

Regulating untaxed liquor in the moonshine capital of the world has proved challenging, especially because little assistance is provided by Franklin Countians. Deputy director of the Virginia alcohol agency's Bureau of Law Enforcement Allen G. Hudson explains how the local attitude makes his job difficult: "It's an awkward situation. They [moonshiners] are good for the economy. They hire people locally and buy materials locally. We don't get a lot of cooperation, because they see them doing more good than we can do them."[30] The way that the moonshiner is judged differently by insiders and outsiders in this case echoes local perspectives on another regional entrepreneur, the marijuana grower. In Sandra Hafley and Richard Tewksbury's exploration of the rural Kentucky marijuana industry, they note that like residents of Franklin County, locals do not view the growers as criminals but as vital nodes in the social network, filling crucial gaps when the legitimate market fails to provide necessary services and jobs.[31] The authors conclude that "participants in the marijuana industry do not perceive themselves as members of an organized crime network; rather, they perceive themselves and their communities as under siege from the outside world. They do not view their activities as wrong, although they do know they are illegal."[32] The difference between illegal and immoral is key with regard to local regulation in both communities. Hafley and Tewksbury suggest that some growers "bribe and are often protected by law enforcement and political officials."[33] While no evidence suggests outright bribery in Franklin County, it is clear that stamping out illicit liquor is not a high priority for local law enforcement. Following a major federal and state operation of which he took no part, the long-serving sheriff of Franklin County, W. Q. "Quint" Overton, declared, "I'd rather be laying on [watching] a drug house than a still."[34]

The late Morris Stephenson, a longtime reporter for the *Franklin County Times*, is an especially important source for understanding moonshining in the area. He often accompanied Virginia ABC agents on their raids in the 1960s and wrote numerous pieces on illicit liquor. Unlike the generally reviled federal agents, these Virginia ABC officials were assigned to Franklin County on a full-time basis and were not seen as outsiders. In *A Night of Makin' Likker*, Stephenson relays this general lack of animosity between the hunters and their prey: "In Franklin County, agents and moonshiners generally had respect for each other. In most cases, the two groups were on a first name basis, just because they lived in the tight-knit county."[35] This disconnect in the views held by federal and state law enforcement and those held by local officials, is also found in the marijuana case: "Marijuana growers strongly resent interference by both government and outside individuals in their and their community's activities. They feel as though they and their community are under siege by outsiders, who remove marijuana growers from their families and homes . . . [state and federal] agencies are viewed with hostility and distrust; they are staffed by outsiders and are perceived as failing to appreciate fully cultural norms and values."[36] All that said, it does bear noting that these communities are not monolithic. Franklin County is well within the Bible Belt and some locals have opposed "Demon Rum."[37] The important point here, however, is that regardless of their opposition to the practice of moonshining, these community members typically do not desire outside interference in trying to rid the county of alcohol.

Nevertheless, those outsiders who did believe it was within their purview to regulate moonshine mounted numerous attacks on illegal distilling in the county, which appear to have decimated this once vibrant industry. Two operations carried out by federal and state law enforcement are particularly important for understanding the current state of liquor affairs in today's Franklin County. The first, Operation Dry Up, signaled a reprioritization of stopping illegal whiskey production, while the second, Operation Lightning Strike, would all but end Franklin's claim to being the moonshine capital of the world.

Operation Dry Up

Before dawn on January 21, 1980, Operation Dry Up commenced with more than sixty Virginian and federal agents raiding a still site in Franklin County. Thirty-three suspected moonshiners were arrested, more than sixty stills were eventually dynamited, and federal and state liquor enforcement officials claimed they had destroyed the largest moonshining operation in the nation as part of their increased focus on illicit liquor.[38] In the previous six months, they had seized sixty-three stills in southwest Virginia, but according to retired ABC enforcement officer Jack Powell, Operation Dry Up was more of a publicity stunt than anything:

> The government drew sharp criticism of the way it handled publicity prior to the start of the operation. The procedure for the way the government had national news media on hand to cover the events was very immature. Word was that the stills were seized several days before the action began and guarded by government and state agents until the *Washington Post* and other high-powered news media arrived. The rumor was that moonshine

in one-gallon plastic jugs were seized from other locations and held and brought to the location of the stills where the news media were to set a record.[39]

Powell goes on to portray the "Blitz" as "ill-conceived and poorly orchestrated," and likely a "show put on by desk jockeys in Washington" irked by a newspaper report that Franklin County led the nation in illegal whiskey production.[40] Though all of this may have been true, these actions marked an important shift. In an interview with the *Washington Post*, an ATF official remarked that the agency had "deprioritized" moonshine during the 1970s to focus on firearms and explosives investigations.[41] For the ATF, this needed to change, and Operation Dry Up was a first step in that reprioritization. According to ATF agent Nolan E. Douglas, moonshining activity had slowed across the United States, but Franklin County had "gotten out of hand." When asked whether the raid would cripple illicit liquor industry in the area, Douglas tellingly replied, "No. I really don't."[42]

This raid tells us much about the priorities of outside law enforcement at this time, but Blaine Harden's 1980 *Washington Post* article, "'Revenooers' Return to Form, Bust 12 Va. Stills," reveals to us even more about the social construction of crime and insider-outsider dynamics in the county. First, a legendary Franklin County moonshiner, Cecil Love, tells Harden that he was tipped off about the raid from a Franklin County sheriff's deputy. Such contact, if Love's statement was true, would certainly point to a disconnect between local and state and federal enforcement. Second are the complaints issued by Cecil's brother, Walter Love, who, rather than being told to report to the local judge the following day as was customary for liquor offenses, was handcuffed and treated, in his words, "like a criminal."[43] Indeed, it would be hard to find more telling examples of differing understandings of criminality at the local and federal level than those provided by the Love brothers.

Although Operation Dry Up signaled the ATF's reprioritization of stopping illegal whiskey production, it was but an opening salvo in a broader war, as moonshining remained a robust industry in the 1980s. Stills continued to increase in size, ramping up output to urban, northern markets, and an August 1982 *New York Times* piece described the industry as "flourishing."[44] After the destruction of a still made up of nine eight-hundred-gallon tanks, the Virginia

ABC Board's assistant director of enforcement, F. W. Enroughty, noted, "We're seeing more illegal whisky now than we've seen in the past five years."[45] The causes of this increase were multifaceted, but like the history of moonshine in bygone ages, it was largely about economics. The severe recession of the early 1980s resulted in a high national unemployment rate, peaking at 10.8 percent in December 1982, and as Enroughty notes, "moonshining picks up when the economy goes down. People don't have any work to do, so they go back into the bushes."[46] At the same time that work was drying up, the price of sugar had fallen dramatically, making production less expensive while the price of moonshine on the black market had increased; a shot of liquor at a northern "nip joint" had doubled from twenty-five to fifty cents.[47] Yet another critical factor in this "flourishing" is that despite the ATF's claim of a reprioritization, law enforcement resources for stamping out illegal whiskey had actually been cut. Beginning in 1982, the Commonwealth of Virginia stopped receiving federal funds from the Bureau of Alcohol, Tobacco, and Firearms, which had turned its attention to illegal weapons sales and cigarette smuggling.[48] Finally, if the Virginia ABC's number of illegal still raids and investigations is any indication, the decrease in funding in 1982 may have had some effect (see fig. 4.3). The 1990s, however, brought about significant change as federal agents took a different tactical approach, one that would yield major impacts on the illicit liquor industry in Franklin County.

Operation Lightning Strike

In 1992 the local arm of the ABC Board decided to take a closer look into the machinations of a local agricultural supply center known as a supplier of moonshining products, a significant break from traditional enforcement strategies. When a trailer across the street from Helms Farmer Exchange became vacant, a female officer from out of town rented the home, claiming to be a college student. Surveillance soon followed, and according to Max Watman: "When the ABC Board rented that trailer and turned on the camera, it was as if they'd flipped on the lights in a roach-infested apartment." Farmer Exchange actually sold few farming goods, but from the beginning of surveillance to the eventual raid dubbed Operation Lighting Strike, the business sold 12,096,800 pounds of sugar, enough to make about 2 million gallons of liquor. One estimate concluded that over a three-year period the amount of sugar sold equated

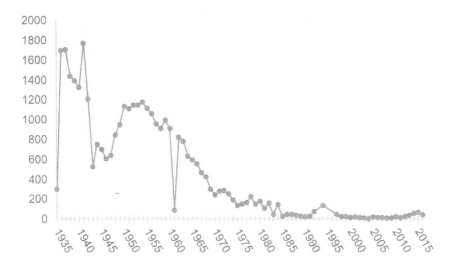

Figure 4.3. Raids and Investigations of Illegal Stills in Virginia from 1935 to 2016. Source: Virginia ABC.

to a quarter ton for every man, woman, and child in the county. Perhaps even more damning were the tens of thousands of heavy-duty one-gallon plastic jugs in the warehouse and the coded receipts. One customer, later revealed to be Ralph Hale, purchased enough supplies to make 276,000 gallons of liquor, estimated to be worth $8.38 million retail.[49]

The prosecuting attorney on the case, Sharon Burnham, took a page from the conspiracy trial of 1935 to broaden the scope of charges beyond liquor violations to conspiracy to defraud the government of taxes. She argued the Helms brothers had conspired *with each other* to keep moonshiners in supplies facilitating their criminal enterprises. This strategy significantly broadened the government's net implicating many locals not directly tied to these activities, such as a suspect's wife who had paid the mortgage on a building containing a still. With federal involvement and Racketeer Influenced and Corrupt Organizations statutes also came the power of civil seizure to take property and assets without a trial, let alone a guilty verdict. As was to be expected, many Franklin County residents did not appreciate the government's intrusion. A local farmer in the area, Jay Lynch, complained to the *Roanoke Times*:

"They talk like a man making a drop of liquor is the worst thing in the world. People don't realize moonshine brings money into the county. When you can't get a job, and there's no other way to feed your family, you'll go to the holler and make some liquor and that beats stealing. Ralph Hale is one of the finer boys to walk this earth. They went up and took all his farm machinery. I can't believe the law's got that much authority." Jay Lynch's words get to the heart of the vastly different understandings of justice and morality locals can hold from those from outside the community. Another local, grocer Mr. Midkiff, reinforces the point, stating, "It's about taxes. That's the only reason. Most are hardworking people. A real bootlegger is as good as his word." These different perceptions came into sharp focus as local law enforcement did not participate in Operation Lightning Strike. Long-serving Sheriff Overton clearly took umbrage at the priorities of state and federal forces, declaring, "We don't have a moonshine problem in Franklin County. We do have a drug problem in Franklin County. There's no comparison. . . . [I've] never heard of kids drinking moonshine, but we do have kids smoking crack and marijuana."[50] Such sentiments only hardened following the suicide of Ramsey Helms, the co-owner of the Helms Farmer Exchange. Operation Lightning Strike had resulted in the seizure of most of his assets and besmirched his reputation, though he was not a moonshiner but merely a merchant of legal goods.

The prosecutor's use of conspiracy and kingpin laws allowed property seizure from not just moonshiners but also from their friends and family members, dramatically upping the stakes. As Morris Stephenson stated, "Nobody is going to take a chance of making liquor when his house is on the line, his cars, his property, his land, everything he owns. There's probably liquor being made here on a small, small basis, but the art is dying."[51] For several decades, moonshine had been an accepted part of the social fabric in the county and a critical safety net during economic downturns. Most observers, however, believed that Operation Lightning Strike had driven the final nail in the local moonshine coffin.

Modern Moonshine and Evolving Norms

As with all illegal activities, it is hard to grasp the true extent of operations. One way is to examine the number of arrests and raids, and only a handful of small-scale busts have taken place in the county since Operation Lightning

Strike. For instance, in 2012 a man from Wirtz, Franklin County, had his fifty-five-gallon still seized and received jail time because of illegal weapons.[52] In 2013 two eight-hundred-gallon stills were destroyed in eastern Franklin County following a tip to Virginia ABC that a man had bought a pallet of sugar. ABC agents called it "a mid-size operation," although the 1,600 gallons of mash would yield just one hundred gallons of liquor. When asked about the case, Stephenson noted that it was one of the largest operations to be busted in recent years but would be just "a drop in the bucket compared to what used to come out of here." Stephenson, a man who had covered the moonshine industry since the early 1960s, concluded: "Most people I talk to now don't know where any is being made. I don't know who to call to get any. I don't know who to see."[53] Similarly, Commonwealth's Attorney Tim Allen contends that illicit liquor production is largely extinct in the county, attributing its decline to Operation Lightning Strike and "the recognition that selling illegal drugs can yield more profit."[54]

Despite these death sentences for moonshine, liquor is front-page news again in Franklin County—not, however, for still raids and bootlegging but for the opening of legal distilleries and cultural tourism. Franklin County has fully embraced its notoriety, evidenced by the high school wrestling tournament called the Moonshine Classic, an annual charity race named the White Lightning Run, and the Moonshine Express, which takes tourists around to several famed sites throughout the county to "see our replica likker still" and "meet local 'characters' associated with Franklin County's infamous liquid industry."[55] In 2016 local promoters organized the two-day Franklin County Moonshine Festival, and for a short time Bootleggers Café served diners in the county seat of Rocky Mount.

The mystique of moonshining in the county certainly grew after the release of the 2012 film *Lawless*, based on Matt Bondurant's novel *The Wettest County in the World*. The movie also benefited the descendants of the highly dramatized Bondurant brothers, who have since opened their own distillery with the motto "Some moonshine is legendary and some is made by legends. Ours is Both!"[56] Similarly, Twin Creeks Distillery is attempting to capitalize on the growing interest in regional moonshine, producing the first legal liquor in the county since Prohibition. Owner Chris Prillaman started the distillery in 2015 because "I figure if they was doing it everywhere else, darn, somebody need to do it around here."[57] Both of his great-grandfathers were in the business, and when

Prillaman notes how painstaking the process of distilling can be, he implicitly acknowledges how changing norms allow him an easier path than his predecessors: "All these people back yonder had to go through all this while looking back over their shoulder." Ironically, the law is still being wrestled with today but in a very different way, for as Casey Fabris of the *Roanoke Times* recently reported, "The 'wettest county in the world' is, in fact, dry."[58] Yet another new business, Franklin County Distilleries, was unaware that liquor by the drink has never been approved at the county level and is now attempting to pass a referendum to allow them to have a tasting room. Regardless, the product is a hit, recently selling out at the local ABC store in thirty-one minutes.[59]

As such, it seems that authentic moonshine is largely gone in the county, but legal liquor is thriving; moonshiners are gone, replaced by distillers. Similar to the laws that turned my ancestors into criminals, the crackdown of Operation Lightning Strike has, perversely, provided numerous opportunities for legal capitalization. Once again, moonshine merits a wink rather than handcuffs. In short, Franklin County moonshining underscores the fluidity of deviance and criminality, the power of the law, and the primacy of economics in the United States.

Conclusion

Moonshiners are criminals. Moonshiners are upstanding citizens. Moonshine is dead in Franklin County. Moonshine is thriving in Franklin County. Somehow all of these statements are true. Cultural criminologists wrangle with such competing understandings, and offer us some insights into how these multiple constructions can coexist.[60] As Mike Presdee explains, "We need continually to remind ourselves of one single simple statement that a criminal act has to be defined through social and cultural processes that are in themselves played out separate from the essence of the act itself."[61] As such, the ebbs and flows of liquor law enforcement by state and federal authorities in Franklin County must be contextualized within broader narratives and priorities in the political and social realms. With hindsight, the crackdown on moonshine production in this small corner of the world nests within a larger "tough on crime" zeitgeist of the 1980s and 1990s. From Ronald Reagan's war on crack and urban youth to Rudy Giuliani's broken windows offensive to Bill Clinton's punitive stance on crime as evidenced by his signing of the Violent

Crime Control and Law Enforcement Act of 1994, we see a nonpartisan quest to convince Americans that crime is a serious problem but one that can be controlled with severe measures and a law-and-order stance. Perhaps Franklin County moonshine production, largely insignificant in the grand scheme of things, served as a symbolic broken window the state could fix to demonstrate its authority and competence.

It is, however, difficult to know how law enforcement priorities are determined. This chapter has attempted to highlight how notions of deviance and criminality can compete dependent upon one's position within a community, but much of the story remains untold. Indeed, it is telling that my plans to include an interview with a current moonshiner in this chapter were not realized. My father had agreed to introduce me to his source, a garage owner who was also a distributor. He told me that this man's shop did not sell tires and that the code to purchase white lightning was "I'd like to buy some used tires." My excitement for this proposed meeting was doused, however, when my father told me we could not carry out the interview as the mechanic was under law enforcement surveillance. As such, I am left to conclude that the federal government is ensuring there is no moonshining renaissance in Franklin County and has not changed its position on *untaxed* liquor, despite society's evolving relationship with legal "moonshine." As we see with marijuana, criminality can melt away with commodification. Perhaps my father and I will just have to go get a nip at one of those legal distilleries—that is, if they can get a liquor license.

NOTES

1. Jack Sullivan, "The DeHarts of Virginia: Moonshine in the Sunshine," *Those Pre-Pro Whiskey Men!*, November 29, 2011, accessed October 9, 2017, http://pre-prowhiskeymen.blogspot.com/2011/11/deharts-of-virginia-moonshine-in.html.

2. Sherwood Anderson, "City Gangs Enslave Moonshine Mountaineers," *Liberty Magazine*, November 2, 1935.

3. Colin Sumner, *The Sociology of Deviance: An Obituary* (Buckingham: Open University Press, 1994).

4. Ian Hacking, "Making Up People," in *Beyond the Body Proper: Reading the Anthropology of Material Life*, ed. Margaret Lock and Judith Farquhar (Durham: Duke University Press, 2007), 222–36.

5. Michel Foucault, *The History of Sexuality* (New York: Random House, 1978).

6. But Foucault dates the invention of the homosexual to the Victorian Era.

7. Wilbur Miller, *Revenuers and Moonshiners: Enforcing Federal Liquor Law in the Mountain South, 1865–1900* (Chapel Hill: University of North Carolina Press, 1991).

8. David W. Maurer, *Kentucky Moonshine* (Lexington: University Press of Kentucky, 2003), 9.

9. Casey Fabris, "Moonshine Express Puts Cars Hauling Liquor on Display," *Roanoke Times*, April 5, 2016.

10. In *Moonshiners and Prohibitionists: The Battle over Alcohol in Southern Appalachia* (Lexington: University Press of Kentucky, 2011), Bruce Stewart shows that mountain residents were not homogenous in their views on alcohol. Those living in urban areas and those identifying as middle class were more likely to embrace the temperance movement and denounce the moonshiner as a criminal. Moonshine expert Roddy Moore of the Blue Ridge Institute and Museum of Ferrum College in Franklin County contends that in this part of the world, support for moonshine was nearly universal (personal communication, December 7, 2017).

11. Donald Edward Davis, *Where There Are Mountains: An Environmental History of the Southern Appalachians* (Athens: University of Georgia Press, 2000).

12. William Wallace Harney, "A Strange Land and a Peculiar People," *Lippincott's Magazine of Popular Literature and Science* 12, no. 31 (1873).

13. Henry D. Shapiro, *Appalachia on Our Mind: The Southern Mountains and Mountaineers in the American Consciousness, 1870–1920* (Chapel Hill: University of North Carolina Press, 1978), 4.

14. Stewart, *Moonshiners and Prohibitionists*.

15. Shapiro, *Appalachia on Our Mind*.

16. Ronald Eller, *Uneven Ground: Appalachia since 1945* (Lexington: University of Kentucky Press, 2008).

17. Allen Batteau, *The Invention of Appalachia* (Tucson: University of Arizona Press, 1990).

18. Franklin County is on the border of Appalachia according to the Appalachian Regional Commission's map of 1965. It is easy to argue, however, that this county is more "Appalachian" than many that are included. Mississippi, for instance, has no mountains, but its politicians fought for inclusion to receive federal funds.

19. Charles D. Thompson, *Spirits of Just Men: Mountaineers, Liquor Bosses, and Lawmen in the Moonshine Capital of the World* (Urbana: University of Illinois Press, 2011).

20. Jess Carr, *The Second Oldest Profession: An Informal History of Moonshining in America* (Englewood Cliffs, NJ: Prentice-Hall, 1972), 114.

21. Blue Ridge Institute and Museum of Ferrum College, "The Franklin County Conspiracy," *Moonshine Blue Ridge Style* (n.d.), 6.

22. Blue Ridge Institute, "The Franklin County Conspiracy," 6.

23. Blue Ridge Institute, "The Franklin County Conspiracy," 6.

24. Thompson, *Spirits of Just Men.*

25. Anderson, "City Gangs."

26. Carr, *Second Oldest Profession,* 115.

27. Ibid.

28. Ibid., 116.

29. Official Records of the National Commission on Law Observance and Enforcement 1935, vol. 4 (1935): 1075.

30. Peter T. Kilborn, "U.S. Cracks Down on Rise in Appalachia Moonshine." *New York Times,* March 23, 2000.

31. Sandra Riggs Hafley and Richard Tewksbury, "The Rural Kentucky Marijuana Industry: Organization and Community Involvement," *Deviant Behavior* 16, no. 3 (1995): 204.

32. Ibid., 206.

33. Ibid., 207.

34. Donald P. Baker, "Raids Attack Mystique of Moonshine Industry," *Washington Post,* July 6, 1999.

35. Morris Stephenson, *A Night of Makin' Likker: Plus Other Stories from the Moonshine Capital of the World* (self-published, 2012).

36. Hafley and Tewksbury, "Rural Kentucky," 210–11.

37. "Moonshine Express," Virginia Is for Lovers, accessed October 10, 2017, https://www.virginia.org/listings/Events/MoonshineExpress/.

38. Blaine Harden, "'Revenooers' Return to Form, Bust 12 Va. Stills" *Washington Post,* January 21, 1980.

39. Jack Allen Powell, *A Dying Art* (Catskill, New York: Press Tige Publishing, 1996), 36.

40. Ibid., 37.

41. Harden, "'Revenooers' Return to Form."
42. Ibid.
43. Ibid.
44. No Author, "For Some, Hard Times Spell 'Moonshine,'" *New York Times*, August 29, 1982.
45. Ibid.
46. Ibid.
47. Ibid.
48. Ibid.
49. Max Watman, *Chasing the White Dog: An Amateur Outlaw's Adventures in Moonshine* (New York: Simon and Schuster, 2011), 150, 154, 156.
50. Ibid., 158, 159.
51. Duncan Adams, "Wirtz Man Pleads Guilty in Moonshining Case," *Roanoke Times*, November 27, 2012.
52. Ibid.
53. Neil Harvey, "Penhook Man Guilty of Making Moonshine," *Roanoke Times*, September 18, 2013.
54. Adams, "Wirtz Man."
55. "Moonshine Express."
56. Bondurant Brothers Distillery, accessed October 21, 2017, www.bondurant brothersdistillery.com/home.html.
57. Casey Fabris, "Franklin Co. Distillery Enjoys Shining Success," *Roanoke Times*, September 18, 2017.
58. Casey Fabris, "Moonshine Express Puts Cars Hauling Liquor on Display," *Roanoke Times*, April 5, 2016.
59. Dan Casey, "The First Rocky Mount Legal Hooch in 95 Years," *Roanoke Times*, January 13, 2016.
60. Jeff Ferrell and Clinton S. Sanders, *Cultural Criminology* (Boston: Northeastern University Press, 1995).
61. Mike Presdee, *Cultural Criminology and the Carnival of Crime* (London: Routledge, 2000).

PART II

The Legalization
and Marketing
of Modern Moonshine

CHAPTER 5

The Rise of "Legal" Moonshine: Breaking Down the Legal Barriers to Craft Distilling in the United States

KENNETH J. SANCHAGRIN

Illegally distilled liquor, more commonly known as moonshine, has largely disappeared from the American landscape.[1] The slow death of large-scale illegal spirits production, however, has corresponded with an explosion in legal distilling of spirits traditionally associated with moonshining as well as other types of liquor, ranging from vodka and rum to tequila and Brazilian cachaça. Indeed, while there were fewer than 100 legal distilleries in the United States in the mid-1990s when the last illicit still was reportedly seized by the U.S. Alcohol and Tobacco Tax and Trade Bureau,[2] as of 2016 there were an estimated 1,100 to 1,300 licensed liquor manufacturers in the country.[3] Most of this growth has occurred within the last decade, as the number of distilleries operating in the United States has increased by 700 percent since 2007.[4] Similar levels of growth has been seen in the Appalachian region, the area many consider to be the traditional home of moonshine in the United States. In both North Carolina and Virginia, for instance, the number of craft distilleries has skyrocketed, and each state can now boast that they have more than forty operations distilling within their borders.

The rapid growth in the number of legal distilleries in the United States corresponds with an equally rapid liberalization of state laws regulating liquor production and sales. Since the end of Prohibition, the majority of regulations governing alcohol production and trade can be found at the state, county, and municipal level. Given the wide variety of state systems, laws, and rules governing the liquor trade, a shocking degree of change has occurred within the last decade as nearly every state has made the production and sale of distilled spirits more accessible to small producers. Notably, as of late 2018 when an Oklahoma law passed in 2016 takes effect, all fifty states will have passed legislation designed to make it easier for distilleries to open and operate within their borders. Interestingly, however, this trend does not apply equally to all types of spirits producers. Rather, many of these laws have been designed to promote and encourage the growth of the craft distillery industry specifically, which is where modern legal moonshine can largely be found today.

The rapid growth in craft distilling, along with the equally rapid change in the legal landscape governing the production of spirits, raises a number of important questions. First, how have state laws changed since the beginning of the 2000s? Second, to what degree have these legal changes affected the craft distilling industry? Finally, given that the evolution of legal rules and regulations often happens slowly, what triggered these quick legal changes?

The Relationship between Law and the Economy

Sociologists studying the relationship between law and the economy argue that industries and the legal rules that govern them reciprocally influence, construct, and affect one another.[5] This means that law is not something that is merely imposed on economic actors and markets from the outside. It also means that legal regulations and norms can facilitate and promote certain kinds of economic interactions, markets, and industries by providing incentives that influence the rational strategizing of industry members while discouraging or prohibiting others.[6] The idea that industries and law make and reshape one another can be traced to studies that seek to explain why most modern organizations within a given industry look so similar to one another. According to these neoinstitutional studies, similarities between businesses are not necessarily due to the efficiency of a given business structure or practice as classical economic theory would predict. Rather, similarities are due to structuration caused by three different forces that drive homogeneity within industries: coercive isomorphism, mimetic isomorphism, and normative isomorphism.[7] The most relevant of these three influences to the analysis of law's connection to organizational behavior is the coercive form, as this type of isomorphism contributes toward homogeneity within a field via coercive pressures felt by industries and their constituent organizations from outside forces such as law, regulations, and political pressure.[8] The other types of isomorphism also drive organizations toward homogeneity. Mimetic isomorphism leads organizations to adopt the practices of other successful organizations in their field as a means to address market uncertainty, while normative isomorphism is driven by professionalization within an industry or field.

It is also important to note that while the vast majority of scholarship examining similarities in business form focuses on the homogeneity of organizational structure and practice, the law also often displays a great deal of homogeneity. Interestingly, a theoretical explanation for legal homogeneity is largely absent in scholarship that explores the reciprocal relationship between law and economic actors. What can be gleaned from the literature, however, is that isomorphic influences possibly affect the promulgation of laws, as some scholars have argued that neoinstitutional ideas and concepts could be applied to actions by judges, regulators, and legislators.[9] More specifically, the abstract notion of structuration could be applied to legislative behavior as well. In this regard, neoinstitutional scholars would predict that the norms and assumptions surrounding what counts as positive, rational, or wise legislation on a given issue would tend toward similar justifications, legal approaches, and even specifics within legal texts. This most likely results from mimetic isomorphism, as legislators attempt to respond to uncertainty within their states and business communities by looking to the approaches taken by other states when crafting legislation.

Figure 5.1 presents a theoretical model that applies the basic premises introduced above to the distilling industry. On the one hand, it is predicted that law will directly influence and shape the distillery industry through coercive isomorphic pressures, as law will dictate certain organizational forms and practices. On the other hand, through the mobilization of political resources and tactics, the distillery industry and indeed the entire alcoholic beverage industry will attempt to influence the laws and regulations that both facilitate and constrain their behavior and business practices. As such, law is embedded within the market for alcoholic beverage and spirits, along with its specific industries and organizations. Finally, while the law is influenced by the political tactics and strategies utilized by the alcoholic beverage and distillery industries, law is also shaped by isomorphic pressures acting on legislators from outside (e.g., other states) as they draft and pass rules and regulations.

Post-Prohibition Development of State Laws and Regulations

The first research question posed in this chapter explored the extent to which law has shaped and structured the distilling industry. Neoinstitutional scholars suggest that coercive pressures from laws and regulations exert significant pressures on industries and their constituent organizations and thus play a substantial role in shaping organizational fields. Certainly, the effect that law has had on the distilling industry is a clear example of the coercive pressure that law can provide. Indeed, from the beginning of national Prohibition in 1920 through 2018, there may be no other influence that has shaped and continues to shape the distillery industry as much as the law, given that the law determines the degree to which the production of alcohol is legally permitted. This is borne out in the history of alcohol regulation post-Prohibition as well as in the recent rapid changes to laws governing the distillery industry.

An important preliminary issue related to the investigation of the relationship between law and the distilling industry is the determination of which law or laws are most relevant to the distillery industry in the United States. The current state of alcohol regulation in the United States can be traced back to the repeal of national Prohibition. In 1933, with the ratification of the Twenty-First Amendment to the U.S. Constitution, states were suddenly and rather unexpectedly forced to revive and redevelop their own alcohol regulations, as the federal government ceded much of the control it had previously held with regard to alcoholic beverage control. Indeed, federal law has little to say about the specifics related to the distillation of alcohol, other than a federal prohibition on the distillation of spirits at home by individual citizens,[10] the existence of federal distilled spirits and federal fuel alcohol permits for commercial distillation,[11] and a range of statutes designed to ensure that appropriate taxes are paid.[12] Thus, as will be described throughout the remainder of this chapter, the business of regulating the amounts of spirits that can be manufactured as well as the amount and manner in which spirits can be sold is left almost entirely up to the individual states. As such, state law will be the primary focus of this chapter.

Following the repeal of Prohibition, states were faced with a monumentally difficult task in crafting regulations regarding the manufacture, sale, and consumption of alcohol. Much of this difficulty can be traced to the fact that state governments needed to craft laws to regulate a newly legalized, previously

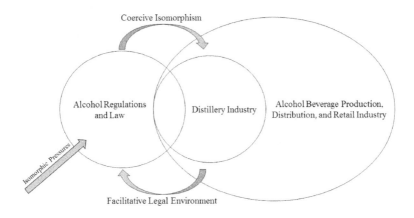

Figure 5.1. Theoretical Model as Applied to the Distillery Industry. Created by author.

underground industry that had been overseeing the manufacture, distribution, and sale of alcohol for thirteen years under Prohibition.[13] In response, many states adopted some variant of the monopoly approach, whereby the state controls all or part of the alcohol manufacture, distribution, or sales process. States favored this approach because proponents argued that it could destroy the connections between alcohol manufacturers and retailers that existed before Prohibition while also discouraging excessive consumption of alcohol by removing much of the profit motive found in private sales. Within two short years after the repeal of Prohibition, twenty states had adopted some form of monopoly system, and all states had enacted some degree of alcohol regulation, though most states focused their monopoly powers on the distribution of alcohol, not on its manufacturing or retail sales.[14]

Since the repeal of Prohibition, states have largely utilized either the *three-tier* or *control* approach to regulating alcohol. A three-tier system, variants of which currently exist in two-thirds of U.S. states, requires alcohol to be sold according to a state licensing regime in which the manufacture, distribution, and sale of alcohol is conducted by wholly separate entities.[15] In a three-tier system, manufacturers (tier one) can only sell to distributors (tier two), who can only sell to retailers (tier three), and the individuals or companies occupying each tier can neither have financial interests in one another nor set up exclusive business relationships across tiers.[16] This allows the state to intervene at each step of the process, breaking the potential ties between levels of production and distribution in a way that reduces the risk of excessive alcohol consumption while also ensuring efficient tax collection.[17]

Like those states using the three-tier approach, control states mandate the separation of the manufacture, distribution, and retail sales of alcohol.[18] In control states, however, some aspect of the distribution or retail sales of alcohol is directly controlled by state or local government. In Iowa, for example, the state oversees the distribution of liquor, which is then sold at retail by privately owned liquor stores. In North Carolina, alternatively, both the distribution and retail sales of liquor are directly controlled by the state and local alcoholic beverage control (ABC) boards, and the state and local boards run their own package stores.

Changes in the Legal and Regulatory Landscape around Craft Distilling

While the general approach dictated by the monopoly systems found within U.S. states has been rather static since the 1930s, since the turn of the twenty-first century, and certainly within the last decade, the entire regulatory approach to distilling has changed in ways that have completely reshaped the industry and led to the current boom in craft distilleries. Before 2000 only three states—Kentucky, Missouri, and Delaware—had laws that provided a regulatory framework that was friendly to commercial distillers, and by 2006 that number had only risen to six (adding Colorado, Montana, and New Hampshire). Then, in the 2010s states began to revise their distillery laws in earnest, and thirty states liberalized their rules and regulations between 2011 and 2015, bringing the total number of states with revised laws to forty-six. This progression can be seen in figure 5.2, which presents a map of the lower forty-eight U.S. states shaded according to the year in which each first enacted legislation that reformed and liberalized its distillery laws.[19]

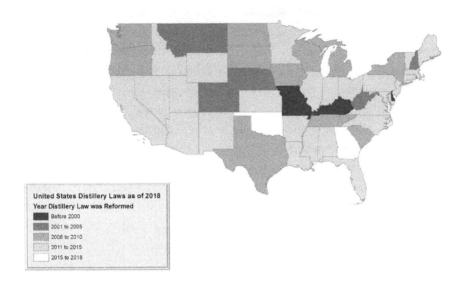

Figure 5.2. Lower Forty-Eight States by Year in which Reformed Distillery Laws Were First Enacted. Created by author.

The effect that this rapid change has had on distilling in the United States cannot be understated. The loosening of the legal regulatory framework surrounding distilling corresponds with the rapid growth in the distilling industry. In 2007, when only 11 states had passed laws friendly to distilleries (or allowed them at all), there were only 146 distilleries operating in the United States.[20] By 2011, when 26 states had reformed their laws, the number of distilleries had jumped to 356, and in 2016, when nearly every state had reformed its distillery laws in one way or another, the number of distilleries jumped to 1,118.[21]

Furthermore, the coercive effects of these laws are related to the number of distilleries found in each state. According to the American Distilling Institute (ADI), for instance, Colorado, which enacted reforms to its distillery regulations early (2001) and has laws that are especially favorable to small producers, has a total of forty-nine craft distilleries, or 8.98 per million residents.[22] Georgia, on the other hand, which only reformed its laws in 2016 and has one of the more draconian regulatory frameworks, has twenty-two craft distilleries, which is only 2.15 per million residents.[23] Finally, at the time the research was conducted for this study, Oklahoma, whose reform laws had yet to go into effect (although they will as of 2018), had no distilleries, according to the ADI.

While every state has elected to reform its laws and rules regarding the distillation of liquor, they have done so in a myriad of ways. On the most basic level, however, states generally fall into one of two categories when it comes to reforms in distillery laws: 1) those that have liberalized their distillery regulations for all producers and 2) those that have privileged certain types of producers, normally "small" craft distilleries. Nineteen states have taken the former approach and elected to liberalize their distillery laws for all producers, regardless of size. This means, for example, that small distillers in Tennessee such as Chattanooga Whiskey or the Corsair Artisan Distillery are subject to the same state regulations as Jack Daniel's,[24] which sold over eleven million cases of its Tennessee Whiskey in 2013.[25]

Alternatively, thirty-one states have elected to establish special rules and regulations for distilleries that meet certain parameters, electing to focus their reforms on smaller distillery operations. Most often, to qualify as a craft distillery, an operation must adhere to a production cap measured by proof gallons, standard gallons, barrels, or cases per year. In Louisiana, for instance, micro-distilleries are limited to producing no more than 12,000 gallons per year.[26] Delaware is quite different, as craft distilleries are permitted to produce 750,000 proof gallons per year (the equivalent of 937,500 standard gallons of liquor at forty proof).[27] Other than production caps, one state, Nevada, classifies craft distilleries according to an annual sales limit of 40,000 cases, while a few others place requirements on distilleries in addition to production caps.[28] Virginia, for example, requires small distillers to operate on farms in areas zoned for agriculture.[29]

Benefits Provided to Craft Distilleries

The difference between these two legal approaches is quite consequential for distillers, as the thirty-one states differentiating between distilleries according to size provide specific benefits to qualifying small distilleries. Some states, such as Kentucky and West Virginia, provide breaks on licensing fees or other taxes, while others, such as California and Montana, provide "sales assistance," which means that only qualifying distilleries are able to provide samples to distillery visitors or engage in retail sales. Furthermore, some states, such as Minnesota and Washington, have particularly friendly regimes whereby distillers get financial breaks through lower fees *and* sales assistance, while still others, including Arizona and New Jersey, provide other additional means of support. Each of these benefits is described in turn here.

Regulations Regarding Product Sampling and Retail Sales

One of the most common benefits states give to small distilleries is the ability to engage in sales practices that differ from their larger competitors. Of the twenty-three states that provide these benefits to small producers, the most common sales practices allowed under the law include the ability to offer samples of spirits to potential customers at the distillery and the ability to sell spirits at the distillery for either on- or off-site consumption. Both of these practices are seen as essential to the success of a craft distillery. First, with regards to the provision of samples, producers claim that samples are the primary, and perhaps only, way to market to and build a clientele for a new distillery operation. For example, Cris Steller, the executive director of the California Artisanal Distillers Guild, argues that distillers "need to be able to sell from [the] distillery tasting room [because] it's the only way to tell your story to consumers and know they understand what you're doing."[30]

Second, direct sales for on- or off-premises consumption is equally important, as small distilleries face steep hurdles when it comes to getting their product to market given the traditional requirements of the three-tier systems found across the United States.[31] This issue was described by Tito Beveridge, the founder of Tito's Handmade Vodka, who said that just because it's "legal to make [liquor,] that doesn't mean you can sell it" because "it's real tough for the little guy to get into the [distributor's] warehouse and out of the [distiller's] warehouse."[32] This is because distributors in many instances are only willing to take on products with a proven sales history, but in states with strict three-tier laws, it can be difficult for distillers to establish the requisite sales history needed to form such a relationship.

In addition to the difficult task of finding a distributor, craft distilleries operating in traditional three-tier systems are often forced to sell their products to distributors at prices so low that they lead to almost impossibly low profit margins. Before the 2013 liberalization of state laws under AB 933 in California, for instance, distillers were forced to sell their products at less than 50 percent of the eventual retail price to account for markups and taxes paid at each step in the three-tier process.[33] Thus, even if a distillery can get on board with a distributor, it can be difficult for small producers, and particularly new small producers, to get off the ground, given the high amount of capital needed to start distilling, the time involved in the distilling process, and the relatively small return per bottle sold.

Given the myriad of regulations and approaches found in the United States, table 5.1 provides a detailed breakdown of a variety of practices that distilleries are allowed to participate in by state. As shown in table 5.1, at present, forty-nine states allow distilleries to offer samples of their products directly to customers, with Oklahoma joining in late 2018. Laws allowing direct sales of bottles of liquor for off-site consumption at distilleries have caught on more slowly than sampling laws, although as of 2017 forty-seven states allow sales by the bottle.[34]

Unsurprisingly, despite the ubiquity of samples and bottle sales, states have elected to regulate both practices in a number of ways. As shown in table 5.1, twenty-eight states regulate how products can be sampled at the distillery. New Hampshire, for instance, limits samples to half-ounce pours and states that customers can consume no more than one sample of each product offered by the distillery.[35] On the other hand, Mississippi law limits samples to four quarter-ounce pours per customer, which means that the total sampled is capped at one ounce.[36] In addition to limiting amounts that can be sampled, some states, such as Kansas, require samples to be provided for free, while others allow distilleries to charge customers.[37] Finally, Utah, unique among the fifty states, requires that distillers "shall establish a distinct area for consumption of a taste outside the view of minors on the premises"[38] and that distilleries "shall have substantial food available that is served on licensed premises to an individual consuming a taste."[39]

Similarly, state laws allowing for bottle sales are also quite diverse. Among states that have legalized bottle sales at the distillery for off-premises consumption, twenty-four place limits on a distillery's sales. In North Carolina, for example, distillery visitors are limited to purchasing a single bottle of liquor *per year*.[40] To abide by this legislation, distilleries are required to provide

Table 5.1. State Laws Regulating Distillery Production and Sales

| State | Small Distiller Production Cap | On-Site Sales | | | Fee Reduction |
		Sampling Allowed (Limit)	Bottle (Limit)	On-Site Consumption (Limit)	
Alabama		Yes	Yes *(750 ml/ person daily)*	Yes	Yes
Alaska		Yes	Yes *(1 G/ person daily)*	Yes	No
Arizona	20,000 PG /yr.	Yes	Yes *(20% of annual production)*	Yes *(20% of annual production)*	No
Arkansas		Yes	Yes	No	No
California	100,000 G/ yr.	Yes *(1.5 oz/ person daily)*	Yes *(2.25 L/ person daily)*	Yes *(1.5 oz/person daily)*	No
Colorado	45,000 L/yr.	Yes	Yes	Yes	No
Connecticut	25,000 G/yr.	Yes *(2 oz/person daily)*	Yes *(1.5 L/ day or 5 G/person over 2 months)*	No	No

Continues on next page

Table 5.1. State Laws Regulating Distillery Production and Sales

| State | Small Distiller Production Cap | On-Site Sales | | | |
		Sampling Allowed (Limit)	Bottle (Limit)	On-Site Consumption (Limit)	Fee Reduction
Delaware	750,000 PG/yr.	Yes	Yes *(1 case/ person daily)*	Yes	Yes
Florida	75,000 G/yr.	Yes	Yes *(4 bottles/ person annually)*	No	No
Georgia		Yes *(0.5 oz/ person daily)*	No *(1 "free" bottle with tour/ person)*	No	No
Hawaii	232,500 G/yr.	Yes	Yes	Yes	No
Idaho		Yes *(0.75 oz/ person daily)*	Yes	No	No
Illinois	35,000 G/yr.	Yes *(0.75 oz/ person daily)*	Yes *(2,500 G annually)*	Yes	Yes
Indiana	10,000 G/yr.	Yes	Yes	Yes	Yes

Continues on next page

Table 5.1. State Laws Regulating Distillery Production and Sales

State	Small Distiller Production Cap	On-Site Sales			
		Sampling Allowed (Limit)	Bottle (Limit)	On-Site Consumption (Limit)	Fee Reduction
Iowa	50,000 PG/ yr.	Yes *(2 oz/person daily)*	Yes *(2 bottles/ person daily)*	Yes	No
Kansas	50,000 G/yr.	Yes	Yes	Yes	Yes
Kentucky	50,000 PG/ yr.	Yes *(1.75 oz/ person daily)*	Yes *(4.5 L/ person daily)*	Yes	Yes
Louisiana	12,000 G/yr.	Yes	Yes	Yes	Yes
Maine	50,000 G/yr.	Yes	Yes	Yes	Yes
Maryland		Yes *(2 oz/person daily)*	Yes *(2.25 L/ person daily)*	Yes	No
Massachusetts	*Fees Increase w/ Production*	Yes	Yes	Yes	Yes
Michigan	60,000 PG/ yr.	Yes	Yes	Yes	Yes

Continues on next page

Table 5.1. State Laws Regulating Distillery Production and Sales

| State | Small Distiller Production Cap | On-Site Sales | | | |
		Sampling Allowed (Limit)	Bottle (Limit)	On-Site Consumption (Limit)	Fee Reduction
Minnesota	40,000 G/yr.	Yes *(45 ml/ person daily)*	Yes *(1 375-ml bottle/ person daily)*	Yes	Yes
Mississippi		Yes *(1 oz/person daily)*	No	No	No
Missouri		Yes *(1 oz/person daily)*	Yes	Yes	No
Montana	25,000 G/yr.	Yes *(2 oz/person daily)*	Yes *(1 750-ml bottle/ person daily)*	Yes *(2 oz/person daily)*	No
Nebraska	10,000 PG/ yr.	Yes *(5 oz/person daily)*	Yes	Yes	Yes
Nevada	40,000 cases/yr.	Yes *(4 oz/person daily)*	Yes	Yes	No
New Hampshire		Yes *(0.5 oz/ person daily per label)*	Yes *(12 9-L cases/ person annually)*	Yes	No

Continues on next page

Table 5.1. State Laws Regulating Distillery Production and Sales

State	Small Distiller Production Cap	On-Site Sales			Fee Reduction
		Sampling Allowed (Limit)	Bottle (Limit)	On-Site Consumption (Limit)	
New Jersey	20,000 PG/ yr.	Yes *(1.5 oz/ person daily)*	Yes *(5 L/ person daily)*	Yes	Yes
New Mexico	150,000 PG/ yr.	Yes	Yes	Yes	No
New York	75,000 PG/ yr.	Yes *(0.75 oz/ person daily)*	Yes	Yes	Yes
North Carolina		Yes	Yes *(1 bottle/ person annually)*	No	No
North Dakota	25,000 PG/ yr.	Yes	Yes *(9 L/ person monthly)*	Yes	No
Ohio	100,000 PG/ yr.	Yes *(1 oz/person daily)*	Yes *(1.5 L/ person daily)*	No	Yes
Oklahoma		Yes *(3 oz/person daily)*[†]	No	No	No

Continues on next page

Table 5.1. State Laws Regulating Distillery Production and Sales

| State | Small Distiller Production Cap | On-Site Sales | | | |
		Sampling Allowed (Limit)	Bottle (Limit)	On-Site Consumption (Limit)	Fee Reduction
Oregon		Yes *(2.5 oz/ person daily)*	Yes	Yes	No
Pennsylvania	100,000 G/ yr.	Yes *(1.5 oz/ person daily)*	Yes	Yes	Yes
Rhode Island		Yes	Yes *(1 375-ml bottle/ person daily)*	Yes	No
South Carolina	124,000 C/ yr.	Yes *(1.5 oz/ person daily)*	Yes *(2.25 L/ person daily)*	No	Yes
South Dakota	50,000 G/yr.	Yes	Yes	No	Yes
Tennessee		Yes	Yes *(5 G/visit)*	Yes	No
Texas		Yes	Yes *(1.5 L/ person monthly)*	Yes	No

Continues on next page

Table 5.1. State Laws Regulating Distillery Production and Sales

| State | Small Distiller Production Cap | On-Site Sales | | | |
		Sampling Allowed (Limit)	Bottle (Limit)	On-Site Consumption (Limit)	Fee Reduction
Utah		Yes (*Must serve out of view of minors; must serve food*)	Yes	Yes	No
Vermont		Yes	Yes	Yes	No
Virginia	36,000 G/yr.	Yes (*4 oz/person daily*)	Yes	No	Yes
Washington	150,000 PG/yr.	Yes (*2 oz/person daily*)	Yes	No	Yes
West Virginia	20,000 PG/yr.	Yes (*"Moderate" quantities only*)	Yes	No	Yes
Wisconsin		Yes (*1.5 oz/person daily*)	Yes	Yes	No
Wyoming		Yes (*3 oz/person daily*)	Yes	No	No

Continues on next page

Table 5.1. State Laws Regulating Distillery Production and Sales

State	Small Distiller Production Cap	On-Site Sales			
		Sampling Allowed (Limit)	Bottle (Limit)	On-Site Consumption (Limit)	Fee Reduction
Total States	31	49[†] (28)	48 (24)	35 (3)	21

† As of October 1, 2018
Abbreviations: PG = proof gallons; G = gallons; L = liters
Source: State distillery laws as listed in table 5.2.

information on all customers to a searchable database, which can be used by other distilleries to determine whether customers have purchased their single bottles during that year. North Carolina also mandates that sales can only occur in wet counties, that bottles first be sold to local ABC boards and then bought back at wholesale prices by the distillery, and that distillers must affix a sticker to each bottle that reads "North Carolina Distillery Tour Commemorative Spirit."[41] Compared with its neighbor to the north, South Carolina represents a much more moderate approach to bottle sales, as distilleries are allowed to sell directly to consumers no more than three 750-milliliter bottles per day.[42] Delaware law, however, is even more permissive than both North and South Carolina, as it permits distilleries to sell up to one case (i.e., twelve 750-milliliter bottles) per customer per day.[43]

While the ability to provide samples and to sell bottles at retail to customers represents the primary way for distilleries to thrive, laws permitting other previously illegal business practices are also becoming more common. Chief among these business practices is the ability to sell spirits at the distillery for on-premises consumption. As shown in table 5.1, thirty-five states currently allow this practice, with Iowa joining on July 1, 2017. While the provision of samples and direct bottle sales are seen as important, many circles view on-premises consumption as equally valuable. For example, within days of the passage of the on-premises sales law in Iowa, but even before it was signed by the governor, the

Cedar Ridge Distillery contracted for a hundred-thousand-dollar bar makeover and had already begun to hire additional staff to handle the expected increase in business.[44] Importantly, by allowing on-premises consumption, distillers argue that they will be more competitive. This is described by Garrett Burchett, the owner of Mississippi River Distilling: "It's such a customer expectation. When you go into a brewery, when you go into a winery, you expect that you can have a glass. And in a distillery, you couldn't" before the new law.[45]

Other Benefits Provided to Distillers

Beyond the ability to provide samples and sell directly to the public, there are a few other ways in which states can provide an advantage to distilleries, one of the most common being through reductions in licensing fees. Most distillers, who face a myriad of taxes and fees at the federal, state, and even local levels, argue that fee reductions help to ease one of the primary barriers to entry into the distilling industry—the startup and continuing costs of operation.[46] Following this logic, twenty-one states provide small distillers with breaks on licensing fees. Some reductions are relatively minor in relative terms, such as in Maine, where large distilleries pay an annual license fee of $1,000 while small distilleries pay an annual fee of $100.[47] In other states, however, the break is larger, such as in Kansas, where large distilleries pay an annual license fee of $5,000 while small distilleries pay an annual fee of $500.[48] The largest break, however, can be found in South Carolina, where large distilleries pay a biannual fee of $50,000, while qualifying microdistilleries only pay $5,000 biannually.[49]

Finally, some states go beyond providing special exceptions to the three-tier or control system and fee breaks to small distilleries by providing other special benefits available only to small producers. In Arizona, for instance, craft distillers are permitted to band together for what is known as cooperative tasting rooms where multiple craft distilleries can provide samples of their products and sell their products via mail order to state residents.[50] In New Jersey craft distillery license holders can get a state-issued label specifying that their product is "New Jersey Distilled" if not less than 51 percent of the raw materials used in the production process came from the state.[51] Finally, New York has a unique approach, as the 2014 Craft New York Act included $2 million of grant funding for the promotion of craft beverages produced in the state.[52]

Sources of Legal Change in Distillery Laws: The Effect of Post-Prohibition Alcohol Regulations on the Current Legal Environment

As described in the previous section, despite the variety in approaches, the liberalization of state laws across the United States has made a significant contribution to the rapid growth of the craft distillery industry. What is less clear, however, is why this liberalization occurred, given that laws regulating the production of spirits remained largely static for seventy-odd years after the repeal of Prohibition in 1933. The answer to this question lies in a long period of gradual normative and cultural change in the alcohol industry from the end of Prohibition until the turn of the twenty-first century, followed by a period of rapid change in the spirits production industry during the late 2000s, which seems to have occurred as a result of increasing political pressures and isomorphic pressures felt by state legislatures.

First, a lengthy period of gradual change occurred within the alcohol industry as a whole and the spirits industry more specifically between the end of Prohibition and the end of the twentieth century. Much of this change was driven by evolving public and regulatory views of alcohol consumption. Historically, the temperance movement advanced a moral argument tying the consumption of alcohol to social ills, including crime, political and social disorder, and public health concerns.[53] In the post-Prohibition years, this moral charge and the desire to limit alcohol consumption remained as both explicit and implicit values of most alcoholic beverage control boards and regulatory agencies. Over time, however, the perception of the role of state regulations and regulators changed and evolved in the minds of legislators and board members themselves. By the 1970s the view that regulators' primary role was to prevent excessive alcohol consumption was largely abandoned by state officials and replaced with the belief that the aim of the legal regulatory framework surrounding alcohol regulation was the generation of government revenue and the maintenance of orderly markets free of criminal elements.[54] During the same period, American opinions about alcohol use and consumption began to moderate, particularly during the coming of age of the World War II generation and the Baby Boomers.[55]

In the seventy or so years after Prohibition, there was also a gradual loosening of alcohol production and retail laws as successive types of beverages began to be deregulated by lawmakers. The first of these beverages was beer, which received symbolic endorsement by regulators immediately following Prohibition, given that it was made widely available by most states, unlike wine and liquor.[56] Within a short time, wine also benefited from decreasing regulation, leaving liquor as the most highly regulated type of alcohol. Importantly, this symbolic endorsement of beer and wine eventually led to the liberalization of regulations surrounding their manufacture, distribution, and retail sale a few decades before the changes in craft distilling laws and the rise of craft distilleries. For example, the craft beer movement can trace its roots to the late 1970s, when the Home Brew Act of 1978 (HR 1337) sowed the seeds of the grassroots movement toward craft beer production.[57] Similarly, the "wine wars" of the 1990s and 2000s, which were a fight about the distribution of wine via mail order across state lines, led to the liberalization of wine distribution laws[58] and have corresponded with a nearly 40 percent increase between 1990 and 2015 in the number of gallons of wine consumed annually by Americans.[59] Both of these movements set the stage for the liberalization of craft distillery laws, as they gave distillers models to follow when fighting for their industry while simultaneously desensitizing both the public and regulators to more lax approaches to alcohol regulation.

The Political Fight to Liberalize Distillery Laws

These gradual changes helped lay the foundation of the craft distilling boom, but the recent rapid changes seen in statehouses and the industry since the turn of the century can be traced to political movements led by distillers as well as mimetic pressures felt by state legislators. In the political aspect of the fight, individual distillers and trade organizations have been the primary voices fighting for more distillery-friendly laws and regulations. In Indiana, for example, Ted Huber, a distiller who is known as "the grandfather of Indiana distilling," has been credited with the creation of the Indiana Artisan Distiller Permit[60] due to his direct lobbying efforts.[61] And in Iowa a group of local distillers fought for five years to win the passage of the most recent reforms to their state's laws allowing for on-site consumption of spirits at distilleries, and, says Jeff Quint, owner of the Cedar Ridge Distillery, he and his fellow distillers look "forward to not hanging out in the [state] Capital anymore."[62]

Beyond lobbying, some distillers have been lucky enough to participate in the legislative process directly. In Idaho, for instance, distillers worked closely with state senators when crafting the state's distillery law.[63] Other liquor manufacturers turn to groups like the American Distilling Institute and the American Craft Spirits Association, which provide model legislation, informative news stories, and calls to action on their websites. Still other efforts, finally, are more indirect and take the form of providing information to the public in the hopes that constituents will continue to demand more access to craft spirits from their legislators. In a review of a distillery tour in Florida, for example, a travel author said that their "tour was more Chamber of Commerce than it was bleeding-hear tutorial on gourmet liquor," given its focus on the positive economic impacts attributable to craft distilling.[64]

Facing these efforts, however, has been powerful groups of distributors and retailers who view direct bottle sales and on-premises consumption at distilleries as threats to their businesses. As explained by Cris Steller of the California Artisanal Distillers Guild, "Distributors are fighting back hard. California is one of the top five markets for spirits in the world, and they think they're going to give up market share if we can sell out of our distilleries."[65] Following this reasoning, distributors in Georgia have spent more than five hundred thousand dollars since 2011 fighting efforts by distillers to reform the state's three-tier distribution system. Similarly, distributors in Florida fought against the expansion of the state's limitations on direct bottle sales by distilleries, which used to stand at four 350-milliliter bottles per year (and currently stand at four 1.75-milliliter bottles), due to the purported damage it would do to distributors' business.[66] Finally, distillers' opponents can sometimes be found within states themselves, and not just from moral crusading legislators. In North Carolina, for example, local ABC boards have fought against expanding on-site sales laws for distilleries due to their own revenue concerns, given that approximately 24 percent of the retail price of each bottle of liquor sold in the state goes to the local boards.[67]

Beyond the effects attributable to political action by multiple stakeholders within the alcoholic beverages industry, it also appears that state legislators have faced isomorphic pressures in their creation of new laws favoring distilleries. Much of this pressure appears to stem from mimetic isomorphic influences, whereby state legislators faced with unclear and at times bleak economic climates in their states following the Great Recession of the late 2000s elected to compete with and look to other states when crafting distillery legislation. Indeed, given the unknowns surrounding state economies and tax revenues, much of the focus of legislators when liberalizing distillery laws has been on the purported economic benefits that accompany distillery operations. New York Governor Andrew Cuomo, in championing a distillery-friendly law in his state, said, "By cutting red tape and easing regulations on farm distilleries, we are supporting the growth and expansion of small businesses that create new jobs and drive economic growth across New York."[68] Similarly, government officials have also focused on the benefits distilleries bring to local economies, as many craft distilleries locally source their ingredients. One Florida state representative, arguing in favor of expanded distillery bottle sales, said that such a move would benefit "small Florida family farms that provide our citrus, corn and sugar cane."[69] Thus, it should not be surprising that the fastest rise in reforms to state distillery laws came after the economic crash in 2007, as thirty-nine states have enacted reforms since that year.

Finally, following the neoinstitutionalist framework, many state legislators have looked to what has been done elsewhere when crafting legislation and justifying the passage of new laws. In New Jersey, for instance, a state assembly member argued that a new law in the state favoring craft distillers "could help create jobs and, as has happened in other states, boost the economy and generate millions in tax revenue."[70] Similarly, in pressing for the passage of a more distillery-friendly law in Florida, state senator Greg Steube argued that other states were passing his state by and grabbing market share from Florida distilleries because of the state's overly restrictive laws.[71] Thus, the response of legislators to these pressures has been to observe what other states have done, adopting their tactics and approaches to regain what legislators see as lost market advantage within their borders.

Conclusion

While much of the illegal moonshine industry has largely disappeared, it has been replaced both nationwide and in traditional Appalachian states by legal moonshine produced by craft distillers. Indeed, in the last decade, the national craft distilling industry has grown exponentially, seeing nearly 700 percent

Table 5.2. State Distillery Laws

Alabama	Code of Ala. § 28-3A-1 et seq. (2017)
Alaska	Alaska Stat. § 04.06.010 et seq. (2017)
Arizona	ARS § 4-101 et seq. (2017)
Arkansas	ACA § 3-1-101 et seq. (2017)
California	Cal. Bus. and Prof. Code § 23000 et seq. (2017)
Colorado	CRS 12-47-101 et seq. (2016)
Connecticut	Conn. Gen. Stat. § 30-1 et seq. (2017)
Delaware	4 Del. C. § 101 et seq. (2017)
Florida	Fla. Stat. § 561.01 et seq. (2017)
Georgia	OCGA § 3-1-1 et seq. (2016)
Hawaii	HRS § 281-1 et seq. (2017)
Idaho	Idaho Code § 23-101 et seq. (2017)
Illinois	235 ILCS 5/1-1 et seq. (2017)
Indiana	Ind. Code Ann. § 7.1-1-1-1 et seq. (2017)
Iowa	Iowa Code § 123.1 et seq. (2016)
Kansas	KSA § 41-101 et seq. (2017)
Kentucky	KRS § 241.010 et seq. (2017)
Louisiana	LA RS § 26:1 et seq. (2017)
Maine	28-A MRS § 1 et seq. (2017)

Continues on next page

Table 5.2. State Distillery Laws

Maryland	Md. Ann. Code art. AB, § 1-101 et seq. (2017)
Massachusetts	ALM GL ch. 138, § 1 et seq. (2017)
Michigan	MCLS § 436.1101 et seq. (2017)
Minnesota	Minn. Stat. § 340A.101 et seq. (2017)
Mississippi	Miss. Code Ann. § 67-1-1 et seq. (2017)
Missouri	§ 311.010 RSMo. et seq. (2017)
Montana	16-1-101, MCA et seq. (2017)
Nebraska	RRS Neb. § 53-101 et seq. (2017)
Nevada	Nev. Rev. Stat. Ann. § 597.120 et seq. (2017) Nev. Rev. Stat. Ann. § 369.010 et seq. (2017)
New Hampshire	RSA Tit. XIII, ch. 175 et seq. (2017)
New Jersey	NJ Stat. § 33:1-1 et seq. (2017)
New Mexico	NM Stat. Ann. § 60-6A-1 et seq. (2017)
New York	NY CLS Al. Bev. § 1 et seq. (2017)
North Carolina	NC Gen. Stat. § 18B-100 et seq. (2017)
North Dakota	ND Cent. Code, § 5-01-01 et seq. (2017)
Ohio	ORC Ann. 4301.01 et seq. (2017)
Oklahoma	37A Okl. St. § 1-101 et seq. (2016)
Oregon	ORS § 471.001 et seq. (2017)

Continues on next page

Table 5.2. State Distillery Laws

Pennsylvania	47 PS § 1-101 et seq. (2016)
Rhode Island	RI Gen. Laws § 3-1-1 et seq. (2017)
South Carolina	SC Code Ann. § 61-6-10 et seq. (2017)
South Dakota	SD Codified Laws § 35-1-1 et seq. (2016)
Tennessee	Tenn. Code Ann. § 57-3-101 et seq. (2017)
Texas	Tex. Alco. Bev. Code § 1.01 et seq. (2017)
Utah	Utah Code Ann. § 32B-1-101 et seq. (2016)
Vermont	7 VSA § 1 et seq. (2017)
Virginia	Va. Code Ann. § 4.1-100 et seq. (2017)
Washington	Code Wash. (ARCW) § 66.04.010 et seq. (2017)
West Virginia	W. Va. Code § 60-1-1 et seq. (2017)
Wisconsin	Wis. Stat. § 125.01 et seq. (2017)
Wyoming	Wyo. Stat. § 12-1-101 et seq. (2017)

growth since 2007. The primary driver behind this explosive growth has been the liberalization of laws regulating the production of spirits, particularly those law governing small producers, as these rules and regulations have been reformed at a rate that rivals only the rapid growth of the industry itself. These changes, however, have not happened in a vacuum, as the evolution of state laws and the growth of the craft distillery industry have occurred in tandem as each has contributed to the growth in the other. While slow changes in attitudes and legal approaches toward alcohol consumption following Prohibition laid the foundation for the state of the industry as it exists today, it was only once craft distillers began to advocate for the liberalization of state laws regarding liquor that these changes began to happen in earnest.

This trend, while likely spurred along by the economic uncertainty caused by the Great Recession, grew over time as more and more states began to reform their distilling laws, which led citizens and producers in neighboring states to demand reforms of their own.

NOTES

1. This chapter examines laws regulating the commercial production of spirits as they existed in July 2017. The discussion of various state and federal laws that follows is not designed, nor should it be considered to be a substitute for formal legal advice regarding the distillation of spirits from a licensed, local attorney who is an expert in local state laws and federal regulations regarding the production of alcohol.

2. "Illicit Liquor (Moonshine)," United States Alcohol and Tobacco Tax and Trade Bureau, accessed July 7, 2017, https://www.ttb.gov/statistics/95newa08.htm.

3. For data on distilleries in general, see "Distilleries: Key Statistics," IbisWorld, accessed July 3, 2017, http://clients1.ibisworld.com/reports/us/industry /keystatistics.aspx?entid=290. For data on craft distilleries, see "ACSA Releases Economic Data Unveiling the State of the Craft Spirits Industry," American Craft Spirits Association, accessed July 3, 2017, www.americancraftspirits.org /2016/10/28/acsa-releases-economic-data-unveiling-the-state-of-the-craft -spirits-industry/.

4. "Distilleries: Key Statistics."

5. Ibid.

6. Neil Fligstein, *The Architecture of Markets: An Economic Sociology of Twenty-First Century Capitalist Societies* (Princeton, NJ: Princeton University Press, 2001).

7. Paul J. DiMaggio and Walter W. Powell, "The Iron Cage Revisited: Institutional Isomorphism and Collective Rationality in Organizational Fields," *American Sociological Review* 48 (1983): 147–60.

8. Ibid.

9. Mark C. Suchman and Lauren B. Edelman, "Legal Rational Myths: The New Institutionalism and the Law and Society Tradition," *Law and Social Inquiry* 21 (1996): 903–66.

10. While 26 USC § 5042(a)(2) allows for the production of wine for personal use and 26 USC § 5053(e) provides for the production of beer for personal use, no statute exists allowing individual citizens to distill spirits for personal use.

11. Federal rules governing distillery permit applications can be found in the Code of Federal Regulations at 27 CFR 19.

12. Punishments for various tax payment failures can be found in 26 USC § 5602, 26 USC § 5615(3), 26 USC § 7201, and 26 USC § 7301.

13. For a discussion of the challenges faced by states immediately following the passage of the Twenty-First Amendment to the U.S. Constitution, see Harry G. Levine and Craig Reinarmen, "From Prohibition to Regulation: Lessons from Alcohol Policy for Drug Policy," *Milbank Quarterly* 69 (1991): 461–94. For a discussion of more modern challenges, see Robin Room, "Alcohol Monopolies in the U.S.: Challenges and Opportunities," *Journal of Public Health Policy* 8 (1987): 509–30.

14. Ibid.

15. Vijay Shanker, "Alcohol and Direct Shipment Laws, the Commerce Clause, and the Twenty-First Amendment," *Virginia Law Review* 85 (1999): 353–83.

16. Andrew Tamayo, "What's Brewing in the Old North State: An Analysis of Beer Distribution Laws Regulating North Carolina's Craft Breweries," *North Carolina Law Review* 88 (2010): 2198–2248.

17. Shanker, "Alcohol and Direct Shipment Laws."

18. Tamayo, "What's Brewing."

19. Both Alaska and Hawaii revised their state laws regarding the commercial distillation of alcohol in 2014.

20. "Distilleries: Key Statistics."

21. Ibid.

22. "Map of American Craft Distilleries," American Distilling Institute, accessed June 22, 2017, http://distilling.com/resources/maps-of-craft-distilleries/map-of -us-craft-distilleries/.

23. Ibid.

24. Tenn. Code Ann. § 57-3-202 (2017).

25. Bruce Schreiner, "Jack Daniels in Legal Fight with Small Distiller," *Kingsport Times News*, October 25, 2013.

26. LA RS § 26:71(A)(3)(d) (2017).

27. 4 Del. C. § 512E(c)(1) (2017).

28. Nev. Rev. Stat. Ann. § 597.235(2)(b) (2017).

29. Va. Code Ann. § 4.1-206(2) (2017).

30. Corie Brown, "The Legal Lowdown on Starting a Brewery or Distillery," Entrepreneur.com, accessed June 20, 2017, https://www.entrepreneur.com/article /246100.

31. Noah Rothbaum, *The Business of Spirits: How Savvy Marketers, Innovative Distilleries, and Entrepreneurs Changed How We Drink* (New York: Kaplan Publishing, 2007).

32. Rothbaum, *Business of Spirits*, 13.

33. Lou Fancher, "Alameda: Bill Changes Landscape for Distilleries," *Contra Costa Times*, November 27, 2013.

34. The approach taken to bottle sales is unique in Georgia, as distillers are allowed to distribute their product but are not allowed to formally charge for it. Specifically, under Georgia law, distilleries can provide a single *free* souvenir bottle of spirits as part of a distillery tour (OCGA § 3-4-180 [2016]). Distillers are allowed, however, to offer tours at several price points, which indirectly allows manufacturers to "charge" for their "free" souvenir products.

35. RSA Tit. XIII Ch. 178:6(IV) (2017).

36. Miss. Code Ann. § 67-1-46 (2017).

37. KSA § 41–305(b) (2017).

38. Utah Code Ann. § 32B-11-210(6)(a) (2016).

39. Ibid.

40. NC Gen. Stat. § 18B-1105(a)(4) (2017).

41. Ibid.

42. SC Code Ann. § 61-6-1150(4) (2017).

43. 4 Del. C. § 512E(c)(4) (2017).

44. Erin Murphey, "Craft Distilleries Toast New Iowa Law," *Quad City Times*, May 9, 2017, accessed June 22, 2017, http://qctimes.com/news/local/government-and-politics/craft-distilleries-toast-new-iowa-law/article_5b9ac2f4-36a6-5470-a6a7-6198cadb7a10.html.

45. Ibid.

46. Erica Sweeny, "Small Batch Spirits," *Arkansas Money and Politics Magazine*, September/October 2015, accessed June 21, 2017, http://amppob.com/cover-story-small-batch-spirits/.

47. 28-A MRS § 1551 (2017).

48. KSA § 41–310 (2017).

49. For the statute governing large distillery fees, see SC Code Ann. § 61-6-1110 (2017). For the statute governing microdistillery fees, see SC Code Ann. § 61-6-1120 (2017).

50. ARS § 4-205.10 (2017).

51. NJ Stat. § 33:1-10 (2017).

52. Brian Mahoney, "Craft Beverage Legislation Goes Down Smooth in NY," Law360.com, December 2, 2014, accessed June 22, 2017, https://www.law360 .com/articles/599348/craft-beverage-legislation-goes-down-smooth-in-ny.

53. Mark E. Lender and James K. Martin, *Drinking in America: A History* (New York: The Free Press, 1987).

54. Room, "Alcohol Monopolies in the U.S."

55. Tamayo, "What's Brewing."

56. Ibid.

57. Nathaniel G. Chapman, J. Slade Lellock, and Cameron Lippard, "Exploring the Cultural Dimensions of Craft Beer," in *Untapped: Exploring the Cultural Dimensions of Craft Beer*, ed. Nathaniel G. Chapman, J. Slade Lellock, and Cameron Lippard (Morgantown: West Virginia University Press, 2017).

58. Shirley Chen, "Craft Beer Drinkers Reignite the Wine Wars," *Loyola Consumer Law Review* 26 (2014): 526–44.

59. "Wine Consumption in the U.S.," Wine Institute.org, last modified July 8, 2016, https://www.wineinstitute.org/resources/statistics/article86.

60. Burns Ind. Code Ann. § 7.1-3-27 *et seq.* (2017).

61. Carson Quinn, "Indiana Is in the Midst of a Distilling Boom," Thrillist.com, October 5, 2016, accessed June 22, 2017, https://www.thrillist.com/drink/ indianapolis/indiana-alcohol-laws-permits-distilling.

62. Murphey, "Craft Distilleries Toast."

63. Tara Morgan, "Whiskey Business in Idaho," *Boise Weekly*, July 9, 2014, accessed June 22, 2017, www.boiseweekly.com/boise/whiskeybusiness/Content?oid =3148024.

64. Beth Kassab, "Craft Distilleries Good for Business, Jobs," *Orlando Sentinel*, January 5, 2017, accessed June 21, 2017, www.orlandosentinel.com/opinion/os -craft-distillery-beth-kassab-20170105-column.html.

65. Brown, "Legal Lowdown."

66. Jim Rosica, "Florida Distillery Bill Put On Hold, Then Passed," FloridaPolitics. com, April 26, 2017, accessed June 22, 2017, http://floridapolitics.com /archives/236845-craft-distillery-bill.

67. Owen Covington, "Craft Distilling Is North Carolina's Next Big Thing," *Triad Business Journal*, March 20, 2015, accessed June 22, 2017, www.bizjournals.com /triad/print-edition/2015/03/20/craft-distilling-is-north-carolinas-next-big-thing.html.

68. "Farm Distilleries Nearly Double in 2 Years of NY Craft Act," *Evening Tribune*,

December 14, 2016, accessed June 22, 2017, www.eveningtribune.com /news/20161214/farm-distilleries-nearly-double-in-2-years-of-craft-ny-act.

69. Nick Evans, "House Panel Approves Three Changes to Alcohol Bill," WFSUNews.com, March 28, 2017, accessed June 22, 2017, http://news.wfsu.org /post/house-panel-approves-three-changes-alcohol-regulations.

70. Jon Offrendo, "New Jersey Distilled: Gov. Chris Christie Signs Craft Distillery Bill into Law," *Times of Trenton*, August 9, 2013, accessed June 22, 2017, www .nj.com/mercer/index.ssf/2013/08/new_jersey_distilled_gov_chris_christie _signs_craft_distillery_bill_into_law.html.

71. Wayne Price, "Are Distilled Craft Spirits the Next Trend in Florida?," FloridaToday.com, February 3, 2017, accessed June 22, 2017, www.floridatoday .com/story/news/2017/02/03/distilled-craft-spirits-next-trend-florida/97373250/.

CHAPTER 6

From the Appalachian Mountains to the Puget Sound and Beyond: Distilling Authenticity in Modern Moonshine

KAITLAND M. BYRD, J. SLADE LELLOCK, AND NATHANIEL G. CHAPMAN

We partook of the region, not just in bread and kernels, but in the purest, potent-est distillations known to man and angels. We leaned back from the table and began to discuss, debate, and imagine exactly what all this food might mean.

—Ronni Lundy

Debates surrounding authentic food products are not intended to establish one product as more authentic than another. Instead, research on authenticity focuses on how producers employ authenticity claims to make their products more marketable and profitable.[1] Modern consumers are surrounded by a plethora of choices, from food, clothing, and automobiles to a multitude of others. Consumers make choices with a limited amount of information; thus, claims of authenticity are a way for consumers to choose a product based on what they believe is a true version of it. Producers are able to use these concerns of authenticity to brand their product as superior to their competitors.[2] Purchasing an authentic product also provides the consumer with cultural capital that can be used to secure and improve their social position.[3]

We begin this chapter by questioning how distilleries use claims of authenticity to create an online identity to market moonshine. We expand this question to address the differences between Appalachian and non-Appalachian distilleries' production of authenticity claims. Our findings suggest that distilleries relied on product sourcing; historical, familial, and geographical identity; product image; and the simplicity of handcrafted products to manage their image as authentic moonshine producers. Overall, distilleries employed authenticity claims to not only differentiate their products but also to market them as superior to their competitors.

Authenticity, Food, and the American South

Authenticity is a contested concept that continues to remain central in studies of music,[4] art,[5] television,[6] and food culture,[7] as well as culture as a whole.[8] While producers actively attempt to manage impressions of their products' authenticities, authenticity itself is not an inherent attribute of any object; rather, it is result of ongoing negotiation between producers and consumers. Producers view their products based on how successful they think the product image will be on the open market, or based on the product's relationship to the audience.[9] Producers rely on both the audience and the image of their product to draw on various claims to manage the impression of authenticity.[10] It is not inherent in a product; instead it is a social product created through interactions between actors in a cultural field.[11]

Johnston and Baumann explain five aspects of food culture that convey authenticity onto a product. First, geographic specificity is a product originating from a specific place. For example, Parmesan cheese from Parma, Italy, is possibly more authentic than Parmesan cheese in the green container found in most grocery stores. Second, history and tradition connect a product to the past through its preparation, appearance, and taste. Third, simplicity highlights food that may be complex but does not appear to be. Simplicity is often found in a product made from scratch. Fourth, ethnic connection reflects the bond between producer and a specific ethnicity. For example, Mexican food prepared by a Mexican chef is viewed as more authentic than Mexican food prepared by a Canadian chef. Fifth, personal connection is the bond between a producer and its past, traditionally through recipes passed down in families or individual creations drawing on a chef's history.[12]

These five aspects of authentic food are combined with a sixth measure of authenticity: exoticism. Exoticism means food that is either socially, culturally, or geographically distant from the consumer.[13] For example, chitterlings appear on menus in five-star restaurants around the country even though they are traditionally a food of the poor rural South and Mexico. The name is also commonly changed to chicharrones, reflecting the Spanish version of chitterlings, even though the two are the same. Exoticism makes it possible for foods to be commodified between cultures and thus appear on elite menus to be consumed by a typically white middle- or upper-class consumer who historically would have expressed disdain at consuming that product.[14] Purchases of exotic and authentic products give the consumer cultural capital because he is consuming authenticity and distinguishing himself from others. This is used as a status marker within social groups, such as foodies, to convey experience, class, and knowledge of food culture that other consumers lack.[15]

Products from the American South are socially, culturally, and in some cases geographically distant and culturally exotic from the rest of the country. John T. Edge explains that although southern food products have steadily risen in popularity in the past two decades, the version of those products available outside of the South is a slightly altered version from what appears throughout the South. This is not to say a southern product such as barbecue cannot be produced in other locales; it may take on a different product image but still be barbecue.[16] The South has been branded through the rise of tourism, food, and souvenirs that make it possible to take a sanitized piece of the South home as a commercialized reminder of the experience. The branding of consumer culture in the South is extremely profitable, but it also commodifies southern identities to make them palatable to outsiders.[17]

Claims of authenticity also have consequences for understandings of the past and historical products. Food and drink, unlike other cultural products, cease to exist once they are consumed but simultaneously offer an imagined connection to the past. Claims of authenticity impact consumers seeking a connection to and understanding of the past. For example, the erasure of black people from historical southern foodways impacts the identity of modern people of color seeking to understand their foodways.[18] Claims of authenticity in modern moonshine, focusing on culture and place, emphasize the beauty of a region that experienced oppressive poverty and inequality. Seeking authenticity for cultural products, especially within southern foodways, must retain the product's connection to its historical roots to prevent the romanticization of the past. This creates the opportunity to move beyond the oppression and commodification of the region by balancing the popularity of southern foodways, including moonshine, with an awareness of the people and conditions responsible for producing them.[19]

Authenticity is not an innate aspect of any product; it is an image carefully created by the producer. The market success of a product depends on the producer's ability to create an image of a product consumers are willing to pay money to consume. As time passes, the desires of consumers change, forcing producers to constantly change a product to meet evolving consumer demands.[20] For example, the changing appearance and accents of country music stars have drifted away from the more rural image and thick accent of the Johnny Cash era to a more modern image of the rural South or the rise of heirloom tomatoes throughout farmers' markets and grocery stores because they are more authentic than industrial-produced tomatoes.[21] As such, authenticity must be carefully managed to ensure the profitability of a cultural product.

What is Authentic Moonshine?

Traditionally, the American South has a reputation for being backward and behind the rest of the United States culturally. The dominant stereotypical image of Appalachian people is "as ignorant, backward people ridiculously out of step with emerging modern America and prone to little more than feuding, moonshining [and] idleness."[22] However, the rising popularity of southern tourism makes Appalachian identities and products marketable (see chapters 8 and 9). The rise of Gatlinburg, Tennessee, and Branson, Missouri, as well as numerous festivals throughout the Ozark and Appalachian Mountains presents Appalachian people and products as something to be experienced and for a price, taken home as a souvenir.[23] In the past two decades, Appalachian foodways, including moonshine, have moved from a low-class product isolated to the mountains to a modern craft beverage with popularity rising around the country.[24]

Moonshine is a product of the rural South, and the rise of legally distilled moonshine is another example of the rising popularity of southern foodways. Following a similar trajectory as other southern foodways, moonshine is no longer isolated to its region of origin. Moonshine does not have to be produced in an illegal still deep in the Appalachian Mountains to be authentic. The legalization of distilling in the South and rise of craft distilleries around the country mean spirits related to illegal moonshine can be created and sold around the country, yet moonshine's origins are distinctly and uniquely southern.[25] The spread of legally distilled moonshine draws on the popularity of modern food movements focusing on authentic products based on the producer's experiences or the sourcing of ingredients.[26]

The question becomes how do producers of a southern foodway like moonshine from Seattle, Washington, for example, claim authenticity compared to moonshine producers in Gatlinburg, Tennessee? How a product claims authenticity varies based on the six aspects of authenticity established by Johnston and Baumann in their research on foodies.[27] However, Peterson describes authenticity as the result of constant impression management on the part of the producers, which provides additional insight into this question that authenticity alone cannot.[28] Impression management is used to navigate social interactions and products. These interactions lack adequate information; thus, participants must make inferences to fill in the gaps. These inferences develop from the appearance, behavior, and nature of a social situation or product. People use these inferences to make conclusions about products, so the inferences must be managed and controlled to ensure the success of a product. For example, the possession of a James Beard award or nomination suggests a chef has a certain skill set that should be respected by other chefs. Individuals or products that signal specific characteristics should possess them. For example, local food is expected to be produced less than one hundred miles from where it is being sold. In a society filled with a multitude of cultural products, authenticity becomes a tool used by producers to manage the impression consumers have by claiming a product has intrinsic value rooted in its group or status identity, originality, and legitimacy. Therefore, producers are creating a niche in the market for their product because it is more authentic than other products.[29]

Current research on food culture and authenticity ignores the role of drinks and alcohol in food culture claims. The study of alcoholic beverages such as moonshine sheds light on how authenticity and impression management operate in another venue. It also makes it possible to study how moonshine producers across the country claim authenticity of a product traditionally produced in the Appalachian Mountains. This brings us to the three main questions guiding this chapter. First, how do distilleries create an online identity to market their products? Second, are there differences between Appalachian and non-Appalachian distilleries, and if so how do non-Appalachian distilleries convey authenticity regarding a traditionally Appalachian product? Third, how do distilleries engage in impression management to convey authenticity within their products?

Data Collection and Analysis
of Moonshine-Producing Distilleries

Using the Google search engine, we identified nearly two hundred unique commercial distilleries producing moonshine across the United States by searching for keywords such as "moonshine" and "distillery." While we could not find an actual official count of distillery operations producing moonshine at the time of writing, we assume significantly more distilleries operate in the United States than we used in our study. Of the nearly two hundred distilleries we found, only a hundred and sixty-eight had official websites.

As a preliminary phase in our data collection, we cataloged each distillery's name, the names of its moonshine products, its location (state, city, and county), and its web address. We then cross-referenced the Appalachian Regional Commission's (ARC) website to determine whether the distilleries in our sample were located within the Appalachian region. According to the ARC website, "the Region includes 420 counties in 13 states. It extends more than 1,000 miles, from southern New York to northeastern Mississippi, and is home to more than 25 million people."[30] The ARC website lists the counties in Appalachia, and we were able to verify whether the distilleries' counties were contained in the region. Of the 168 distilleries, 39 were categorized as located in Appalachia and 129 were not (we refer to these as non-Appalachian distilleries).

The next phase involved collecting data from the distilleries' websites. The data we collected was mostly textual but also included all the web graphics as well as distillery logos and images of the bottles, labels, and the distilleries themselves. All text and images were downloaded and sorted into categories in which each distillery has a unique heading and set of identifiers such as its name, location, and its status as Appalachian or non-Appalachian.

To address our research questions, we conducted a multistage visual and textual content analysis of our self-defined modern moonshine distillery websites; this definition was based on each distillery producing a white whiskey product and claiming it as moonshine, though most distilleries produced numerous other liquors as well. In the first stage of analysis, we read through the entire corpus of data to get an overview as well as to draw sensitizing concepts. After completing the first read-through, we concluded that the analysis of only a fraction of the total sample would yield saturation given the highly repetitive nature of the data. At this point, we randomly sampled our dataset to include only 77 total distilleries: 20 Appalachian and 44 non-Appalachian (see table 6.1). The ratio of Appalachian and non-Appalachian distilleries in our sample is proportional to our original population of distilleries.

In the second phase of our analysis, the authors each reread the data, making note of key concepts and frames. Upon completion of this phase, we developed a code dictionary and categorization scheme. Finally, we methodically examined each website for evidence of the previously identified concepts and frames. To do this, we performed a line-by-line reading of each website and coded it based on the themes and patterns we had found in the previous stage.

Overview of Commercial Distillery Websites

Websites varied in design elements such as color, fonts, imagery, layout, and so on. Likewise, commercial distillery websites showed significant variety in their incorporation of features such as the ability to book distillery tours, shop online, read about the distillation process, or view image galleries or videos. Many distillery websites were simple, sometimes consisting of a single static page containing only the most crucial information, such as distillery name, logo, location or address, brief description, and perhaps a contact email address or phone number. Typically, these more simplistic designs often used only a few different colors in their scheme, and images were scarce.

By comparison, other websites were complex and multifaceted in their design, which was likely indicative of professional web development and marketing. Websites with more complex designs typically contained many more images of the distillery itself but also of their distilleries' spirits, production processes, employees, and even images of the surrounding locale. Further, more complex websites were also more likely to have integrated their web presence across multiple other sites such as Facebook, Instagram, and Twitter. They also had interactive calendars showing upcoming distillery and community events such as live music performances. Many distillery websites, regardless of their complexity, listed any awards their spirits received.

While distillery websites varied dramatically in the aesthetic and functional dimensions discussed above, our visual and textual content analysis revealed several themes recurred repeatedly (see table 6.2). Specifically, the emphasis on the sourcing of local ingredients, handcrafted production processes, environmentally and economically sustainable business practices, a commitment to

Table 6.1. Craft Distillery Study Sample

Distillery	City	County	State	County Rurality*	Appalachian	Other Spirits
Alamo Distilling Co.	San Antonio	Bexar, Medina, Comal	TX	Mostly Urban	Non-Appalachian	Whiskey, Rum
Anchorage Distillery	Anchorage	Anchorage Municipality	AK	Mostly Urban	Non-Appalachian	Gin, Vodka
Batch 206 Distillery	Seattle	King	WA	Mostly Urban	Non-Appalachian	Gin, Bourbon, Vodka
Baton Rouge Distilling	Baton Rouge	East Baton Rouge Parish	LA	Mostly Urban	Non-Appalachian	Brandy, Bourbon
Bear Wallow Distillery	Nashville	Davidson	IN	Mostly Urban	Non-Appalachian	Rye Whiskey, Bourbon
Black Draft Distillery	Martinsburg	Berkeley	WV	Mostly Urban	Appalachian	Moonshine Only

Continues on next page

Table 6.1. Craft Distillery Study Sample

Distillery	City	County	State	County Rurality*	Appalachian	Other Spirits
Black Heron Spirits	West Richland	Benton	WA	Mostly Urban	Non-Appalachian	Whiskey, Vodka, Bourbon, Limoncello, Brandy, Gin, Wine
Blaum Bros. Distilling Co.	Galena	Jo Daviess	IL	Mostly Rural	Non-Appalachian	Bourbon, Gin, Vodka
Bone Spirits	Smithville	Bastrop	TX	Mostly Rural	Non-Appalachian	Bourbon, Gin, Vodka, Whiskey
Bottle Tree Beverage Co.	Gluckstadt	Madison	MS	Mostly Urban	Non-Appalachian	Vodka, Gin, Whiskey, Schnapps
Bouck Brothers Distilling	Idaho Springs	Clear Creek	CO	Completely Rural	Non-Appalachian	Bourbon, Whiskey
Boundary Oak Distillery	Radcliff	Hardin	KY	Mostly Urban	Non-Appalachian	Bourbon

Continues on next page

Table 6.1. Craft Distillery Study Sample

Distillery	City	County	State	County Rurality*	Appalachian	Other Spirits
Broad Branch Distillery	Winston-Salem	Forsyth	NC	Mostly Urban	Appalachian	Whiskey
Carolina Moon Distilling	Edgefield	Edgefield	SC	Mostly Rural	Non-Appalachian	Vodka, Bourbon, Whiskey, Rum
Claremont Distilled Spirits	Fairfield	Monmouth	NJ	Mostly Urban	Non-Appalachian	Vodka, Whiskey
Clayton Distillery	Clayton	Jefferson	NY	Mostly Urban	Non-Appalachian	Vodka, Gin, Bourbon
Climax Moonshine	Asheville	Buncombe	NC	Mostly Urban	Appalachian	Whiskey
Copper Run Distillery	Walnut Shade	Taney	MO	Mostly Urban	Non-Appalachian	Whiskey, Rum
Coulter and Payne Farm Distillery	Union	Franklin	MO	Mostly Rural	Non-Appalachian	Bourbon

Continues on next page

Table 6.1. Craft Distillery Study Sample

Distillery	City	County	State	County Rurality*	Appalachian	Other Spirits
Country Hammer Moonshine Distillery	Pittsburgh	Allegheny	PA	Mostly Urban	Appalachian	Moonshine Only
Crown Valley Distillery	Sainte Genevieve	Sainte Genevieve	MO	Mostly Rural	Non-Appalachian	Whiskey
Dark Corner Distillery	Greenville	Greenville	SC	Mostly Urban	Appalachian	Whiskey, Gin, Bourbon
Davis Valley Distillery	Rural Retreat	Wythe	VA	Mostly Rural	Appalachian	Vodka, Whiskey
Doc Collier Moonshine Distillery	Gatlinburg	Sevier	TN	Mostly Rural	Appalachian	Moonshine Only
Dragon Distillery	Frederick	Frederick	MD	Mostly Urban	Non-Appalachian	Vodka, Gin, Rum, Bourbon
Dusty Barn Distillery	Mount Vernon	Posey	IN	Mostly Rural	Non-Appalachian	Rye Whiskey, Whiskey

Continues on next page

Table 6.1. Craft Distillery Study Sample

Distillery	City	County	State	County Rurality*	Appalachian	Other Spirits
East Tennessee Distillery	Piney Flats	Sullivan	TN	Mostly Urban	Appalachian	Moonshine Only
Firefly Distillery	Charleston	Charleston	SC	Mostly Urban	Non-Appalachian	Vodka
Five and 20 Spirits	Westfield	Chautauqua	NY	Mostly Urban	Appalachian	Rye Whiskey, Bourbon, Limoncello, Brandy, Schnapps
Flag Hill Distillery	Lee	Strafford	NH	Mostly Urban	Non-Appalachian	Vodka, Gin, Rum, Brandy, Grappa, Wine
Fog's End Distillery	Salinas	Monterey	CA	Mostly Urban	Non-Appalachian	Rye Whiskey
Four Flights Distillery	Corning	Steuben	NY	Mostly Rural	Appalachian	Vodka, Bourbon, Gin
Great Notch Distillery	Wyckoff	Bergen	NJ	Mostly Urban	Non-Appalachian	Gin, Vodka, Whiskey

Continues on next page

Table 6.1. Craft Distillery Study Sample

Distillery	City	County	State	County Rurality*	Appalachian	Other Spirits
Gristmill Distillers	Keene	Essex	NY	Mostly Rural	Non-Appalachian	Bourbon, Cider
Hard Times Distillery	Monroe	Benton	OR	Mostly Urban	Non-Appalachian	Moonshine Only
Hatfield and McCoy Moon-shine	Gilbert	Mingo	WV	Mostly Rural	Appalachian	Moonshine Only
Hewn Spirits	Pipersville	Bucks	PA	Mostly Urban	Non-Appalachian	Rum, Bourbon, Rye Whiskey, Single Malt Whiskey
Hollow Creek Distillery	Leesville	Lexington, Saluda	SC	Mostly Urban	Non-Appalachian	Moonshine Only
Howling Moon Distillery	Asheville	Buncombe	NC	Mostly Urban	Appalachian	Moonshine Only
Ironroot Republic Distillery	Denison	Grayson	TX	Mostly Urban	Non-Appalachian	Vodka, Gin

Continues on next page

Table 6.1. Craft Distillery Study Sample

Distillery	City	County	State	County Rurality*	Appalachian	Other Spirits
Jakal Distillery	Lexington	Lexington	SC	Mostly Urban	Non-Appalachian	Rum
Jake's Creek Distillery	Sevierville	Sevier	TN	Mostly Rural	Appalachian	Moonshine Only
Kings County Distillery	Brooklyn	Kings	NY	Mostly Urban	Non-Appalachian	Bourbon, Single Malt Whiskey
KO Distilling	Manassas	None (Independent City)	VA	Mostly Urban	Non-Appalachian	Gin, Whiskey
Lake George Distilling Company	Fort Ann	Washington	NY	Mostly Rural	Non-Appalachian	Whiskey, Bourbon, Rye Whiskey
Last Shot Distillery	Skaneateles	Onondaga	NY	Mostly Urban	Non-Appalachian	Bourbon, Whiskey, Vodka
Loon Liquor Co.	Northfield	Dakota, Rice	MN	Mostly Urban	Non-Appalachian	Gin, Vodka

Continues on next page

Table 6.1. Craft Distillery Study Sample

Distillery	City	County	State	County Rurality*	Appalachian	Other Spirits
Mastermind Distillery	Pontoon Beach	Madison	IL	Mostly Urban	Non-Appalachian	Vodka
McLaughlin Distillery	Sewickley	Allegheny	PA	Mostly Urban	Appalachian	Bourbon, Whiskey, Vodka
Mid-Best Distillery	Gravois Mills	Morgan	MO	Completely Rural	Non-Appalachian	Rum
Mill Street Distillery	Utica	Licking	OH	Mostly Urban	Non-Appalachian	Bourbon, Grappa
Mountain Laurel Spirits	Bristol	Bucks	PA	Mostly Urban	Non-Appalachian	Rye Whiskey, Whiskey
Mountain Moonshine	Morgantown	Monongalia	WV	Mostly Urban	Appalachian	Moonshine Only

Continues on next page

Table 6.1. Craft Distillery Study Sample

Distillery	City	County	State	County Rurality*	Appalachian	Other Spirits
Mount Baker Distillery	Bellingham	Whatcom	WA	Mostly Urban	Non-Appalachian	Vodka, Gin
Mystic Mountain Distillery	Larkspur	Douglas	CO	Mostly Urban	Non-Appalachian	Whiskey, Vodka, Gin
Oakley Brothers Distillery	Anderson	Madison	IN	Mostly Urban	Non-Appalachian	Moonshine Only
Old Town Distilling Co.	Fort Collins	Larimer	CO	Mostly Urban	Non-Appalachian	Vodka, Gin, Bourbon, Whiskey
Ole Smoky Distillery	Gatlinburg	Sevier	TN	Mostly Rural	Appalachian	Moonshine Only
Onyx Spirits	East Hartford	Hartford	CT	Mostly Urban	Non-Appalachian	Whiskey
Ozark Distillery	Osage Beach	Camden, Miller	MO	Mostly Rural	Non-Appalachian	Whiskey, Vodka

Continues on next page

Table 6.1. Craft Distillery Study Sample

Distillery	City	County	State	County Rurality*	Appalachian	Other Spirits
Pinchgut Hollow Distillery	Fairmont	Marion	WV	Mostly Urban	Appalachian	Whiskey
Port Chilkoot Distillery	Haines	Haines	AK	Completely Rural	Non-Appalachian	Gin, Bourbon, Rye Whiskey, Vodka
Ridge Runner Distillery	Chalkhill	Fayette	PA	Mostly Urban	Appalachian	Vodka, Whiskey
Rock Town Distillery	Little Rock	Pulaski	AR	Mostly Urban	Non-Appalachian	Vodka, Bourbon, Rye Whiskey, Rum, Gin
Rusted Crow Spirits	Dearborn Heights	Wayne	MI	Mostly Urban	Non-Appalachian	Vodka, Rum, Gin
Short Mountain Distillery	Woodbury	Cannon	TN	Mostly Rural	Appalachian	Bourbon

Continues on next page

Table 6.1. Craft Distillery Study Sample

Distillery	City	County	State	County Rurality*	Appalachian	Other Spirits
Skunk Brothers Spirits	Stevenson	Skamania	WA	Completely Rural	Non-Appalachian	Brandy, Whiskey, Bouron, Cordial
Smoky Quartz Distillery	Seabrook	Rockingham	NH	Mostly Urban	Non-Appalachian	Vodka, Rum, Bourbon
Southern Grace Distillery	Mount Pleasant	Cabarrus	NC	Mostly Urban	Non-Appalachian	Moonshine Only
Still Pond Distillery	Arlington	Calhoun, Early	GA	Mostly Rural	Non-Appalachian	Gin, Vodka
Straw Hat Distillery	Timmonsville	Florence	SC	Mostly Urban	Non-Appalachian	Whiskey, Limoncello
Sugarlands Distilling Company	Gatlinburg	Sevier	TN	Mostly Rural	Appalachian	Whiskey

Continues on next page

Table 6.1. Craft Distillery Study Sample

Distillery	City	County	State	County Rurality*	Appalachian	Other Spirits
10th Mountain Whiskey and Spirit Co.	Gypsum	Eagle	CO	Mostly Urban	Non-Appalachian	Rye Whiskey, Bourbon, Vodka, Cordial
Van Brunt Stillhouse	Brooklyn	Kings	NY	Mostly Urban	Non-Appalachian	Whiskey, Rum, Grappa

* County rurality is based on 2010 Census data. According to the County Classification Lookup Table (2017), "Counties with less than 50 percent of the population living in rural areas are classified as mostly urban; 55 to 99.9 percent of the population living in rural areas are classified as mostly rural; 100 percent rural are classified as completely rural."

Table 6.2.
Authenticity Themes in Appalachian and Non-Appalachian Distillery Websites

Theme	Appalachian (%)	Non-Appalachian (%)
Handcrafted	25	39
Local Ingredients	35	55
Family Identity	65	46
Distillery Identity	45	22
Historical Identity	65	27
Legality	40	30
Flavors (yes)	55	33
Moonshine Only	10	1
Small Batch	20	37

the local community, and the distilleries' family identity and history, as well as the broad use of well-styled branding and imagery, were significant recurring themes across a substantial number of distillery websites. Overall, there were few stylistic differences between Appalachian and non-Appalachian distilleries in the websites themselves; the differences arose in how the distilleries discussed their products.

Distillery Themes of Authenticity

"Handcrafted" White Whiskey

Many distilleries in the present study devoted significant portions of their websites (sometimes multiple pages) to highly detailed descriptions of their distillation processes. Twenty-five percent of Appalachian distilleries and 38 percent of non-Appalachian distilleries in our sample explicitly mentioned handcrafted processes, which is more than one-third of our entire sample. For example, Appalachian distilleries mention the traditional copper still used in the distilling process, while non-Appalachian distilleries focus on the small staff—artisanal nature of production and ingredients and small batch size.

While scholars are not in perfect agreement as to what constitutes the essential defining characteristics of craft products, there are some key overlaps: in general, craft products are typically made by hand. Extending this definition, craft goods are designed by a single person or small group of people who carefully source or select the raw materials themselves and finally create the product by hand.[31] According to Colin Campbell, "the artist craftsman (or craftswoman) is still set against a division of labor that involves the separation of design and manufacture—a dichotomy that carries with it the implied, if not explicit, contrast between inalienable, humane, authentic, and creative work, on the one hand, and purely mechanical, unfulfilling, and alienating labor, on the other."[32] McLaughlin Distillery emphasizes the handcrafted nature of its spirits by drawing attention to its small staff and rejection of expensive machinery: "McLaughlin Distillery is not your typical distillery. Each spirit is crafted to perfection by hand. We do not have expensive machinery or a large staff"[33] (non-Appalachian, Pennsylvania). Distilleries seem to make claims to authenticity by simultaneously downplaying the role of extensive mechanization on the one hand and emphasizing the handcraftedness of their production processes on the other.

Johnston and Baumann argue the concept of simplicity (understood here in terms of the production process) goes hand in hand with authenticity. The notion of simplicity in relation to handcraftedness evokes perceptions of honesty and sincerity separating a product from mass-produced objects.[34] The mass production of moonshine, beginning after legalization, was a contrast to the inherently simple, handcrafted product prevalent in the Appalachian Mountains.[35]

Distilleries also often express not only the specific phases of their distillation processes that are done by hand but also the *artistry* involved. Coulter and Payne Farm Distillery's description of its distillation process exemplifies this aspect of handcraftedness: "We focus on the 'craft' in craft distillation. We consider ourselves to be *artisans* first, and beverage producers second. Everything we do revolves not only around the finished product, but how it comes into being. . . . We still do most everything by hand. From choosing and malting our own grain, to hand labeling our bottles, to actually stirring our mash, we focus on what is best for our product"[36] (non-Appalachian, Missouri, emphasis added). The rising concerns surrounding mass-produced products have made it possible for artisanal producers such as craft distilleries across the country to separate their product as simple and handcrafted in comparison to their mass-produced counterparts.[37]

Other distilleries, when discussing the handcrafted nature of their spirits and distillation processes, focused on the benefits of small batch sizes. The appealing factors resulting from small batch sizes such as increased flexibility and creativity stand in stark contrast to the impersonal soulless products resulting from industrial system of production. For, as Five and 20 Spirits explains, "working with small batches allows for greater attention to detail, and it also allows us to be creative and flexible with our products so we can offer you exciting and unique beverages"[38] (non-Appalachian, Pennsylvania). The importance of simple handcrafted products arises in contrast to industrial-produced products, making it possible for distilleries to claim authenticity through their production process.

Lastly, when discussing the handcrafted dimensions of moonshine distillation, distilleries often made note of not only the increased quality of handcrafted products, but also the required expertise that goes into making the perfect moonshine. As Pinchgut Hollow Distillery explains, "We are craft distillers who care deeply about quality. We distill our moonshine and whiskey using a traditional copper still that requires skill and expertise. We care deeply about the ingredients that we put into their stills, about where they are harvested, how they are transported and stored, and how they are made into distilling material because it's all so important for the quality of what we make. We use small, old-fashioned, hand-operated equipment because that puts them directly in touch with how the spirit is actually being transformed from raw material into something a person wants to drink"[39] (Appalachian, West Virginia). Consumers demand handcrafted products be imbued with the personality and humanity of their creators, unlike mass-produced products. One potential outcome of understanding craft objects in this way is the augmentation of perceived authenticity of the product. It makes sense that contemporary moonshine distillers would emphasize the handcrafted nature of their spirits because handcrafted products are typically viewed by consumers to be higher quality, more unique, and more memorable compared to their industrially mass-produced counterparts.

Overall, both Appalachian and non-Appalachian distilleries rely on claims of simplicity to legitimate their products in a market overflowing with competitors' products. Simplicity connects a product to the producer and calls to mind images of small-scale production facilities or home distilling instead of industrial processing plants.[40] Handcrafted products claim artistic style through the process of production in the same way that art is more legitimate based on the background and process employed by the artist.[41]

Distillery Identity Management

Distilleries actively work to create an identity, or an impression of their products, conveying authenticity to the consumer, roots in tradition, personal connection, or geographic specificity.[42] Authenticity is neither inherent in a product nor static, thus forcing producers to constantly manage the impression consumers have of their products. Distilleries focus on the interrelation of geographic specificity, personal connection, and history to create an impression of authenticity within their products. On their websites, 65 percent of distilleries within and 27 percent of distilleries outside of Appalachia focused on the history of the community in which they were located as a source of authenticity.

Distilleries focusing on historical identity are able to connect their personal history with the history of a region: "Dragon Distillery is a small, veteran-owned business strongly rooted in the local Frederick, Maryland community. In the mid-1700s our family settled on a 200-acre tract of land about 25 miles away from the current distillery location. We are continuing the tradition of supporting and enjoying Frederick through our craft distillery"[43] (non-Appalachian, Maryland). Dragon Distillery draws on family history dating hundreds of years to connect their products to a specific location: Frederick, Maryland. The connection between the distillery and the community is a source of authenticity for the producers because they are able to showcase a deep history in the town. The emphasis on a small, veteran-owned business also separates the distillery from its competitors.

Other distilleries draw on family experiences distilling moonshine before Prohibition in the same area the current distillery is located: "Our family had arrived in the Monongahela River valley just before the revolutionary war. Settling below Pittsburgh, the Heston boys were known from Fredricktown to

Opekeski to Goose Run to Mudlick to Pinchgut Hollow. We had a proud history of serving our country in wartime, and making farm whiskey. However, all the distilling ended on that day in 1932, that is, until now"[44] (Pinchgut Hollow Distillery, Appalachian, West Virginia). Pinchgut Hollow Distillery, like those outside of Appalachia, relies on a construction of family history in a specific location to embed its product with authenticity. The reference to making farm whiskey, also known as moonshine, before Prohibition shows the family has experience producing moonshine.

On their websites, 65 percent of distilleries within Appalachia and 46 percent of those outside of Appalachia focus on a family connection between the producers and the product. This can be achieved through recipes and equipment passed down from previous generations: "The same equipment that William 'Doc' Collier and his family have used for generations to make their moonshine up in the mountains. Doc's Shine Shop is set up just like an old-fashioned country Mercantile Store, like the one his daddy first sold 'shine"[45] (Doc Collier Moonshine, Appalachian, Tennessee). This distillery focuses on the exhibition of a traditional still and Mercantile Store transporting customers back to the Appalachian Mountains during a time when country stores were the norm and moonshine was a hallmark of the uniqueness of the Appalachian lifestyle.[46] The experience of shopping in a country store immerses customers in the past, making Doc Collier's moonshine a souvenir from a different time period. The country store markets the rural South as an experience, while the moonshine is something that can be purchased as a reminder of the past and a piece of the mountain lifestyle to be taken home.[47]

Legality also plays a role in the impressions of authenticity distilleries use for their products: "This here is the real thing. Just like Pappy used to make. Only this batch and every batch we make is guaranteed legal and certified. It might whiff a little dangerous and taste a mite sinful but the taxes are paid on this jar"[48] (Davis Valley Distillery, Appalachian, Virginia). Moonshine's history is one of illegal production, bootlegging across state lines, and tax evasion. Although moonshine is legal today, the ability to draw on family traditions and geographic specificity implies production before it was legal: "we started with a recipe that has more experience than the law allows and built this business from the ground up with the sole intention of providing high quality spirits to a market thirsty for old-fashioned moonshine"[49] (Hollow Creek Distillery, Appalachian, South Carolina).

The history of legal production connects to the imagery of mountain men using stills hidden deep in the hollows of the Appalachian ranges to support their families while avoiding lawmen. This imagery, while now passé, is a source of authenticity for distilleries that can trace their recipes and experiences back to the days of illegal production, unlike their counterparts who seek out other sources of authenticity because they do not have access to the traditions and experiences prevalent in the Appalachian Mountains.

Distilleries within Appalachia are more likely to rely on family, history, and geographic identity to claim authenticity in comparison to their non-Appalachian counterparts, who are unable to tap into the same regional history and experiences. Whether claiming tradition, geographic specificity, or family experience, moonshine distilleries actively engage in impression management to create an image of their products that is authentic to a consumer. Authenticity within and outside of Appalachia takes on similar appearances to food culture in general. The fabrication of authenticity allows producers to focus on one or two aspects of their product that can be used to claim authenticity, thus making it superior to a competitor's product.

Sourcing Products

The current dominant food movement places an emphasis on locally sourced products. The idea behind this is that products from local sources are more environmentally friendly because they do not have to be transported long distances, thus reducing greenhouse gas emissions and keeping the revenue within the community to support small-scale farmers.[50] Distilleries also support the local food movement when possible:

> "Grain to Glass" is a philosophy that places importance on buying all the grain used in the production of a distilled spirit directly from the farmers that grow it. In most cases, they try to source everything within 50–100 miles of their distillery. This helps to support the local economy, reduces emissions from the transportation of ingredients, and increases the control the distillery has over the quality of their products. It also builds a sense of community. To help fulfill our Vision and Mission, we have expanded the Grain to Glass idea into a Field to Glass philosophy. We grow everything we use on site at our own family farm, Shawnee Bend Farms outside

Union, Missouri, located on the same ground as our distillery. Every glass you drink comes 100% from ingredients grown, harvested, cleaned, processed, mashed, distilled, blended and bottled by our family on our farm.[51] (Coulter and Payne, non-Appalachian, Missouri)

The idea of grain to glass or field to glass is used to set a distillery apart from competitors who rely on industrially produced products, deemed inferior by the local food movement.

Overall, 55 percent of non-Appalachian distilleries, compared to 35 percent of Appalachian distilleries, mentioned sourcing ingredients from local farmers. Other distilleries, while not completely invested in the local food movement, are still concerned about the sourcing of their products. Instead of sourcing everything from within fifty or one hundred miles, they focus on heirloom ingredients and being able to trace a product to a specific location: "Handmade from heirloom corn, rye, and malted barley mash, hops, Louisiana cane sugar, and Blue Ridge Mountain artesian well water"[52] (Broad Branch Distillery, Appalachian, North Carolina). Local food products and heirloom ingredients are a draw for foodies, who seek out these products because they are seen as simple, local, and healthier than their industrial-produced counterparts.

Other distilleries focus on the organic and sustainability aspects of the food movement. Organic and sustainable products offer another draw for customers who are interested in products produced with minimal chemicals and environmental impact: "Committed to locally-sourced organic ingredients & environmentally conscious production methods Loon Liquor Company aims to craft the most delicious spirits from organic, local suppliers while quantifiably improving social and environmental sustainability"[53] (Loon Liquor Company Distillery, non-Appalachian, Minnesota). Although the product may not visibly differ from its competitors, the consumers of organic and sustainable moonshine are buying an ethically sound product in line with current trends in food culture as a whole.

The emphasis on locally grown and sustainable ingredients places distilleries, especially those outside of Appalachia, into the larger food movement, making it possible to draw on the same clientele that frequents farm-to-table restaurants and has disposable income to spend on craft liquors.[54] Moonshine's ability to tap into these same markets capitalizes on business practices already effective and influential across the country, making their appeal more general than claims of history and tradition within the Appalachian Mountains.

Branding and Imagery

Those who distill legal moonshine use packaging, branding, and imagery to create a more authentic product. Our data shows moonshine distillers typically package their moonshine in one of four distinct vessels: jugs with a small handle, clear mason jars, short bourbon- or whiskey-style bottles, and tall and slender vodka-style bottles (see table 6.3). These vessels represent distinct marketing strategies. The most stereotypical vessels, the jug and the mason jar, were used by a total of 44 percent of non-Appalachian distilleries; of Appalachian distilleries, 16 percent used the jug and 42 percent the mason jar. The short bourbon-style bottle was the most popular for non-Appalachian distilleries: 39 percent used it. This seems to suggest non-Appalachian distilleries seek to distinguish their product by imitating high quality, small-batch whiskey, which already has a consistent following in the market. The least popular is the tall, slender vodka-style bottle with only 11 percent of Appalachian distilleries and 17 percent of non-Appalachian distilleries using it, even though both moonshine and vodkas are clear liquors.

In addition to vessel shape and size, we also coded for content and brand imagery. The most common imagery themes to emerge from our data were mountain scenes, mountain culture (e.g., miners, prospectors, log cabins in the mountains, hunting scenes), state imagery (e.g., flags, iconic buildings), animals, and simple labels with only the brand name. Mountain and mountain culture imagery was the most common among Appalachian distilleries, with a total of 47 percent using it. The most common images across Appalachian distilleries were mountain culture images such as miners, old-fashioned pickup trucks, horse-pulled plows, or a hound dog sitting on a porch next to a pottery jug marked XXX. One such distillery, Twin Creeks Distillery in the Appalachian Mountains of Virginia, uses a mason jar with mountain imagery on the label. Appalachian distillers used mountain culture imagery on moonshine packaged in mason jars or the shorter, small-batch-whiskey-style bottles.

Non-Appalachian distilleries were more likely to use text only, 30 percent, on their bottles. For example, Virginia Lightning Distillery uses a jug style bottle but does not have any significant imagery aside from the lightning bolt that is

Table 6.3.
Bottle Styles and Label Imagery for Appalachian and Non-Appalachian Distilleries

	Jug		Mason Jar		Short/ Bourbon Bottle		Tall/Vodka Bottle		Total (%)	
	A	NA	A	NA	A	NA	A	NA	A	NA
Mountains	1	3	2	1	2	1	1	1	32	11
Mountain Culture	0	2	3	3	0	3	0	1	16	17
State	0	2	1	1	0	2	0	1	5	11
Animals	0	1	0	1	1	4	0	0	5	11
Text Only/ No Imagery	1	1	1	3	2	9	0	3	21	30
Other	1	3	1	3	1	2	1	3	21	20
Total (%)	16	22	42	22	32	39	10	17		

Note: A is Appalachian; NA is Non-Appalachian.
No image was available for one Appalachian distillery.

part of its brand name. Only 27 percent of non-Appalachian distilleries used mountain or mountain culture imagery on their bottles. Overall, mountain imagery was not as relevant to non-Appalachian distilleries; instead they focus on the brand name or other imagery, such as a devil or a hipster. The most common form of branding and packaging is the short, small-batch whiskey style bottle with no imagery other than brand name and logo.

Discussion and Conclusions

Overall, the differences between Appalachian and non-Appalachian distilleries reflect the constant impression management on the part of the producers. A distillery claiming authenticity must be able to tap into an accepted measure of authenticity such as geographic specificity, the local food movement, tradition, and personal connection.[55] The location of the distillery makes it possible for producers to draw on the various facets of authenticity. Appalachian distilleries rely on their identity as Appalachian by focusing on the geographic specificity and personal connection to the history of the region. Non-Appalachian distilleries may lack the historical provenance, and therefore, must rely on tapping into preexisting food trends, more directly by focusing on local, sustainable, and handcrafted products and ingredients. Both types of distilleries attempt to claim authenticity through the production of their moonshine. This does not suggest one type of moonshine is more authentic than the other; instead it shows the malleability of authenticity.

The changes occurring in Appalachian foodways, such as moonshine, mirror the increasing popularity of exotic cuisines in recent decades. Southern and Appalachian foodways are experiencing a rise in popularity across the country. For example, Marcie Cohen Ferris identifies the current period in southern food as a food renaissance drawing on the agrarian past of the region, modern techniques, and individual chefs and artisans who work to make southern food modern.[56] The spread and adaptation of regional foodways is not new or unique to the U.S. South. These changes are a common occurrence as consumers seek out new experiences and products. For example, there has been a rise in ethnic restaurants across the United States. Thirty years ago pad thai, sushi, dim sum, and ceviche were rarely seen in the United States, but now restaurants in urban areas across the country are dedicated to these types of cuisines, and grocery stores regularly carry sushi in their delis.[57]

The rising popularity of craft distilleries and moonshine makes the study of authenticity increasingly relevant. In a market crowded by consumer choices, producers must find a way to make their products stand out above their competitors. Although authenticity claims impact consumers' purchasing decisions, there is no true authentic representation of a cultural product. Claiming there is one static authentic representation is placing a value judgment on the product that is irrelevant to the study of authenticity. Authenticity does not necessarily delineate one true version of a product; rather, it is the constant negotiation of interactions between producers and consumers to meet the changing demands of the market. Authenticity is a tool used by producers to successfully market their products. As researchers we can identify the themes and frames used by cultural producers, and we can discuss the effectiveness of those themes in the marketing of their products. Moonshine produced within or outside of Appalachia is not more or less authentic, and the continued existence and increasing numbers of these distilleries suggest their strategies are working from a market standpoint. As in the early days of country music, claims of authenticity are a marketing tool that can increase the profitability of small-scale producers making it possible for them to compete with the large-scale producers who lack access to authenticity claims.[58]

Although the sample employed by this study is not inclusive of every distill-ery, the breadth of distilleries makes it possible to overcome the shortcoming. By drawing on other methodological techniques, such as interviewing dis-tillery owners and employees, future research could expand and refine our understanding of the relationship between producers, consumers, and authenticity in the cultural and economic field of moonshine production and consumption. Future research may also focus on how producers claim moonshining as an art form, drawing on sociological concepts such as status hierarchy and processes of legitimation. This would facilitate the use of au-thenticity as a culturally appropriate measurement.

Authenticity and impression management are successful marketing tools used to adapt a cultural product to consumer demands. The lack of static or true authentic products suggests the success and validity of claims of authen-ticity is found in their longevity and the longevity of the cultural product. Legal moonshine is a relatively new cultural product, and as such claims of authenticity and the associated impression management are in the earliest stages of development. As consumer demands and the structure of the market change, moonshine's claims of authenticity must follow if they hope to remain effective. As Peterson's work on the fabrication of authenticity suggests, in order to understand the effectiveness of authenticity claims one must study the same cultural product over an extensive period of time.[59] Our work on claims of authenticity among moonshine distilleries provides a snapshot into the techniques used by producers to foster an image of artisanal nature, local sourcing, and product history. The success of these claims reflects the success of the distilleries, but success is not simply measured by profit margins or size; as some distilleries have no desire to become large, their success is instead measured by the reception of their products.[60]

While the use of authenticity in the study of cultural products can explain the profit margins of restaurants, artists, and record companies, authenticity also has real consequence and meaning for people's understanding of their identity. For example, the role of slaves in the creation of southern foodways is often erased in modern conversations regarding authentic southern food. This is a disservice to the slaves who were responsible for the iconic southern dishes we enjoy today and a disservice to people of color today who seek inspiration from their culinary heritage. The erasure of people of color from modern southern foodways also does little to dispel the negative image of the racist and oppressive South.[61] Moonshine, like southern food as a whole, is steeped in a South filled with irony and contradiction; the use of geography and culture to create claims of authenticity highlights the beauty of a region that has suffered from stark poverty, violence, and oppression.[62] These images and claims present a commodified version of Appalachia that can be marketed and consumed as a piece of southern or Appalachian identity without acknowledging the underlying inequalities that first pushed moonshine into prominence. Moonshine will continue to evolve as people modify their claims of what constitutes an "authentic" product and as we move further away from the historical roots of moonshine and into a consumer driven market with producers responding to these claims.

NOTES

Epigraph. Ronni Lundy, "Introduction," in *Cornbread Nation 3: Foods of the Mountain South*, edited by Ronni Lundy (Chapel Hill: University of North Carolina Press, 2005), 1.

1.   Josée Johnston and Shyon Baumann, *Foodies: Democracy and Distinction in the Gourmet Foodscape* (New York: Routledge, 2010), 27; Richard A. Peterson, *Creating Country Music* (Chicago: University of Chicago Press, 1997), 207.

2.   Michael B. Beverland, "Crafting Brand Authenticity: The Case of Luxury Wines," *Journal of Management Studies* 42, no. 5 (2005): 1026–28; Shun Lu and Gary Alan Fine, "The Presentation of Ethnic Identity: Chinese Food as a Social Accomplishment," *Sociological Quarterly* 36, no. 3 (1995): 540–43; Peterson, *Creating Country Music*, 207.

3.   Pierre Bourdieu, *Distinction: A Social Critique of the Judgment of Taste* (Cambridge, MA: Harvard University Press, 1984), 12.

4.   David Grazian, "The Symbolic Economy of Authenticity in the Chicago Blues Scene," in *Music Scenes: Local, Translocal, and Virtual*, ed. A. Bennett and

Richard A. Peterson (Nashville: Vanderbilt University Press, 2000), 32; Richard A. Peterson, "In Search of Authenticity," *Journal of Management Studies* 42, no. 5 (2005): 1089; Richard A. Peterson and Roger M. Kern, "Changing Highbrow Taste: From Snob to Omnivore," *American Sociological Review* 30, no. 1 (1996): 321.

5. Gary Alan Fine, "Crafting Authenticity: The Validation of Identity in Self-Taught Art," *Theory and Society* 32, no. 2 (2003): 176.

6. Herman Gray, "Equity and Diversity in Media Representation: Desiring the Network and Network Desire," *Critical Studies in Media Communication* 18, no. 1 (2001): 103.

7. Johnston and Baumann, *Foodies*, 34; David Kamp, *The United States of Arugula: The Sun-Dried, Cold-Pressed, Dark-Roasted, Extra Virgin Story of the American Food Revolution* (New York: Broadway Books, 2006), 7; Jennifer A. Jordan, *Edible Memory: The Lure of Heirloom Tomatoes and Other Forgotten Foods* (Chicago: University of Chicago Press, 2015), 15; David Sax, *The Tastemakers: Why We're Crazy for Cupcakes but Fed Up with Fondue* (New York: Public Affairs, 2014), 12.

8. Bourdieu, *Distinction*, 13.

9. Herbert J. Gans, "The Creator-Audience Relationship in the Mass-Media: An Analysis of Movie-Making," in *Mass Culture*, edited by Bernard Rosenberg and David Manning White (New York: The Free Press, 1957), 319; John Ryan and Michael Hughes, "Breaking the Decision Chain: The Fate of Creativity in an Age of Self-Production," in *Cybersounds: Essays on Virtual Music Culture,* ed. M. D. Ayers (New York: Peter Lang, 2006), 240; and John Ryan and Richard R. Peterson, "The Product Image: The Fate of Creativity in Country Music Songwriting," in *Individuals in Mass Media Organization Creativity and Constraint,* ed. James S. Ettema and D. Charles Whitney (Thousand Oaks, CA: Sage, 1982), 15.

10. Peterson, *Creating Country Music*, 218–19.

11. Peterson, *In Search of Authenticity*, 1092; Peterson, *Creating Country Music*, 159.

12. Johnston and Baumann, *Foodies*, 74–90.

13. Ibid., 97–101.

14. John T. Edge, *The Potlikker Papers: A Food History of the Modern South* (New York: Penguin Press, 2017), 187.

15. Bourdieu, *Distinction*, 21; and Johnston and Baumann, *Foodies*, 30.

16. Edge, *Potlikker Papers*, 295.

17. Anthony J. Stanonis, "Introduction: Selling Dixies," in *Dixie Emporium: Tourism, Foodways, and Consumer Culture in the American South*, ed. Anthony J. Stanonis (Athens: University of Georgia Press, 2008), 2.

18. Michael W. Twitty, *The Cooking Gene: A Journey Through African American Culinary History in the Old South* (New York: Harper Collins, 2017), 14–17.

19. Mary Rizzo, "The Café Hon," in *Dixie Emporium*, 283; Twitty, *Cooking Gene*, 408.

20. Peterson, *Creating Country Music*, 178.

21. Peterson, *Creating Country Music*, 178; Jordan, *Edible Memory*, 42.

22. Patrick Huber, "The Riddle of the Horny Hillbilly," in *Dixie Emporium*, 73.

23. Huber, "Riddle of the Horny Hillbilly," 74; Aaron K. Ketchell, "Hillbilly Heaven: Branson Tourism and the Hillbilly of the Missouri Ozarks," in *Dixie Emporium*, 121; and Emelie K. Peine and Kai A. Schafft, "Moonshine, Mountaineers, and Modernity: Distilling Cultural History in the Southern Appalachian Mountains," *Journal of Appalachian Studies* 18, nos. 1/2 (2012): 94.

24. Edge, *Potlikker Papers*, 9; Elizabeth Engelhardt, *A Mess of Greens: Southern Gender and Southern Food* (Athens: University of Georgia Press, 2011), 27.

25. Edge, *Potlikker Papers*, 9.

26. Johnston and Baumann, *Foodies*, 141.

27. Ibid., 73.

28. Michael Hughes, "Country Music as Impression Management: A Meditation on Fabricating Authenticity," *Poetics* 28 (2000): 189.

29. Erving Goffman, *The Presentation of Self in Everyday Life* (Garden City, NY: Anchor Doubleday, 1959), 253; and Hughes, "Country Music as Impression Management," 189.

30. "The Appalachian Region," Appalachian Regional Commission, accessed July 19, 2016, https://www.arc.gov/appalachian_region/TheAppalachianRegion.asp.

31. Tanya Harrod, *The Crafts in Britain in the Twentieth Century* (New Haven: Yale University Press, 1995), 53.

32. Colin Campbell, "The Craft Consumer: Culture, Craft, and Consumption in a Postmodern Society," *Journal of Consumer Culture* 5, no. 2 (2005): 25.

33. "Who We Are," McLaughlin Distillery, accessed July 20, 2017, www.mclaughlin distillery.com/about.html.

34. Johnston and Baumann, *Foodies*, 141.

35. Edge, *Potlikker Papers*, 9; Engelhardt, *A Mess of Greens*, 27.

36. "Our Story," Coulter and Payne Distillery, accessed July 20, 2017, www.coulter andpaynefarmdistillery.com/discover.html, emphasis added.

37. E. Melanie DuPuis and David Goodman, "Should We Go 'Home' to Eat?: Toward a Reflexive Politics of Localism," *Journal of Rural Studies* 21, no. 3 (2005): 361; Johnston and Baumann, *Foodies*, 76.

38. "Small Batch Distilling," Five and 20 Spirits and Brewing, accessed July 20, 2017, www.fiveand20.com/our-story.

39. "Heston Farm's Pinchgut Hollow Distillery," Pinchgut Hollow Distillery, accessed July 20, 2017, www.hestonfarm.com/pinchgut-hollow-distillery.html.

40. Johnston and Baumann, *Foodies*, 76; Sax, *Tastemakers*, 32.

41. Fine, "Crafting Authenticity," 176.

42. Johnston and Baumann, *Foodies*, 74–86; Hughes, "Country Music as Impression Management," 189; Peterson, *Creating Country Music*, 55–89.

43. "Who We Are," Dragon Distillery, accessed July 20, 2017, www.dragondistillery.com/about-us.html.

44. "Our History," Pinchgut Hollow Distillery, accessed July 20, 2017, www.hestonfarm.com/pinchgut-hollow-distillery.html.

45. "Doc Collier Moonshine Distillery," Doc Collier Moonshine, accessed July 20, 2017, https://doccollier.co/.

46. Engelhardt, *Mess of Greens*, 27.

47. Huber, "Riddle of the Horny Hillbilly," 71.

48. "Appalachian Moon Corn Whiskey Moonshine," Davis Valley Distillery, accessed July 20, 2017, www.appalachianmoon.com/distillery.html.

49. "About the Barn," Hollow Creek Distillery, accessed July 20, 2017, http://hollowcreekdistillery.com/about-the-barn/.

50. DuPuis and Goodman, "Should We Go 'Home,'" 361.

51. "Our Story," Coulter and Payne Distillery.

52. "Nightlab 1.0," Broad Branch Distillery, accessed July 20, 2017, www.broadbranchdistillery.com.

53. "Our Mission," Loon Liquor Company, accessed July 20, 2017, http://loonliquors.com/story-and-mission/.

54. Kamp, *United States of Arugula*, 269.

55. Johnston and Baumann, *Foodies*, 74–86; Hughes, "Country Music as Impression Management," 189; Peterson, *Creating Country Music*, 55–89.

56. Marcie Cohen Ferris, *The Edible South: The Power of Food and The Making of an American Region* (Chapel Hill: University of North Carolina Press, 2014), 325–27.

57. Kamp, *The United States of* Arugula; Sax, *Tastemakers*.

58. Peterson, *Creating Country Music*, 10.

59. Peterson, *Creating Country Music*, 5–6.

60. Shyon Baumann, "A General Theory of Artistic Legitimation: How Art Worlds are Like Social Movements," *Poetics* 35 (2007): 53.

61. Twitty, *Cooking Gene*, 5–7.

62. Stanonis, "Introduction," 5.

CHAPTER 7

Entrepreneurial Family Values and the Modern Moonshiner: Appalachian Craft Distilling beyond Its Neoliberal Frame

JASON EZELL

By 2013 the word was out. As Ken Teusch, reporter for the Russellville, Arkansas, *River Valley Leader*, put it, "white lightning may be . . . shedding its outlaw image."[1] Based on this news, the writer offered advice to his Ozark neighbors: "So tell your friends and relatives up in the hills to get wise to themselves. Don't hide that still out in the chicken house and whip up a batch now and then for special occasions. That's illegal! Instead, go mainstream, slap the words 'craft' or 'artisanal' on that mason jar and start peddling it to Yankees with more money than sense."[2] For Teusch, transcending outlaw status hinged on a couple of moves. First, moonshiners just needed to start using the word "craft" to describe what they do. Second, Teusch implied that covert behavior is what makes this craft illegal; thus, openly making moonshine, treating it like a business, would turn it into a legal practice. What is interesting about the Arkansas reporter's humorous characterization of the recent rise of the legal moonshine or craft distilling industry is that, while the figure of the moonshiner remains at center stage, the roles of the entrepreneur, marketer, and lawmaker are conspicuously obscured.

This chapter makes the case that, while the marketing of newly legal moonshine heavily depends on the figure of the moonshiner, modern moonshine is better understood in a broader context as an industry that provides an economic stimulus produced by the neoliberal collaborations of lawmakers and marketers. Attending to this particular frame is important for two reasons.

First, as explained below, neoliberal ideology hinges on a traditional family form; the traditional neoliberal family form is one that adheres to strict norms of sexuality, gender, and ability. These norms are reinforced materially by law and representationally by moralistic marketing codes. Second, as an industry that generates regional tourism, neoliberal craft moonshine could redefine regional tradition in ways that reify these norms, thereby further enabling an image of Appalachia as a place that is unaccommodating to LGBT, feminist, and disabled persons. This situation does not make modern moonshine a uniquely heterosexist, sexist, or ableist industry; however, because the neoliberal context of its emergence often promotes such values, it is important to imagine ways the fledgling industry can articulate itself beyond its particularly exclusive frame.

The chapter begins by outlining some key critiques of neoliberalism by queer and disabilities theorists before couching the newly legal Appalachian moonshine industry—modern moonshine—as a neoliberal economic stimulus effort focused on boosting regional tourism through neolocal craft branding. In so doing, the chapter also calls attention to the relevant legal and marketing measures that support the neoliberal family form within both the region and the industry. Then, two case studies of new moonshine distilleries' web presence (Short Mountain Distillery in Tennessee and Asheville Distilling in North Carolina) are offered to show how regional distillers cultivate brands, which foreground new entrepreneurial moonshiner figures within neoliberal parameters. The essay closes by using these defined neoliberal limits to point to other possible moonshiner figures, ones that hold potential both to highlight regional craft traditions *and* to promote a more socially diverse Appalachia.

The Compulsory and Traditional Family Form of Neoliberalism and the Modern Moonshine Industry as Neolocal Craft

Gender and sexuality scholar Lisa Duggan has described the 1990s ascendance of neoliberalism in the United States as predicated on the false assertion that the economic sphere is somehow separate from political and cultural arenas such as local governments or family norms.[3] She explains that this illusion allowed lawmakers and corporate lobbyists to 1) make economic policies that enabled a "free market" that was less and less accountable to government and citizenry and 2) to trivialize many sociocultural issues as mere "identity politics," even as the market distributed wealth unevenly across different social demographics. Duggan describes how, in the 1990s, even during the Clinton presidency, neoliberalism evolved to pay lip service to multiculturalism and diversity, usually only in the context of expanding demographic markets. At the same time, legislators passed laws that facilitated free-market practices that perpetuated material inequalities. (For example, the North American Free Trade Act marked an increase in Mexican maquiladoras, factories that U.S. companies use to make products cheaply to sell at a greater profit margin in the United States. This free-market practice depends on paying the mostly Mexican female laborers far less than what would be paid a U.S. worker. It is a free market that takes advantage of inequalities.)

From this description of neoliberal practice, a few central aspects of neoliberalism become clear. The first is that neoliberalism's mantra of "smaller government" means, in practice, diminished social programs for citizens and expanded policy design to support corporate growth. Second, the neoliberal focus on the economy obscures how the government works *with* business leaders to achieve mutual goals. Finally, that same focus on the economy also obscures how industry and government make use of culture and identity both to perpetuate patterns of unevenly distributed wealth and to generate illusions of equality.

In an earlier essay, Duggan described the kinds of pressures neoliberalism put on LGBT cultures, referring to those pressures as "homonormativity."[4] She defined homonormativity as "a politics that does not contest dominant heteronormative assumptions and institutions—such as marriage and its call for monogamy and reproduction—but upholds and sustains them while promising the possibility of a demobilized gay constituency and a privatized, depoliticized gay culture anchored in domesticity and consumption."[5] Dugan's definition highlights how much neoliberalism depends on its normative family form based on monogamous, childbearing heterosexual marriages that figure the family as private in terms of being apolitical and public in terms of market participation. Within such a neoliberal context, LGBT equality can only be achieved to the degree this normative family can be approximated.

Queer and disabilities theorist Robert McRuer has additionally pointed out that, not only does the neoliberal political economy make heterosexuality compulsory, but that it also makes able-bodiedness compulsory.[6] There are a couple of reasons for this. First, the family must be able to work to take care of itself since the neoliberal government prefers to reduce social programs that support poor families. Second, families must reproduce to create children who will be workers and consumers in the economy. According to neoliberal logic, aberrations from this traditional family form could sacrifice self-sufficiency and risk dependency on the state; theoretically, the absence of such highly productive families could result in masses of citizens unable to provide for themselves, unable to build sustaining relationships between themselves, and unable to remake themselves as future generations of economic workers and consumers.

Queer theorist Jasbir Puar has expanded on the concept of homonormativity by further describing a neoliberal "homonationalism."[7] By this term, Puar describes how some gay citizens (usually white, middle-class men) who are able to approximate the neoliberal traditional family form are offered nominal inclusion (marriage and military service rights, for example) as a way for the state to win support from them for its own expansionist projects which are often racist, classist, sexist, and nationalist. Although Puar's argument has been taken as a critique of the gay citizens who embrace their own inclusion in the state at the expense of others, Puar's main critique is of the state that sustains itself on such divisive mechanisms. In other words, her critique is aimed at the neoliberal strategy of social justice lip service, which Duggan identifies as emerging in the 1990s. Given these definitions, this chapter addresses in what ways the modern moonshine industry is a neoliberal phenomenon.

Linking Neoliberal Values to Modern Moonshine

As Teusch's article points out, two key aspects distinguish the modern moonshine industry from its earlier illicit forms: its legitimization as a legal enterprise and its makeover as a craft brand. Its legitimization should be understood to operate within a neoliberal frame as described above. First, as a loosening of legal barriers to economic productivity, the legalization of moonshining reflects neoliberal values in that it presents itself as a gesture of smaller government in the name of a freer market. Following the U.S. economic recession of 2008, the newly legal industry emerged as an economic stimulus. As a government act to spur economic growth, stimulus events expose just how much the economy depends on the political in the neoliberal context. In 2009 Tennessee passed a bill that would allow counties to approve local commercial distilling of moonshine.[8] North Carolina began licensing craft distilleries in 2005, but the business really took off in 2007 with the partnership of NASCAR star Junior Johnson and Piedmont Distillers.[9] Far from state governments' simply stepping out of commercial moonshiners' ways, lawmakers set the terms for commercial licensing, charging for permits. Permission has actually required additional legal intervention.

Historian Bruce Stewart has shown how Appalachian prohibition efforts depended on vilifying the manufacture of moonshine.[10] This prohibition discourse expanded the temperance movement's condemnation of individual consumption to one of blame for production as well. This moral climate painted the earlier moonshiner as an impediment to modern, national progress *and* as a provincial outlaw. If the neoliberal context restores honor to moonshiners by walking them through a legal permit process and positioning them as forces of needed economic stimulus, it still does not wholly abandon its moralism. Neoliberal moralism is carried out in at least two ways: by the self-regulation of liquor marketing practices and by the passage of laws to reinforce the traditional family so essential to the neoliberal ideology.

Critics of neoliberalism like Duggan have pointed out how important media manipulation is to redirect or shape public opinion around political-economic change. As she shows, this dynamic allowed Clinton-era politicians to invoke civil rights language and imagery in media practice as their policy practice disinvested in social programs in order to support freer trade. Public relations and policy design worked together but deployed different messaging to achieve the larger neoliberal goal. In the case of legal substances such as alcohol and tobacco the government appears to distance itself from moralism in order to embrace the higher value of market freedom. In the broader context, though, neoliberal moralism simply shifts its focus from production to marketing; therefore, advertising for cigarettes and liquor is compelled to take on less glamorous or sexy forms and to appear only in childfree spaces. Production is permitted while consumption is assiduously circumscribed by the regulation of marketing practices.

An example of such a phenomenon in the liquor industry is the 2011 "Code of Responsible Practices for Beverage Alcohol Advertising and Marketing."[11] The Distilled Spirits Council endorses its member commercial brewers and distillers for following the proscribed marketing practices. Billed as a form of self-regulation, this code promotes itself as an example of neoliberal smaller government by setting itself up as an instrument by which an autonomous industry morally regulates itself when in reality it is entangled with government policy as part of the liquor industry lobbyist network, not only submitting regular reports to the government but courting politicians' endorsements.[12] In fact, in 2005 the director of the Federal Trade Commission commended the code as a more efficient regulatory tool than legal means because, as such, it did not have to answer formally to First Amendment concerns.[13]

As a form of self-regulation, the code remains extralegal in order to sidestep some aspects of law; at the same time, as a tool of a lobbyist organization, it maintains close reporting lines with lawmakers. As such, it gives lie to the idea that, where law does not regulate an activity, that activity goes unconstrained.[14] In addition, according to the most current (2011) code, "members hold themselves to a standard higher than mandated by any law or regulation" and "agree to observe the spirit, as well as the letter, of this *Code*."[15] By this language, the code invokes not a legal but a moral authority that is faintly religious.

The primary moral element of the code is to limit marketing of liquor to adults. While this moral stance is itself largely uncontroversial, it depends on a child protectionism that assumes the specific traditional family form discussed by the above queer critics of neoliberalism. Child protectionist rhetoric has played an important role in historical anti-LGBT political movements. For example, this rhetoric was crucial to the success of Anita Bryant's 1977 Save Our Children campaign, which overturned Miami-Dade County LGBT anti-discrimination ordinances and which also inspired both the 1978 California Briggs Initiative (a proposition to prohibit openly lesbian and gay educators from teaching in public school) and the 1979 formation of the pro-family Moral Majority by Jerry Falwell.[16] Although emerging in a different context, the liquor marketing code invests in a respectability associated with a traditional family model understood to be "naturally" heterosexual.

In its section on "Social Responsibility," the code conveys permissiveness: "Beverage alcohol products and drinkers may be portrayed as responsible personal and social experiences and activities, such as the depiction of persons in a social or romantic setting, persons who appear to be attractive or affluent, and persons who appear to be relaxing or in an enjoyable setting." Elsewhere, the code prohibits depictions which defy "good taste"; the code defines this taste by avoiding representations of lewdness, "graphic or gratuitous nudity," "overt sexual activity," or "promiscuity."[17] The Council seems at pains to define maturity by the images it permits and prohibits. Romantic, good-looking, and wealthy drinkers register appropriate maturity, whereas those who are openly sexual do not. Although it is surely not the express intent of the code, maturity is associated with a certain sexual propriety that is only fully accessible to those who either share this sense of propriety or can afford the privacy to emulate it. Such portraits might easily be seen to exclude many, including certain gay cultures and the poor.

Further, as a form of *self*-regulation, the council and its code support a view of the government as not ultimately responsible in these matters. In fact, the absolutist distinctions between child and adult also imply that, while the child is not capable of a mature choice, the adult always is. What such a construction denies is the possibility that adults may be differently able to make such choices. Not only does this framing exclude adults with various decision-making abilities from the picture, but it also risks framing addiction and abuse as the responsibility of neither industry nor government but of the individual adult who will demonstrate natural maturity or not. This sort of construction renders certain campaigns unimaginable; for example, a movement to lobby the government to expand medical insurance to better cover alcoholism surely would not occur to the neoliberal moral imagination of this industry marketing code. Responsible drinking falls within the natural domain of the mature adult whose measure of maturity reflects access to privacy, moderation (especially sexual), and rational decision-making. In the neoliberal context, these qualities are the province of the middle-class, heterosexual, able-bodied family. Because of the 2011 code, media representations will visually associate liquor consumption, including new moonshine, with these bodies, along with their values.

Extralegal marketing regulation is one way neoliberalism preserves its moralistic support for the traditional family even as it legitimizes the production of moonshine. Another way it achieves this goal is to pass parallel anti-LGBT state legislation. For example, Tennessee has been active against gay rights. In 2004 "Rhea County commissioners unanimously voted to ask state lawmakers to introduce legislation amending Tennessee's criminal code so that the county [could] charge homosexuals with crimes against nature" and expel them from the county.[18] In 2011 the Tennessee Senate approved the "Don't Say Gay" bill, a measure that would prohibit discussion of homosexuality in public school classrooms. The bill was ultimately defeated, but it was quite popular in the state.[19] This bill calls to mind California's 1978 Briggs Initiative in that both bills deployed child protectionist rhetoric to prohibit LGBT visibility within public educational contexts. Also in 2011 the Tennessee governor approved a law that nullified city laws against LGBT antidiscrimination as being in excess of the protections offered by the state.[20] Finally, in 2013 the state of Tennessee legally established August 31 as Traditional Marriage Day.[21] These examples show that the same state government which permitted moonshine production also made consistent legal effort to prohibit LGBT visibility and equality.

North Carolina's March 2016 House Bill (HB) 2 caused a national furor by making it law that in government buildings people may only use the bathroom for the sex that matches the one on their birth certificates.[22] As in Tennessee, this bill trumped city antidiscrimination laws, like the one in Charlotte, which allowed transgender persons to use the bathroom of their identified gender.[23] This bill did not only affect LGBT citizens, but it also disadvantaged the disabled community. For example, Disability Rights North Carolina protested that under HB2 persons with a disability would not be able to enter a restroom with a caregiver of a different sex.[24] The assumption that people need no assistance from others in using a restroom is itself an ableist position, which prevents lawmakers from seeing the possibility that those caregivers may be of a different gender than those they assist. Concerns over gender and ability overlap.

In such cases, alliances between LGBT and disability politics are not unusual. Transgender and disability activists have agitated for safer bathroom access for some time.[25] Further, as we have seen, theorist Robert McRuer has shown how connected compulsory able-bodiedness and heterosexuality are in U.S. society.[26] Both are essential to reproduce the economically productive, working family at the heart of American neoliberal myths of success. Neoliberalism in particular depends on them both in that, in its disavowals of government responsibility for social welfare, it transfers that responsibility to individuals and their families, demanding that they be economically productive and that they care for their own bodies. This political context facilitated the rise of the modern moonshine industry. That context is one in which state governments promote heterosexism and ableism as part of the landscape of their support for business.

Therefore, modern moonshine should be understood as the product of neoliberal states particularly invested in enacting heterosexist and ableist legislations and in supporting traditional sexual, gender, and family forms. A further troubling synchronicity stems from the fact that as a product heavily associated with Appalachia, modern moonshine has come to represent the region at the same time these heterosexist and ableist laws do. To the outsider, the geography doubles down on its bigotry along with its craft. This is particularly true because modern moonshine depends on a form of craft branding that succeeds by using the sociality of a particular place to sell the product to its consumers.

The modern moonshine industry models itself on the successes of craft beer. As secretary of the North Carolina Distillers Association, Esteban McMahan, said in 2015, "We're continually surprised that after a huge craft beer movement, it doesn't seem intuitive to some that the same thing will happen for craft distilling."[27] Studies show how craft breweries have already stimulated rural tourism in Appalachia, particularly in North Carolina, and new moonshine seems poised to do the same thing (see chapter 9).[28] Geographer Wes Flack has attributed the tourist appeal of craft beer to neolocalism.[29] He defines "neolocalism" as a phenomenon by which consumers reject national (and global) mega-brands, understood as indistinctive, in favor of local brands, which cultivate a unique sense of place and allow consumers to express their individuality by association with that place through their embrace of the brand. Such consumers of neolocalism are not merely provincial. They are aware of global brands and associate them with the flattening of individuality and local culture—with, for example, the "McDonaldization" of the world—and choose instead to situate their own identities in the specificity of a place by buying local.[30] The brands themselves must amplify their unique local qualities in order to appeal to the neolocal consumer.

By its long association with Appalachian culture, moonshine virtually hummed with neolocal potential. What's more, marketing scholars Anne-Marie Hede and Torgeir Watne have shown how craft alcohol branding tends to facilitate consumers' human identification with the brand by incorporating the stories of local heroes and legends into marketing strategies.[31] This strategy has been deployed in the new moonshine industry since its inception: in 2007 North Carolina's Piedmont Distillers partnered with NASCAR legend Junior Johnson in order to sell its Midnight Moon 'shine based on the Johnsons' and stock car racing's roots in historical moonshine running.[32] Such marketing approaches foster neolocalism by inviting consumers to express affinities with such local, legendary moonshining figures like Johnson when drinking his liquor. Wes Flack has cautioned that consumers of neolocalism become disenchanted with formulaic branding and marketing; new brands have to demonstrate unique takes on the local.[33] As new moonshine ages, its branding requires newer moonshiner figures. What happens when younger brands offer moonshiner figures who stretch the bounds of the traditional family so essential to the neoliberal states that produced new moonshine in the first place? The following two case studies examine the internet and social media presence of two such new moonshine brands and how they walk this fine line.

Out Shine: Short Mountain Distillery, Genetic Entrepreneurialism, and Niche Sexuality

In 2009, as part of an economic stimulus strategy, Tennessee passed a bill easing restrictions on moonshine production, and the following year, Cannon County passed a referendum to allow its Short Mountain Distillery to begin production.[34] One local reacted online with "Great news! Maybe some of us unemployed can finally get a job in the county again!"[35] Although in the 1960s and 1970s, the Appalachian Regional Commission (ARC) had classed Cannon County as economically "distressed," by the time the referendum passed, it was considered "transitional."[36] At least according to locals like the internet user above, local jobs were still scarce; work was elsewhere. While Short Mountain Distillery billed itself as artisan craft, it also committed itself to a sustainability that would revitalize Cannon County farming, business, and tourism.[37] In these ways, Short Mountain Distillery followed the model of craft beer to position itself as a viable, rural economic stimulus. What is different about Short Mountain Distillery is the fact that it is gay-owned. Owner Billy Kaufman has stated that, following on the passage of new laws, modern moonshine quickly became a hyper-competitive market in the region and that thirty new distilleries followed on the heels of his own.[38] However, as of 2017 Short Mountain remains the only member distillery listed with the LGBT Chamber of Commerce of the Nashville area.[39]

Despite this distinction, the gay-owned distillery still followed market conventions. Leveraging marketing strategies like those described by Hede and Watne, the new company cast itself as an extension of a local moonshining tradition, citing the fact that Cannon County itself had eighteen stills after the Civil War and that legendary Prohibition-era shiner Cooper Melton used the springs on distillery property.[40] Further, they profile the traditional moonshiners who contributed their craft to the modern moonshine: Ricky Estes and Ronald Lawson ("retired from their days of illegal wildcatting"), with antiqued photos designed to look like mugshots and with arrest placards bearing the script "Living Legends of Moonshine."[41] Employing a very effective visual irony, these photos actually maintain the outlaw image of the moonshiner while framing it as an honorable distant history. Arguably, though, the success of this irony depends on an erasure of any real enmity between government and shiner. To that effect, owner Kaufman claimed in a local news interview that previously local moonshining had been a "gentleman's game" with authorities forewarning shiners of raids.[42] Kaufman's history of Cannon County moonshining preserves the playful competition of the outlaw but drains that status of any real risk or violence and repackages it as a matter of refinement. Casting the outlaw as gentleman naturalizes the refined craft of moonshining by obscuring its dangerous and illicit elements; it also mutes the area's specific histories of poverty.

For example, instead of crediting the traditional moonshiners themselves with boosting the local economy, area journalists framed the new Short Mountain Distillery owners as part of a legacy of rescuing the region from economic crisis. Writing for the nearby *Murfreesboro Post*, columnist Mike Vinson portrayed Kaufman as coming from a line of legendary entrepreneurs: "It appears that Kaufman is of the blood line to adequately assess the situation at hand, peer down the Stream of Time, and oversee a business (Short Mountain Distillery) that could prove beneficial to the collective good of Cannon County and surrounding counties: Kaufman is the great grandson of Jesse Schwayder, who founded Samsonite in 1910. Still, it was Kaufman's grandfather, Louis Degan, who brought Samsonite to Murfreesboro, a move that provided jobs and security to a number of families for decades."[43] Vinson portrayed entrepreneurship as, at once, a matter of good genes and mystical vision, and he further cast the Kaufman family as friends of the region. Owned by the four Kaufman brothers, Short Mountain Distillery does not make such mythical claims about itself, but it does corroborate the theme: "Billy proposed an idea to his brothers (David, Ben, and Darian) to start a distillery called Short Mountain Distillery. It would create jobs, help keep local farmers in business and bring another unique Tennessee brand to America and the world. Most important to the Kaufman brothers, Short Mountain Distillery would be a locally owned and family funded business that's a productive part of the community generating needed revenue that will stay in the county."[44]

Hede and Watne show how neolocal craft marketing strategies broadly reference local legends so that consumers and journalists can elaborate on the myth, essentially entangling themselves into the brand story. The above are examples of just such journalistic and marketing collaborations; what is interesting about the neoliberal-era story is that the new moonshine *entrepreneur* achieves a legendary status that rivals that of the traditional moonshiner. It is important to recognize that the two figures are a crucial pairing in the branding of modern moonshine. Whereas the shiner, as a "wildcat," has a kind of rogue loner association, the innovative entrepreneur is firmly part of a family. On the Short Mountain Distillery website, a black-and-white photo of the Kaufman brothers echoes the mugshots of Estes and Lawson but distinguishes itself by posing the brothers with their arms on each other's shoulders, wearing dressy attire.[45] Separate from the shiners' photo, we can still imagine the brothers as a core family, which the shiners belong to as part of an extension of the refinement on display here.

In the brothers' photos, Billy stands out. His brothers wear dark jackets and white shirts, but Billy himself is dressed more quirkily. He wears no jacket; instead, he sports a bow tie, a handlebar mustache, suspenders, a lighter and more tactile pant, and work boots. His style evokes a more playfully anachronistic gentleman—a gentleman farmer, to be exact. Billy's image is central to the branding of this modern moonshine in a couple of ways. First of all, for the company to be seen as locally owned, as the website claims, the owners must be recognizably local. Billy Kaufman is that sign. Second, then, not only is Kaufman a new local, relocated there from Los Angeles more than fifteen years prior, but he also ethically innovates the local practice of farming as a way of sustaining it.[46] It is important, then, that he stands somewhere between tradition and innovation, shiner and entrepreneur, local and outsider; the image of the gentleman farmer gracefully performs that balance. At the same time, other photos show Kaufman in everyday work clothes, actively farming, while others show him hosting tastings as a gentleman host. In image and work, Kaufman performs the flexibility critical to success in the neoliberal environment.

Short Mountain and the Terms of Being a Gay Moonshiner

Short Mountain Distillery exhibits this kind of performative nimbleness in another crucial way, though. On August 1, 2012, Ben Rock wrote for the website *Out & About Nashville* that "with more character than vodka and a smoother flavor than tequila, gay-owned Short Mountain Shine is ready for its grand

105-proof entrance into Nashville's GLBT community."[47] With no mention of Billy Kaufman's sexuality on the distillery website or in general local media, the fact that the moonshine distillery is gay-owned only functions as part of a niche marketing strategy that—in the context of Tennessee's contemporary anti-LGBT law-making—is better described as circumscribed marketing. While Short Mountain Distillery might be openly "gay-owned" in the gay media of a nearby city and it might come out in the gay bar launch party that Rock's article announces, to be loudly gay everywhere would surely be a liability. In many ways, the openly anti-LGBT state of Tennessee forces Kaufman into a certain flexibility around where and when he markets his company with his own image. His is a kind of market-enforced "passing" that pushes him into several forms serially: farmer, gentleman, "family" man, entrepreneur, anachronist, gay businessman, and so on.

At the same time, on the website, Kaufman's sexuality is interestingly tacit. Arguably, it is plain in his quirky difference from his brothers, in the very plasticity he performs, in his photos at work or with animals (rather than with wife and children). In many ways, it is Kaufman's queerness that provides the "twist" to update traditional moonshine; it is a somewhat unspoken but somehow recognizable gayness that modernizes the traditional regional product. To the degree this is true, Tennessee benefits from a muted gayness that innovates the moonshine image and boosts the local economy; what mutes that gayness is a neoliberal geography that aggressively associates tradition with heterosexuality—in marriage, school, and family form. The overall message is clear: A *gay* entrepreneurial family should not feel at home here.

The phenomenon functions as a neolocal, regional variation on what Puar has called homonationalism in a couple of ways. First, it is an example of how certain relatively privileged gay citizens are allowed to enjoy highly circumscribed freedom and inclusion where it benefits the state. Second, as a neolocal industry, modern moonshine also ironically endorses the national by positioning its local product as an important alternative to the foreign. In fact, U.S. nationalism is consistently raised as an ethical motivation for the sale and purchase of modern moonshine. This is no less the case with gay-owned Short Mountain Distillery.

For example, local journalist Melinda Hudgins stressed the uniquely American spirit of Short mountain moonshine when she reported that the distillery owners claimed they wanted "to slap American flags on everything to prove a point."[48] Underscoring the truly neolocal character of the enterprise as Flack defines it—a sense of the local re-entrenched against more global industry—Hudgins further quotes Kaufman to say of Short Mountain's distilling that "China is not involved" and "we want to make moonshine the American vodka."[49] Such statements implicitly pose Appalachian moonshine as an entrepreneurial measure within a kind of extended economic Cold War against "red" Russia and China. Furthermore, the homonationalist aspect of this global free-market patriotism is underscored by remembering that anti-Russian sentiment spiked around this time in response to reports of homophobia there.[50] The composite dynamic is a strange one. New moonshine allows consumers to express their Americanness by buying American and not foreign spirits, especially not Russian or Chinese liquors. There is an irony in the media landscape, though: at the same time U.S. journalists critiqued Russia's homophobia, its uniquely American moonshine was itself being produced domestically in a homophobic state.

In the case of Short Mountain Distillery, then, politics shapes the figure of the modern moonshiner in several ways. First, the moonshiner is necessarily yoked to a legendary entrepreneurial family, which transmutes the outlaw into the innovator. The figure of the entrepreneur subtly takes the foreground from the moonshiner proper so that "craft" better describes the business than the liquor production. Second, the emphasis on the family is important. While the actual focus on moonshine production is shifted from shiner to the entrepreneurial family, the work of the lawmaker remains invisible. The focus on the new moonshiner family carries the message that social good is the responsibility of the private citizen and *not* of the government—a core neoliberal tenet. This might explain why regional poverty and violence must be erased from marketing histories of new moonshining.

Finally, the modernization of moonshine depends on a flexible figure who not only embodies both tradition and innovation but who also must perform differently for various markets. In the case of Short Mountain Distillery, that flexibility is associated with a tacitly gay entrepreneur within a culture whose markets clearly constrain him from addressing them all as an openly gay man. In this case, that flexibility can be understood as a form of regional homonationalism within a homophobic environment. However, as the next case study shows, the neoliberal entrepreneurial family values at work in modern moonshine marketing not only manifest in terms of sexuality; they also exert their influence in matters of gender and ability.

Working Hearts: Asheville Distilling and the Mother as Exceptionally Capable Entrepreneur

In 2015 Marlo Thomas profiled North Carolina modern moonshiner Troy Ball, who shared an early insight about the liquor: "I realized that even though this quality white whiskey was an American tradition, it was unrepresented in the market. . . . People all over the country were drinking Russian vodka when we had our own white spirit right here. It was the hole in the doughnut."[51] Echoing the specifically non-Russian distinctiveness of Appalachian moonshine also touted by Short Mountain moonshiners, Ball went on in Thomas's interview to cite entrepreneur-politician Ross Perot as inspiration. Elsewhere, Ball referenced the "ability to make American cocktails with an American spirit, rather than a Russian vodka, or a Mexican tequila."[52] Cultivating a similar U.S. patriotic neolocalism powered by Appalachian disavowals of global products, Ball, like Kaufman, positions the Appalachian as uniquely American and frames international liquors as inherently foreign. Unlike Short Mountain's serially masculine neolocal entrepreneurial figure, though, the *Troy* behind Asheville Distilling's Troy & Sons moonshine is a woman. And she was the first woman in the United States to be given legal license to distill whiskey in the male-dominated industry.[53]

On her website, Troy Ball credits her older moonshining neighbors in North Carolina with introducing her to "keeper" moonshine—the high quality, smooth liquor saved for personal use and typically not for sale.[54] As a transplant from Austin, Texas, Ball demonstrated patience and loyalty in winning her neighbors' confidence. Although her relationship with shiners is clearly important, Ball's entrepreneurial character is built squarely around two other qualities: research and motherhood. Collecting and comparing recipes from neighbors everywhere was an ongoing part of her research method, but Ball extended it by, according to the website, "testing recipes acquired from the North Carolina State Archives."[55] Later, when she found an heirloom white corn grown for over two hundred years by the local McEntire farming family, she took it to the University of Tennessee to have its unique property analyzed by scientists.[56] With a Vanderbilt degree in business, Ball took a scholarly approach to developing her moonshine business. Ball and farmer John McEntire began experimenting with distilling his corn. As Marlo Thomas described it, "Tucked away in a small barn in the Great Smoky Mountains of North Carolina, Troy Ball and her friend John McEntire were like a pair of mad scientists—mixing, boiling, adding ingredients, then taking them out again—trying to achieve just the right formula for their precious concoction."[57]

While this studied approach is central to Ball's entrepreneurial image, it is ultimately inseparable from the motherhood evoked by the very name of her moonshine. As a further example, Thomas's article is titled "Mom of Special Needs Sons Supports Her Family by Bringing This Rare Product to Market." Ball's two oldest sons, born with, in Thomas's words, "a still-undiagnosed genetic disease," were key to their mother's realizing her entrepreneurial potential: "After many years of caring for Marshall and Coulton, I achieved a certain peace of mind when I realized that the skills I learned raising my boys—to be resourceful, tireless, and adaptable—were the very same skills that would help me be successful in business. And that's a good feeling."[58] Her adaptability may very well reference the kind of entrepreneurial flexibility that Kaufman had to employ. As an educated and ambitious woman, Ball was surely challenged to find a way to present herself—as both a mother and an entrepreneur. Not only was the work of both too all-consuming to manage simultaneously, but also a sexist society makes reconciling both roles additionally demanding. Being a woman moonshiner in the overwhelmingly male liquor distilling business only added to the challenge.

Ball brought her motherhood and her sons with her to work in ways that went beyond putting their name on the shingle. As the above quote shows, her entrepreneurial skills were lifted straight from her mothering experiences. On the website, Ball adds that, of her sons, Luke, the youngest, who was born without the genetic condition of his older brothers, "is the only one who physically works at the distillery with us, but the hearts and spirits of all our boys infuse everything we do."[59] This emphasis on heart is mirrored in her moonshining craft: "The heads are the very first liquids to be distilled, while the tails are the very last. Our whiskeys are strictly made from neither of these, but rather, the pure hearts. Only the hearts have the desired strength and quality to become a full and flavorful whiskey."[60] There is a sense that, even though the sons do not figure visually on the website and that only Luke "physically" works at the distillery, the real *body* of Troy & Sons' entrepreneurialism is emotional. According to Ball, the real work is in the marketing: "Building a brand is a marathon, not a sprint. It takes large sums of money and constant work to spread the word about your products. I think many people underestimate just what that means, personally and for their families. I did, but am fortunate to have a family that believes in me and supports what I do!"[61] Asheville Distilling's success not only hinges on marketing and the entrepreneurial family, but as a member of the Distilled Spirits Council's small distillers program, the company also follows the council's marketing code discussed earlier, subscribing to its larger moral sense of respectability.[62]

Inasmuch as her entrepreneurial figure sells the product, Troy Ball's website image functions in a way that is similar to Kaufman's gentleman farmer. Her site pictures her walking a mountain field in tall grass—in jeans, a white flowing shirt, and riding boots, with a wide-brimmed hat topping her long blond curls. The hat, boots, and jeans mark her as a rural woman, lending her feminine appearance the hint of a stylish and anachronistic masculinity. Usually pictured alone, she looks comfortable in her natural environment—appearing more like an explorer or surveyor than a farmer. With this look, she makes tradition fashion-forward, even manages a playful but inoffensive androgyny and evokes the fearless inquiry that is also a hallmark of her entrepreneurial image. Even though she is alone, she exudes an air of happiness in her solitude, as if it, like her moonshining business, is a singular gift afforded her by her ever-supportive family who believe in her personal projects.

At first glance there is little evidence of the limits imposed on this figure that might parallel Kaufman's niche sexuality. There is little trace of constraint on what Ball can show of herself on her site and in her publicity. She is forthcoming about her challenges as a businesswoman and mother, and her family has apparently met those challenges. It is possible that the visual absence of her sons represents a limit in terms of wider cultural readiness to see the *dis*abled as absolutely able to perform entrepreneurial work. In addition, while those are certainly limits facilitated by a state that demands and only rewards certain forms of work, Ball makes a lot of effort to counter that narrative by centering her sons' affective contributions to the enterprise, within the parameters of the marketing code. (Additionally, since her son Marshall is a published author with his own business, it makes more sense to think of the distillery as her work and of writing as his.)[63] However, there is one fleeting reference on the

Troy & Sons website that points to critical limits in how Ball can represent her experience.

In the origin story of her modern moonshining business, Ball says, "As the boys got older and we qualified for assistance with their care, I finally felt I could start something outside the home for myself."[64] So seamless is the entrepreneur's success story, emotionally converting challenge into entrepreneurial fitness with the help of a legendarily supportive family, that it is easy to miss the acutely specific challenges that a neoliberal small-government political culture lays at the feet of the disabled. In so many cases, the discrete nuclear family is simply not enough to address the needs of a body that the system classifies as outside the norm, thereby rendering its support "special"—i.e., too extraordinary and costly. The neoliberal state often defines such bodies as outside the routine system of care, making it especially difficult to qualify for assistance. In saying that after years her family qualified for government assistance, was Ball confessing they had reached a certain poverty threshold scary enough for the state to help? In saying this assistance allowed her to work for herself, is Ball subtly registering the powerful state disinvestment in costly childcare that forces mothers into full-time responsibilities? If so, such stories can only be obliquely referenced in Troy & Sons' entrepreneurial story of modern moonshine, and only as a passing footnote to the greater inspiration of the family's "doing it for themselves." Within the neoliberal context that gave rise to new moonshine, Ball can*not* represent her family as state-dependent. Such a story would compromise the compulsory ability of the entrepreneurial family at the heart of neoliberal values.

Conclusions: Imagining Modern Moonshine Pushing Its Neoliberal Frame

In both these case studies, the family story is crucial to the web presence of the modern moonshine distilleries. This should come as no surprise since modern moonshine is an industry produced by a neoliberal context that itself depends on the myth of the traditional enterprising family. Also in both cases, the companies market the entrepreneurial owner associated with such a family as legendary, more so than the wildcat moonshiners. With Short Mountain, that legendary status is depicted as the result of mythical, entrepreneurial genes. In the case of Asheville Distilling, the entrepreneurial legend is characterized by two elements: scientific research and endlessly resourceful motherhood. In order to amplify these legends, lived narratives of sexuality, gender, and ability must be muted. However, this muting does not stem from savvy marketing sense alone; it is also the product of wider neoliberal systemic forces. Moralistic market regulation and harsh laws in the host states maximize the positive visibility of the traditional family and limit the visibility of apparent deviations from that family form.

To reiterate: this is not to say that modern moonshine is a uniquely neoliberal industry. Neoliberalism shapes all contemporary business in one way or another. Nor is it to say that new moonshine distilleries like Short Mountain and Asheville Distilling have a special responsibility to make sexuality, gender, and ability cornerstones of their marketing campaigns. However, as a formerly illicit production, moonshining may face more acute market pressures to reflect neoliberal morals centered on a traditional family form characterized by respectable and compulsory heterosexuality and able-bodiedness. Also, as a neolocal craft industry, new moonshine may also be compelled to use its marketing practices to tacitly associate a morally conservative sense of tradition with the region. When such marketing associations coincide with the passage of aggressive laws that deny protections to LGBT and disabled persons, a composite media image of contemporary Appalachia solidifies around a sense of welcome for one sort of family and a sense of *un*-welcome for others.

If the preceding analysis exposes this possibility, then it also becomes possible to look to alternative moonshine traditions that can promote a different Appalachia. For example, moonshining legend Popcorn Sutton's suicide to avoid prison in the months preceding Tennessee's legal moonshine production defies comfortable neoliberal narratives.[65] First, his suicide underscores rather than obscures the violence in moonshining history. Second, the insistently impudent, crass, and working-class figure Sutton presented in the media defies the kind of respectability embraced by neoliberal entrepreneurship. Sutton's is a narrative that exaggerates a certain traditional moonshiner figure who is an entrepreneur at odds with law and state. While centered on a tragic story, the marketing for the distillery now bearing Sutton's name will find it difficult to whitewash certain aspects of moonshine history.

Further, although it has not been the focus of this chapter, the questions raised hopefully oblige us to also interrogate the whiteness of white lightning. Appalachia has long been assumed a racially white geography. In 1985

William H. Turner's and Edward J. Cabbell's book *Blacks in Appalachia* questioned this assumption by calling attention to the history of African Americans in the region.[66] Similarly, Frank X. Walker's 2000 book of poetry *Affrilachia* not only pointed out similar histories but led to the formation of the Affrilachian Poets, dedicated to describing the experiences of people of color in Appalachia, "to render the invisible visible."[67] In light of such important work, it is also exciting to imagine the ways by which modern moonshine could also generate new visibilities. Historical work like that of Shane Hand, whose scholarship traces black moonshining traditions in Mississippi, raises the possibility of black-owned modern moonshine distilleries which might pull from such traditions for their marketing narratives and make clear that Appalachia is no more a white place than it is a straight or able-bodied place.[68] Startup monies might be offered black entrepreneurs interested in such projects.

Although this essay is rooted in a critique of neoliberalism and its impact on the Appalachian region, its goal is to shine light on opportunities for modern moonshine to market a new Appalachia rooted in its own often neglected traditions rather than in the harsh moralism of its neoliberal frame. If figures like Popcorn Sutton and African American moonshiners present other legends as possibilities to the marketing of modern moonshine, so do Short Mountain and Asheville Distilling in the stories they have yet to tell. Moreover, it is possible that these stories are just beginning to make their rounds. For example, Billy Kaufman now names his business's contributions to gay-related causes, such as local AIDS/HIV initiatives and Nashville's Sisters of Perpetual Indulgence fundraisers.[69] Troy Ball has begun to speak frankly about how close to financial devastation her family became.[70] If modern moonshine can go further to articulate a loudly LGBT or disabled moonshine family, then the richness of Appalachian tradition could very well strain the stereotypes within which neoliberal forces would confine it. Such voices could very well reflect a much more open and authentic Appalachian spirit.

NOTES

1. Ken Teusch, "Moonshine Mainstream?" *River Valley Leader* (Russellville, AR), January 10, 2013, www.rivervalleyleader.com/opinion/blogs/likely_stories /article_edd5fb78-5b51-11e2-b8b2-0019bb30f31a.html.

2. Ibid.

3. Lisa Duggan, *The Twilight of Equality?: Neoliberalism, Cultural Politics, and the Attack on Democracy* (Boston: Beacon Press, 2004).

4. Lisa Duggan, "The New Homonormativity: The Sexual Politics of Neoliberalism," in *Materializing Democracy: Toward a Revitalized Cultural Politics*, ed. Russ Castronovo and Dana D. Nelson (Durham, NC: Duke University Press, 2002), 175–94.

5. Ibid., 179.

6. Robert McRuer, *Crip Theory: Cultural Signs of Queerness and Disability* (New York: NYU Press, 2006).

7. Jasbir Puar, *Terrorist Assemblages: Homonationalism in Queer Times* (Durham, NC: Duke University Press, 2007).

8. "A bill was drafted that would permit distilleries in any county in Tennessee where there are both operating liquor stores and liquor by the drink, which opens up much of the state" (Walker Duncan, "Local Distillers Carry on Tennessee's Whiskey History," *City Paper*, March 11, 2012, http://nashvillecity paper.com/content/city-news/local-distillers-carry-tennessees-whiskey-history).

9. Owen Covington, "Craft Distilling Is North Carolina's Next Big Thing," *Charlotte Business Journal*, March 23, 2015, www.bizjournals.com/charlotte/blog/morning -edition/2015/03/craft-distilling-is-north-carolinas-next-big-thing.html.

10. Bruce E. Stewart, *Moonshiners and Prohibitionists: The Battle over Alcohol in Southern Appalachia* (Lexington: University Press of Kentucky, 2011).

11. Distilled Spirits Council, Code of Responsible Practices for Beverage Alcohol Advertising and Marketing, 2011, accessed July 31, 2017, www.discus.org/assets /1/7/May_26_2011_DISCUS_Code_Word_Version1.pdf.

12. See reports and "What Others Are Saying about the Code," Discus.org, accessed July 31, 2017, www.discus.org/responsibility/code/.

13. Distilled Spirits Council, Semi-Annual Code Report, 2010, accessed July 31, 2017, www.discus.org/assets/1/7/2010-Jan-Jun.pdf.

14. Robert I. Reynolds, "Response to Semi-Annual Code Report: Distilled Spirits Council of the United States, March 2005," Distilled Spirits Council, accessed July 31, 2017, www.discus.org/assets/1/7/PIRECodeReleaseStatement3_8_05 .pdf. In response to the 2005 Council report, Robert I. Reynolds, Director of Alcohol Policy Initiatives at the Pacific Institute for Research and Evaluation, wrote that "clearly, additional proactive steps will help encourage expanded public participation in the complaint process and achieve 100% company compliance" with the code.

15. Distilled Spirits Council, Code of Responsible Practices.

16. For more on the Save Our Children campaign, see Gillian Frank, "'The Civil Rights of Parents': Race and Conservative Politics in Anita Bryant's Campaign against Gay Rights in 1970s Florida," *Journal of the History of Sexuality* 22, no. 1 (January 2013): 126–60. Frank shows how the campaign's child protectionism focused on white Christian children and that the Save Our Children leadership included those who also led campaigns against school desegregation and the feminist ERA.

17. Distilled Spirits Council, Code of Responsible Practices. The other quotes in this paragraph come from this same source.

18. Associated Press, "Tenn. County Officials Seek to Ban Gays," *Fox News*, March 17, 2004, www.foxnews.com/story/2004/03/17/tenn-county-officials-seek-to -ban-gays/.

19. Tom Humphrey, "'Don't Say Gay' Bill Clears Senate Panel," *Knox News*, April 21, 2011, www.knoxnews.com/news/2011/apr/21/dont-say-gay-bill-clears-senate -panel/.

20. Mae Beavers, "Tennessee Prohibits Local Governments from Imposing LGBT Anti-discrimination Policies," Freedom Legislation Forum, April 16, 2012, http://republicanstates.wordpress.com/2012/04/16/tennessee-equal-access -to-intrastate-commerce-act/.

21. SJR 134, OpenStates.org, accessed April 15, 2014, http://openstates.org/tn /bills/108/SJR134/.

22. House Bill 2, North Carolina General Assembly, accessed July 31, 2017, www .ncleg.net/Sessions/2015E2/Bills/House/PDF/H2v4.pdf.

23. "Charlotte's Nondiscrimination Ordinance and N.C. House Bill 2 (HB2)," Charlotte, NC, accessed July 31, 2017, http://charlottenc.gov/NonDiscrimination /Pages/default.aspx.

24. Disability Rights North Carolina, "HB2 Harms North Carolinians with Disabilities," April 20, 2016, accessed July 31, 2017, www.disabilityrightsnc.org /sites/default/files/HB2%20response%20DRNC.pdf.

25. For an example of this activist alliance, see Simone Chess, Alison Kafer, Jesse Quizar, and Mattie Udor Richardson, "Calling All Restroom Revolutionaries!," in *That's Revolting!: Queer Strategies for Resisting Assimilation*, ed. Mattilda Bernstein Sycamore (Berkeley: Soft Skull Press, 2008), 216–36.

26. McRuer, *Crip Theory*.

27. Quoted in Covington, "Craft Distilling."

28. Alison Murray and Carol Kline, "Rural Tourism and the Craft Beer Experience:

Factors Influencing Brand Loyalty in Rural North Carolina, USA," *Journal of Sustainable Tourism* 23, nos. 8–9 (2015): 1198–1216.

29. Wes Flack, "American Microbreweries and Neolocalism: 'Ale-ing' for a Sense of Place," *Journal of Cultural Geography* 16, no. 2 (1997): 37–53. Flack dates the rise of craft brewery neolocalism to the 1990s. An interesting line for further research would be how neolocal and neoliberal ideologies—the latter of which, according to Duggan, reached a new ascendancy in the 1990s—emerged together.

30. George Ritzer, *The McDonaldization of Society: An Investigation into the Changing Character of Contemporary Social Life* (Thousand Oaks, CA: Pine Forge Press, 1993).

31. Anne-Marie Hede and Torgeir Watne, "Leveraging the Human Side of the Brand Using a Sense of Place: Case Studies of Craft Breweries," *Journal of Marketing Management* 29, nos. 1–2 (2013): 207–24.

32. "The Legacy of Junior Johnson," *Junior's Midnight Moon,* accessed September 4, 2017, www.juniorsmidnightmoon.com/legacy/.

33. Flack, "American Microbreweries."

34. I have written elsewhere on Short Mountain Distillery's web profile in contrast to the local Radical Faerie subculture that often protested it. Some of the analysis here was also outlined in that project. See Jason Ezell, "Signs and Spirits: The Intimate Politics of Tennessee Moonshining and Queer Space at Short Mountain," *Powerlines* 2, no. 1 (2014). Walker Duncan, "Local Distillers Carry on Tennessee's Whiskey History," *City Paper,* March 11, 2012, http://nashvillecitypaper.com/content/city-news/local-distillers-carry-tennessees-whiskey-history; "Cannon County Voters Say 'YES' to State's First Distillery Referendum," *Cannon Courier,* November 2, 2010, www.cannoncourier.com/cannon-county-voters-say-yes-to-states-first-distillery-referendum-cms-3899.

35. "Cannon County Voters Say 'YES,'" see comment by tngram, November 2, 2010, 10:17 p.m.

36. Appalachian Regional Commission, "Maps," 2010, accessed July 14, 2017, www.arc.gov/maps.

37. Short Mountain Distillery, "Short Mountain Distillery: Short History," accessed July 15, 2017, http://media.wix.com/ugd/0cf933_1c5c07bfd1236fd9f8c788316a80b80d.pdf. Further positioning itself as a specifically rural tourism project, the website's home page as of July 2017 runs the tagline "Escape to the country."

38. Quoted in James Grady, "Distilling the Spirit of Short Mountain: Billy Kaufman Brings a Storied Tradition to a New Age," *Out and About Nashville*, December 31, 2015, https://www.outandaboutnashville.com/story/distilling-spirit-short -mountain/51023#.Wb16SbKGNdg.

39. Nashville LGBT Chamber of Commerce, Member Directory: Restaurant, Food and Beverage, Accessed September 16, 2017, https://www.nashvillelgbtchamber .org/list/ql/restaurants-food-beverages-21.

40. Short Mountain Distillery, "About Us," accessed July 15, 2017, www.shortmoun taindistillery.com/about-us.

41. Ibid.

42. Melinda Hudgins, "There's Moonshine in Them There Hills," *Murfreesboro Post*, November 6, 2011, www.murfreesboropost.com/theres-moonshine-in-them -there-hills-cms-29097.

43. Mike Vinson, "Lifting 'Spirits' in Cannon County," *The Murfreesboro Post* (Murfreesboro, TN), September 12, 2010, www.murfreesboropost.com/mike -vinson-lifting-spirits-in-cannon-county-cms-24399.

44. "About Us," accessed July 15, 2017, www.shortmountaindistillery.com/about-us.

45. Ibid.

46. Grady, "Distilling the Spirit."

47. Ben Rock, "Short Mountain Distillery to Shine at Tribe, PLAY," *Out and About Nashville*, August 1, 2012, www.outandaboutnashville.com/story/short-moun tain-distillery-shine-tribe-play#.UrSYwuKAHsZ.

48. Hudgins, "There's Moonshine."

49. Ibid.

50. For an example of contemporary journalistic coverage of Russian homophobia, see Olga Khazan, "Why Is Russia So Homophobic?," *The Atlantic*, June 12, 2013, https://www.theatlantic.com/international/archive/2013/06/why-is-russia-so -homophobic/276817/.

51. Marlo Thomas, "Mom of Special Needs Sons Supports Her Family by Bringing This Rare Product to Market," *Huffington Post*, January 8, 2015, www.huffington post.com/2015/01/08/mom-of-special-needs-sons_n_6437868.html.

52. Mackensy Lunsford, "Asheville Moonshine Maker Diversifies," *Citizen-Times*, July 5, 2014, www.citizen-times.com/story/local/2014/07/05/asheville-moon shine-makers-diversifies/12249265/.

53. Lilly Knoepp, "The 'Pure Heart' of the First Woman Legally in the Moonshine Business," *Forbes*, February 8, 2017, https://www.forbes.com/sites

/lillyknoepp/2017/02/08/the-pure-heart-of-the-first-woman-legally-in-moon shine-business/#e809d1e6a70a.

54. Asheville Distilling Co., "Our History," accessed July 15, 2017, www.ashevilledis tilling.com/our-history/.

55. Ibid.

56. Stephanie Stewart-Howard, "The Whiskey Talking—Troy and Sons Distillery," *Buttermilk Trace: A Southern Creative Consortium*, October 26, 2012, www .buttermilktrace.com/the-whiskey-talking-troy-sons-distillery/.

57. Thomas, "Mom of Special Needs."

58. Ibid.

59. Asheville Distilling Co., "Our History."

60. Asheville Distilling Co., "The Craft," accessed July 15, 2017, www.asheville distilling.com/the-craft/.

61. Asheville Distilling Co., "Our History."

62. Distilled Spirits Council, "Small Distiller Affiliate Members," accessed September 17, 2017, www.discus.org/about/small-distiller-members/.

63. See Marshall Ball's writing website *Marshall Ball: The Messenger of Love*: http:// marshallball.com/.

64. Asheville Distilling Co., "Our History."

65. Campbell Robertson, "Yesterday's Moonshiner, Today's Micro-Distiller," *New York Times*, February 20, 2012, www.nytimes.com/2012/02/21/us/popcorn -suttons-whiskey-once-moonshine-is-now-legal.html?mcubz=1.

66. William H. Turner and Edward J. Cabbell, *Blacks in Appalachia* (Lexington: University Press of Kentucky, 1985).

67. Frank X. Walker, *Affrilachia: Poems* (Lexington, KY: Old Cove Press, 2000); Affrilachian Poets, accessed September 17, 2017, www.theaffrilachianpoets. com/.

68. "Library Exhibit Examines Moonshine Tradition in South Mississippi from 1900–1966," *Southern Miss Now,* April 20, 2012, http://news.usm.edu/article /library-exhibit-examines-moonshine-tradition-south-mississippi-1900-1966.

69. Joey Amato, "Billy Kaufman: King of the Mountain," *UNITE,* June 23, 2016, http://unitemag.com/billy-kaufman-king-of-the-mountain/.

70. Troy Ball, with Maria Carter, "Making Moonshine Saved My Family from Financial Ruin," *Country Living,* February 16, 2017, www.countryliving.com/life /a41768/moonshine-saved-my-family/.

CHAPTER 8

The "Uncatchables": A Case Study of Call Family Distillers in Wilkes County, North Carolina

CAMERON D. LIPPARD

Junior and Clay Call had '59 Dodges. You could hear them comin' down the road about four or five miles from my home. . . . There wasn't nothin' that could catch 'em.

—Roscoe "Doc" Combs,
Wilkes County Moonshiner and NASCAR Driver

Moonshiners, revenuers, and journalists have called Wilkes County, North Carolina, the world capital of moonshine since the 1940s. For most of the twentieth century, moonshiners and bootleggers ran jars and jugs of moonshine in their modified stock cars across the South and up into the "Yankee" cities of New York and Chicago. These illicit entrepreneurs often outran or evaded local law enforcement and federal revenuers. Of course, Joe Carter, a federal Bureau of Alcohol, Tobacco, and Firearms agent for more than twenty years in Wilkes County, suggested that plenty of moonshiners were caught and sentenced to jail time, or at least saw their cash flow reduced to barely a trickle.[1]

While many Wilkes County families participated in making or running moonshine, the Call family represented the stuff of legend for the Wilkes County moonshiner in the Appalachian Mountains.[2] They embodied the no-nonsense and familial need to run illegal liquor to make ends meet in an economically depressed rural South. In addition, to evade capture when running liquor, Willie Clay Call built and used souped-up stock cars that later inspired the world-famous racing sport of NASCAR. In fact, revenuers called Willie Clay "uncatchable" due to his fast-moving Fords, Dodges, and Chryslers.[3] This family became even more legendary when blockbuster movies like *Thunder Road* portrayed Appalachian moonshiners as *real* American heroes: outrunning and outsmarting the oppressive big government in fast cars in the rural and rebellious American South. This chapter, however, is not about the fantastic tales of moonshining in Wilkes County. Instead, it provides a case study of how a family tradition of making illegal moonshine started by Willie Clay Call became an accepted and legitimate distilling company run by his son, Brian Call, as of 2015.

Today, Call Family Distillers uses the same distilling methods and recipes as Willie Clay Call, which had been passed down to him over several generations and date back to the family patriarch in Tennessee, the Rev. Daniel Houston Call.[4] The company also sells its products in signature mason jars and puts a caricature of Clay's face right on the label (fig. 8.1). The Call family also uses its distillery as an unofficial museum to Wilkes County moonshine, displaying the tools of the trade from the past to show the direct lineage to the industrial and government-regulated production of today. As Helen Rosko suggests in chapter 9, the family has capitalized on the history and culture of Wilkes County moonshining to start a legitimate and authentic craft distillery. The only main difference between what Willie Clay did from 1930s to 1960s and what his son, Brian Call, is doing in the twenty-first century is that the family spirits are taxed and sold by the North Carolina Alcoholic Beverage Control (ABC) store system. As Brian Call stated in an interview with a local news station, "I think my dad would be real proud of what we have done . . . except for having to pay taxes."[5]

Wilkes County, North Carolina: Moonshine Capital of the World

In 1950 journalist Vance Packard called Wilkes County the "Moonshine Capital of the World," a title previously held by Franklin County, Virginia.[6] While illicit distilling in Wilkes County had existed for decades, its notoriety and volume hit a fevered pitch during the mid-twentieth century. According to Packard, moonshiners there produced around five hundred thousand gallons of illegal liquor in 1949 alone, netting a profit of nearly $2 million.[7] Consequently, revenuers scrambled to crack down on the illicit distillers, many of whom had begun to use large submarine stills to produce as much as a thousand gallons of whiskey in a single run. In fact, between 1949 and 1958, the Alcohol, Tobacco, and Firearms office in Wilkes County would seize more stills than any other ATF post in the nation, solidifying the county's reputation as the moonshine capital of the world.[8]

These law enforcement measures, however, failed to curtail moonshining in Wilkes County, at least during the 1940s and 1950s. For one, alcohol distilling had deep historical roots in the county. Famous local moonshiners like Junior Johnson often argued in their courtroom testimonials that making whiskey was a family tradition that reached backed several generations, and as such the government had no right to impose a tax on them.[9] More importantly, many residents continued to view alcohol manufacturing as an economic necessity. By the 1950s the county's two leading legitimate industries—farming and furniture manufacturing—had declined, causing some locals to increasingly engage in moonshining.[10] Indeed, profits from illicit liquor allowed struggling farmers to earn a living. As Willie Clay Call remembered in a local television interview, "They would grow their corn in the summer time and mash it in the winter time to make liquor. . . . It was to pay the bills and get by."[11] The moonshine industry also supported and propped up local businesses that sold mason jars, sugar, corn, car parts, and other items used in the production and distribution of illegal alcohol.[12] "Most of the county's hardware stores, garages, tinsmiths, sugar dealers, and other merchants prosper directly or indirectly from this secret wealth-producing industry," Vance Packard wrote, explaining why many residents tolerated moonshining, a profession that helped them survive during tough economic times.[13]

The use of modified stock cars to run illicit liquor further helped Wilkes County gain fame as the moonshine capital of the world. To meet consumer demand and evade capture, many local moonshiners and bootleggers increasingly began to soup up their family cars and farm trucks. In an interview with *Hot Rod Magazine*, Junior Johnson detailed the ways in which these Wilkes County residents modified their cars to haul moonshine: "The cars we ran on the road, you could modify 'em to the tip. Plus, they were supercharged and turbocharged. We could just do anything we wanted to 'em. . . . A supercharger or turbocharger just packs so much power in that motor, it's unbelievable. And we had no limitations on cubic inches. We could bore and stroke 'em all we wanted. We'd run 500 cubic inches a lot of the time."[14] In addition, these cars had heavier springs to deal with the weight changes in shipping cases of moonshine and even included switches to manually turn off brake lights so

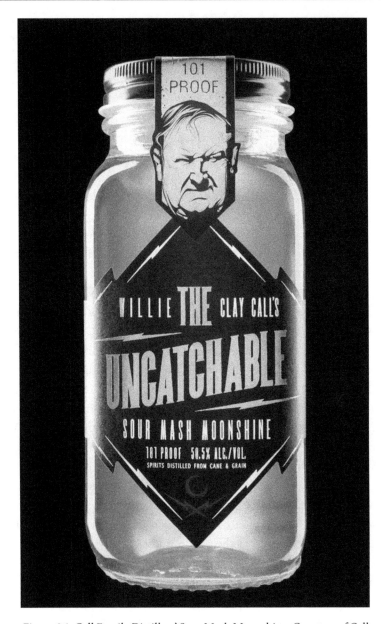

Figure 8.1. Call Family Distillers' Sour Mash Moonshine. Courtesy of Call Family Distillers.

law enforcement could not see them coming at night. Able to exceed speeds of one hundred miles an hour, they were also faster than the standard-issue patrol cars of the time.[15] "It was kind of an intriguing thing to work on them and make them run," Johnson recalled; "you almost wanted the law to run you because you had such an advantage over them."[16]

Media coverage of Johnson and other daredevil drivers in Wilkes County evading revenuers not only reinforced the county's reputation as the moonshine capital of the world but also helped to popularize a new American pastime, the National Association for Stock Car Auto Racing (NASCAR). By 1950 local boosters had constructed the North Wilkesboro Speedway, a five-eighth-mile track that hosted NASCAR races until 1996. Local bootleggers such as Johnson, Dean Combs, and Roscoe "Doc" Combs soon became NASCAR legends, and moonshiners such as Willie Clay Call gave NASCAR drivers and mechanics tips on how to drive and build their cars to go faster.[17]

By the 1960s, however, moonshining began to decline in Wilkes County. This was in part due to improved liquor law enforcement. Throughout the 1960s, local and federal revenuers such as Joe Carter, Charlie Weems, and Charlie Felts launched an aggressive campaign to combat moonshining in Wilkes County, one that resulted in the confiscation of several hundred stills and the arrest of a number of "big-time" moonshiners.[18] In his autobiography, *Shortcuts to Justice*, Carter recalled that he often destroyed twenty stills a week during the decade.[19] Meanwhile, Felts, who served as an ATF agent in Wilkes County for thirty years, made several hundred moonshine-related arrests.[20] This crackdown convinced a growing number of illicit distillers to quit the business. While there were several busts during the 1970s and 1980s, the number of law enforcement and ATF agents in the county dropped to fewer than five by the 1990s. In 2009 the ATF office in Wilkes County closed its doors after making only a single arrest in the previous five years.[21]

In addition to improved law enforcement, several other forces helped to curtail moonshining in Wilkes County. During the 1960s Holly Farms and Tyson Foods arrived in the region, enabling many locals to begin earning decent wages from farming and processing chicken.[22] The arrival of other companies, such as Lowes Foods and Lowe's Hardware, further provided employment outside of moonshining—as well as health and retirement benefits—to local residents.[23] In 1965 Wilkes County also opened its first ABC store. This gave residents access to cheap and legal liquor, causing the demand for moonshine to plummet.[24] Meanwhile, some moonshiners—unable to make a profit from illegal alcohol—switched to transporting and selling marijuana, heroin, cocaine, and other illicit drugs. By the 1980s it appeared that moonshining had vanished in Wilkes County.[25]

Call Family History of Moonshining

A history of moonshining in Wilkes County would be incomplete without including the Call family. Indeed, the Call family is to Wilkes County history of moonshine as Junior Johnson is to the history of stock car racing and NASCAR. Stretching back seven generations, the Call family first began to produce whiskey in Tennessee with the Reverend Daniel Houston Call. Below is a description of Reverend Call and his work with the American whiskey legend and twenty-first-century industry giant Jack Daniels (Jasper Newton Daniels):

> Call Family Distillers represents a deep-rooted heritage of whiskey making, beginning in the 1800's in Lynchburg, TN. Reverend Daniel Call was a Lutheran minister that lived in Lynchburg. At a young age, Jack Daniels began working at the general store owned by Rev. Call. Behind the store, Call operated a whiskey still. During the 1860's as the Civil War swept through America, Reverend Dan Call taught Jack Daniels the art of distilling whiskey. They partnered up together and formed a distillery named Call & Daniels Distillery No. 7, District #4. As the temperance movement began to sweep throughout America, the Reverend was called to make a serious decision: choose his church congregation or the whiskey business.[26]

The reverend ultimately opted to keep his ministry and sold his share of the whiskey business to Daniels. Shortly thereafter, he moved his family to North Carolina and settled in the Wilkes County area.

In Wilkes the Call family resumed making whiskey. While few records on their production or arrests remain extant, the Call family emerged as a household name in Wilkes County when it came to moonshine.[27] They also became legendary to revenuers, largely due to the exploits of Willie Clay's father, Willie Simon Call (fig. 8.2).

Willie Simon Call (1908–68) had several run-ins with the law while attempting to support his family by making and transporting moonshine.[28] According

Figure 8.2. Mugshot of Willie Simon Call, father of Willie Clay Call and grandfather of craft distiller Brian Call. Courtesy of Call Family Distillers.

to his great-grandson Brian Call, "He spent a lot of time in jail. He was always running from the law and never really was around much.[29] The Call family was a community that law enforcement both respected and feared. As the Call Family Distillers' website describes the area where many Calls lived in Wilkes County, "Known in some parts of the world as Hells Half Acres—[the] Call Section is a place that was once home to some of the toughest individuals in western North Carolina. It was due to the high volume illegal whiskey production in this area that led federal revenue officers to dub Wilkes County, NC—The Moonshine Capital of the World."[30]

Kyle Hayes, a Wilkes County attorney, remembered that Simon and his seven brothers had been arrested and convicted several times for running liquor. He stated, "I reckon I represented all the Call boys, one time or another. Julia Call, their mother, was the most like my mother. . . . so I couldn't help but think of my mother when she'd be up there at the Courthouse trying to help her boys."[31] However, these arrests and convictions failed to dissuade Simon Call from teaching Willie Clay and his other children how to make and run liquor.

Figure 8.3. 1961 Chrysler New Yorker owned by Willie Clay Call. Courtesy of Call Family Distillers.

Willie Clay took on the family tradition as a teenager.[32] Under his father's and uncles' tutelage, he learned how to make sour mash, run the liquor, and drive the jars of moonshine to various points throughout Wilkes County and beyond.[33] Call soon became friends with Junior Johnson and Millard Ashley, all of whom worked together to run liquor and build cars to evade law enforcement and race on the backroads of Wilkes County. The three men helped to solidify operations, conjure up recipes for the moonshine, and soup up cars that could outrun the law enforcement to deliver the product. They also watched out for each other when it came to revenuers snooping around and helped to find customers.

Call also began to modify his family's traditional distilling methods to make what he thought was a better liquor. He used steam injection to distill his mash so as not to burn any grains in the fermented beer or liquid, which would have made an off-taste in the liquor.[34] He also ran his mash through a 300-gallon still that produced 13 to 14 gallons of 100-proof liquor in a single run. In addition, Clay used copper worms instead of copper radiators and—in honor of Junior Johnson's number 11 racecar—operated eleven barrels of mash at one time. His liquor recipe included mostly corn or rye, depending on what he wanted to run, as well as sugar to increase the levels of fermentation and alcohol production. He also used limber twig apples and other local ingredients to make a variety of brandies.[35] Like his ancestors, Clay produced his liquor in the backwoods of Wilkes, purposing his mule, Kate, to pull the liquor out to his car to run it to cities throughout North Carolina.

Call modified several cars to deliver his moonshine to and from Winston-Salem and Charlotte at night, including a 1961 four-door Chrysler New Yorker (fig. 8.3).[36] He recalled, "It'd run 180 miles an hour loaded or unloaded, uphill or downhill." Call logged three hundred thousand miles in this car, delivering two or three loads a night of about 130 jugs of moonshine.[37] Because revenuer cars were slow, many revenuers actually bought souped-up cars from Clay and other moonshiners, including Joe Carter, an ATF revenuer in Wilkes County, who purchased a 1960 Dodge built by Willie Clay Call.[38] Carter later arrested Call twice and sent him to jail.

By the late 1960s, Call and many other Wilkes County moonshiners had ceased making large amounts of moonshine. Call lamented that his prison time and the fact that revenuers were catching "30 to 40 boys a week" made him reconsider the benefits of running liquor.[39] He also saw that the demand for moonshine had begun to decline due to the arrival of North Carolina's ABC stores in the mid-1960s.[40] Although Willie Clay continued to make small batches of liquor, he increasingly relied on cattle farming to make a living. He also began to spend significant time at local events and libraries telling people about the history of Wilkes County moonshining from his perspective.[41] Starting in 1957, he worked with Joe Carter on the *Thunder Road* movie, which told the story of moonshining in Kentucky. Between 2009 and 2011, Clay also participated in several moonshiner and revenuer reunions where each side recalled stories of past adventures. In 2009 the *Winston-Salem Journal* described the first of these reunions:

> Several hundred people gathered in a field near the weathered wooden house where Benny Parsons was raised. They sat on hay bales to listen to the stories as smoke curled from a moonshine still set up across the creek. Sitting in rocking chairs on one side of the stage were bootleggers Junior Johnson, Willie Clay Call, Millard Ashley, Don Call, Dean Combs, James Willard Shew and Clarence Benton. On the other side were retired revenue

agents Bob Powell, Bob Gram, Charles Mercer, Will Blocker and Tommy Chapman. They had shared a meal earlier, eating barbecue. But dinner wasn't filled with the kind of backslapping reminiscences that people saw during the stage show. The moonshiners and revenuers mostly segregated themselves, Powell said later, with no laughter or storytelling. He described it as more a relationship of tolerance than camaraderie.[42]

Although Willie Clay Call passed away in 2012, he left a rich legacy of distilling liquor for his son, Brian Call, and the rest of the family to carry on into the twenty-first century.

Call Family Distillers

In 2015 Brian Call and his family opened Call Family Distillers in Wilkesboro, North Carolina. Brian learned his skills to make liquor from his father, Willie Clay. He also gained some experience in distilling by running an ethanol plant and working as the head distiller for Piedmont Distillers, one of state's first post-Prohibition distilleries founded in 2005. While at Piedmont Distillers, Brian soon recognized the economic opportunities of opening his own distillery. "Distilling liquor was surely growing across North Carolina," he recalled.[43] "I was also surprised how well moonshine was selling from places in Tennessee. . . . I knew that with my dad's recipe and history we could do something big." Thus, Brian decided to produce legitimate and taxed whiskey in Wilkes County for the first time in his family's history.

Brian was correct about the sudden increase in craft distilleries across the South and other parts of the United States. While the definition is fuzzy, a craft distillery can be an independently owned distillery that manufactures small batches (fewer than 52,000 cases a year), using recipes and ingredients to physically produce and bottle a unique spirit on-site.[44] As of 2016 the American Craft Spirits Association identified 1,315 craft distillers active in the country.[45] These distillers produced more than 5 million cases of liquor and had retail sales around $2.5 billion in 2015. Similar to the craft beer industry, craft distillers represent 5 to 7 percent of the market share of big liquor. Most of these new distilleries have only opened within the last twenty years. In addition, many of them have been concentrated in five states outside of the American South, including California, New York, Washington, Colorado, and Texas. Finally, many distillers have produced a variety of spirits, focusing mostly on vodka, gin, and whiskey. Others also have begun to make more unique flavors such as bourbon, scotch, brandy, or grappa.[46]

Craft distilleries opening in Appalachia and other parts of the South were slow to start. This was in part due to the reluctance of Georgia, Tennessee, North Carolina, and South Carolina to allow liquor production based on their past heritage and dogged acceptance of Prohibition.[47] In fact, these states had passed state prohibition laws well before the federal law took effect in 1920.[48] Even after the repeal of national Prohibition, they continued to rely heavily on pre-Prohibition restrictions, permitting counties and towns to decide whether to ban alcohol in their area (i.e., dry versus wet areas).[49] In North Carolina, for instance, several mountain counties voted to remain dry after 1933, prohibiting liquor by the drink and encouraging crackdowns on illicit distilling well into the twenty-first century.

By the early 2000s, however, the situation changed. Largely due to the economic recession of 2008, southern legislators—hoping to increase tax revenue—began to loosen their states' alcohol manufacturing laws, resulting in the first significant boom in distilleries throughout the South.[50] Most of these new distilleries, such as Ole Smoky in Tennessee and Top of the Hill in North Carolina, initially manufactured unaged whiskey (marketed to the public as moonshine) or vodka, both of which do not have to be aged (like bourbon) and thus can quickly bring in capital.[51] They also bought and blended neutral spirits, which took them somewhat out of the traditionally defined craft distillery category.

North Carolina, in particular, has witnessed a significant rise in craft distilling over the past decade. In *Still and Barrel,* John Trump pointed out that there are more than forty craft distilleries operating in the state as of 2016.[52] There is also the Distillers Association of North Carolina, in which members exchange ideas about the industry and assist new distilleries with local and state regulations. Collaborating with the North Carolina Department of Agriculture, the Distillers Association recently created a Craft Distiller's Trail (similar to Kentucky's Bourbon Trail) for tourists and enthusiasts to track down unique spirits across the state. In addition, the Distillers Association supports efforts to use local ingredients from farms to make gin, rum, whiskey, bourbon, moonshine, and other spirits. However, most of these fairly new distilleries cluster in the urban areas of Raleigh-Durham, Charlotte, and

Winston-Salem-Greensboro, where there are less strict building codes, more industrial spaces to choose from, and a larger potential customer base.

According to Brian Call, legal distilling failed to take off immediately in Wilkes County. "Making liquor was not something everybody thought about or considered early on as a money-maker for the area," he recalled. "The County and town [Wilkesboro] did not know what to do or how to regulate a distillery. I had to show them how to make it okay, safety-wise, and how making liquor would not lead to huge explosions and fires. . . . I helped them understand that warehouses were good locations."[53] In addition, Brian mentioned, "Getting a license to distill from the [federal] government was fairly simple and just a lot of paperwork. Even North Carolina was pretty simple. . . . It was just convincing people around here that it was a good investment and safe to do." He also lamented that part of the challenge of owning a distillery in North Carolina was distributing the product in a state that still used an ABC dispensary system: "The hard part is, we had to do it the hard way. We had to meet with all the boards in every county. Talk to 'em and get your product in there. That is a lot of work in 100 counties with 240 individual ABC boards. You have to meet with each one of them. It's one of the hardest states to work with. . . . Other distillers don't even want to come to North Carolina because of the system." While the legal process proved challenging, it was clear that the Call family distillery had a rich history to back up and market their products. Distillery partner and marketer Brad Call suggested that this history is very unique to the Call Family Distillers. "We are lucky, really," he explained. "We have Willie Clay Call's legacy to really inspire our line of products. He also left us some great recipes that we use today to make all of our moonshine. I think people really like the fact that we are the true makers of moonshine unlike others out there."[54] Brian also stated, "We are different from distillers in Tennessee because we don't need to make up a history to get our liquor out there. . . . Ole Smoky or Thunder Road Distillery just say they have a mountain tradition, but they really don't. They just happen to be in the right area where moonshining happened"—the Appalachian Mountains.

The Call family distillery differs significantly from other distilleries in North Carolina because it remains family owned and operated. Many new distilleries in North Carolina, especially in the western part of the state, have started with out-of-state craft distillers and investors. For example, Asheville Distilling Company, located outside of Asheville, was founded by Texas native Troy Ball. Another Wilkes County distillery, Copper Barrel, was the result of a partnership between Vermont entrepreneur George Smith and Buck Nance, a Wilkes County moonshiner. Meanwhile, Southern Distillery, one of the largest and newest distilleries operating in North Carolina, is owned and operated by investors from Kentucky.[55]

The Call distillery, however, is a family business. Brian Call, who personally funded the entire distillery from savings and other investments, continues to serve as master distiller. His wife, Laura, works in the office and helps with the operations and accounting. She also assists with bottling and labeling, handwriting the batch number on every bottle sold since 2015. Brad Call, Brian's cousin, helps with distilling and marketing, traveling to ABC commissions and various festivals to promote the product. Other family members give tours of the history of the family business and distillery during the week. As Brad Call stated, "It is a family affair because that is what it always was for us. It also keeps us more in the tradition of Wilkes County and North Carolina moonshine-making."

The distillery's liquor also remains "traditional," in that Brian Call continues to strictly follow family practices and recipes for distilling spirits. The Call family distillery has a custom-built 2,100-gallon still designed by Brian and named the "Bull," one of Willie Clay Call's nicknames. It can produce up to 600 gallons a day, running liquor off at about 150 proof, or 75 percent alcohol. Brian also uses reverse osmosis to deionize the water, which lowers the proof to about 101, or 50.5 percent alcohol. Brian explained, "This proof is at the level my Dad liked and I think it works well with our flavored moonshine." Like his ancestors, Brian also ferments his mash in eight open white pine barrels that can hold up to 1,000 pounds of mash each. To meet health code standards, he uses all food-grade stainless still equipment in a clean facility. Brian commented, "That's a difference I see [between my Dad and me]. . . . You ain't pullin' no damn possum out of your mash barrel, a squirrel or something that's got in there."[56] Moreover, the distillery uses only family recipes to produce their straight white liquor and uses flash-frozen strawberries and cherries to make flavored liquors. It also manufactures a family-inspired and award-winning apple pie moonshine and a recreation of Clay's limber twig apple brandy.

Other craft distilleries such as Top of the Hill have begun to turn away from North Carolina– and Appalachian-inspired flavors by producing vodka and rum. In addition, Wilkes County's Copper Barrel has attempted to make odd flavors of moonshine such as cotton candy and coffee. Brad Call stated, "We already knew we had a great product because it had been tested by Clay for decades, so we used the same recipes. . . . This distillery is different from other craft distilleries because we have tradition on our side. We also don't buy neutral-grain spirits to produce other types of liquors to make ends meet. We are really all-in with our moonshine."[57]

A final difference is that Call Family Distillers has embraced a factual history instead of embellishing moonshiner and hillbilly stereotypes to market its liquor. As Brad Call explained, "Our history is true. Willie Clay Call did make illegal shine. He raced his liquor at night to customers. . . . Our family went to jail for things related to moonshine. It is all true." Other distilleries in the Appalachian Mountains have trouble making such claims. More often than not, they attach their branding to the legend of Appalachian moonshining. For example, Ole Smoky Distillery states in its marketing campaigns that it comes from a tradition of moonshining but cannot provide the same factual and personal stories as the Call family distillery. Ole Smoky vaguely attempts to acknowledge a moonshining legacy on its website by saying, "We're Appalachian born and bred. The Ole Smoky families are among the first to step foot in the Smoky Mountains. Like other families, we have honed the art of whiskey making in order to survive during tough economic times. We're among friends here, neighbors with folks who have moonshine stories and traditions of their own. We are proud to share some of ours."[58] Another example is Mountain Airy's Mayberry Spirits Distillery, which uses the popular television series *The Andy Griffith Show* and the fictional town of Mayberry to link its product with an idealized past full of hillbillies making 'shine in a good ole southern and family-friendly town.[59]

One problem that Call Family Distillers faces, however, is that its "moonshine" comes with a stigma. In their research of southern Appalachian moonshine, Emelie Peine and Kai Schafft argued that moonshine assisted in popularizing the negative stereotypes of mountain residents as "gun-toting, cousin-slaying, cock-fighting, impoverished whites" to the American public.[60] Speaking to this issue, Brad Call stated, "I go out to various bars and venues to convince bartenders and restaurants to use our products. Sometimes, they think it is going to taste terrible because moonshine is supposed to be terrible with a burn and it's been run through radiators. . . . However, when they try ours they see that it is a quality product. They really do like it, but because it has the word moonshine on it, some folks won't even put it on the shelf at their nice bar." In some respects, the Call family liquor is not fully moonshine since it is taxed. However, the recipe is the same, and the history the distillery embraces gives it legitimacy. As Brad Call pointed out, "People can argue the usage of the word 'moonshine' and the semantics of what that may mean . . . but ultimately, I guess, the point is that Brian learned how to make this liquor from one of the most famous moonshiners. He carries the expertise in there and makes the same great liquor regardless if it is bootlegged or not. What makes it moonshine to us is that it is just as Willie Clay made it, not whether we pay taxes or not."

Another potential problem for the Calls is that the liquor market is constantly evolving. Brian lamented that moonshine sales have begun to decline. "The market really changed since we got in it," he observed. "There is now people doing bourbon, brandy, but moonshine is kind of dropping off." However, they do have a plan for the future. As Brian Call stated, "We plan to use an old family recipe to make the Reverend, a whiskey using barrels from a South Carolina company in Bamberg. I knew the moonshine would work to make a bourbon, but I want something different. We can use our ancestors' Tennessee sour mash recipe and possibly filter it through charcoal or some sugar maple." Brad Call continued, "We have to keep up with demand on the shine production, but we know things will have to evolve for the future."

The Calls have also discovered that few people come to Wilkes County to visit the distillery. While the county has a small display in its local history museum discussing moonshining in the area, the Call family actually has more information and informal exhibits for tourists to admire at their distillery. Brad Call suggested, "We get some people to come and tour and try our product. . . . However, our business is really to get it out there to the public as much as we can. The tourist thing in Wilkes isn't that big yet but we hope it will increase." Unfortunately, their distillery is also located on the outskirts of the town in an industrial park, limiting their exposure to potential tourists. As Brian pointed out, "I think we need a presence somewhere downtown or on the main drag near Wal-Mart to get more people to stop and try our liquor . . . but I don't worry about that too much right now." Brad also proposed that getting tourists to visit the distillery and sample its products was difficult because North Carolina allows customers to only purchase one bottle of liquor per year at a distillery. As he lamented, "People have to do a tour to taste the liquor. Then, they can only buy one bottle of liquor, we have to register them for state records, and then they can't buy another bottle from us for another year. Of course, we tell them to go to the ABC store, and they can buy all they want but that does limit us a little."

Conclusion

Call Family Distillers represents a clear marriage between illicit moonshine history and the rise of craft distilling. By embracing their family history, the Calls have successfully created a craft spirit that is unique and true to their heritage and community. This family history pushes their distillery to use only local ingredients and family-tested recipes to make spirits that have distinctive Appalachian roots. This shows in the distillery's production of its unaged, 101-proof liquor to its special apple brandy made from fruit grown in the area. Like craft beer enthusiasts, many liquor consumers now want something unique in their cocktails, a niche that the Calls—capitalizing on their family history—seek to fill. In addition, the Call family distillery's heritage helps to preserve a way of life and culture unique to Wilkes County and southern Appalachia.

Surely, making moonshine in the backwoods of Appalachia and evading taxes was and continues to be a criminal offense. However, we can see that craft distilleries such as Call Family Distillers are spurring on economic development that brings tourism dollars and a new industry to the mountain region. Moreover, craft breweries and distilleries have created a boon in new tax revenue across North Carolina and other parts of the South. More important, the Call family's distillery has brought Wilkes County back to the national stage as the distillery has won awards for its spirits and been featured in several newspapers across the country. Whether realized or not by the Call family, this illicit legacy becoming legitimate will challenge the misconceptions of Appalachian culture by bearing the truth behind moonshiners and demonstrating how illicit traditions can become celebrated, money-making crafts.

NOTES

Epigraph. Quoted in Alex Gabbard, *Return to Thunder Road: The Story behind the Legend* (Lenoir City, TN: Gabbard Publications, 2014), 39.
1. Joe Carter, *Shortcuts to Justice* (Albemarle, NC: SSI Publications, 1999), 52–71.
2. Gabbard, *Return to Thunder Road*, 25–26.

3. Gabbard, *Return to Thunder Road*, 64–96; Brad Call, interview with the author, April 2017.

4. Frank Stephenson Jr. and Barbara N. Mulder, *North Carolina Moonshine: An Illicit History* (Charleston, SC: American Palate, 2017), 132; Brad Call, interview with the author, April 2017.

5. Roy Ackland, "Wilkesboro Family Opens Distillery in Heart of Moonshine Country," Fox 8, May 16, 2016, accessed August 20, 2018, http://myfox8.com /2016/05/16/wilkesboro-family-opens-distillery-in-heart-of-moonshine -country/.

6. For more on moonshining in Franklin County, see Charles D. Thompson Jr., *Spirits of Just Men: Mountaineers, Liquor Bosses, and Lawmen in the Moonshine Capital of the World* (Urbana: University of Illinois Press, 2011).

7. Vance Packard, "Millions in Moonshine," *American Magazine* (September 1950): 46–47, 100–105. Later researchers have also found that during the 1950s, Wilkes County moonshiners were probably manufacturing around 200 to 1,000 gallons of moonshine in one run of distilled mash, suggesting that many operations had gone from small pot stills to 1,000- to 5,000-gallon submarine stills. See Stephenson and Mulder, *North Carolina Moonshine*, 79–97.

8. Aaron Lancaster, "Chasing the Good Ol' Boys and Girls of Wilkes County, North Carolina" (MA thesis, Appalachian State University, 2013), 98–99; Michael Tomsic, "Wilkesboro, Former 'Moonshine Capital,' Losing its Federal Courthouse," WFAE, October 17, 2012, accessed September 21, 2017, http:// wfae.org/post/wilkesboro-former-moonshine-capital-losing-its-federal -courthouse.

9. Gabbard, *Return to Thunder Road*, 48–59.

10. Lancaster, "Chasing the Good Ol' Boys," 77. Moreover, while sugar was rationed significantly during World War II, by 1950 it was plentiful and cheap, leading many farmers to combine their corn and sugar to make liquor.

11. Ackland, "Wilkesboro Family Opens Distillery."

12. Stephenson and Mulder, *North Carolina Moonshine*, 116–31.

13. Quoted in Daniel S. Pierce, *Real NASCAR: White Lightning, Red Clay, and Big Bill France* (Chapel Hill: University of North Carolina Press, 2010), 19.

14. W. Pengine, "Moonshiner Runners, History, and Their Cars," *Hot Rod Magazine*, January 10, 2006, http://hotrod.com/articles/moonshine-runners-cars -history/.

15. Gabbard, *Return to Thunder Road*, 140–43.

16. Quoted in Pierce, *Real NASCAR*, 28.

17. For more on Wilkes County and NASCAR, see Pierce, *Real NASCAR*.

18. Gabbard, *Return to Thunder Road*, 73–77.

19. Carter, *Shortcuts to Justice*, 52–71.

20. Throughout his career as an ATF agent in Wilkes County, Felts confiscated millions of gallons of mash and made more than 2,500 moonshine-related arrests. See Stephenson and Mulder, *North Carolina Moonshine*, 68.

21. Jeremy Markovich, "Ghosts of North Wilkesboro," *SB Nation*, March 4, 2015, accessed September 21, 2017, https://www.sbnation.com/longform/2015/3/4/8126311/north-wilkesboro-speedway-after-nascar.

22. Gabbard, *Return to Thunder Road*, 90; and Brad Call, interview with the author, April 2017. Gabbard notes that wrangling chickens paid $100 a week in the late 1950s, which was a high-paying (and legal) wage in the area.

23. Markovich, "Ghosts of North Wilkesboro."

24. Stephenson and Mulder, *North Carolina Moonshine*, 118–19; Lancaster, "Chasing the Good Ol' Boys," 103.

25. Lancaster, "Chasing the Good Ol' Boys," 103.

26. "Moonshine History," Call Family Distillers, accessed July 27, 2018, www.callfamilydistillers.com/new-page/.

27. Brad Call, interview with the author, April 2017.

28. Ibid.

29. Brian Call, interview with the author, May 2017.

30. Call Family Distillers," Rev. Daniel H. Call and Jasper Newton Daniel," July 31, 2017, www.callfamilydistillers.com/reverend-dan-call-jack-daniels-tribute-to-a-true-craft-distiller/.

31. Gabbard, *Return to Thunder Road*, 77.

32. Brad Call, interview with the author, April 2017.

33. Brad Call, interview with the author, April 2017; Brian Call, interview with the author, May 2017.

34. Brad Call, interview with the author, April 2017.

35. Ibid.

36. Ibid.

37. Stephenson and Mulder, *North Carolina Moonshine*, 134.

38. Gabbard, *Return to Thunder Road*, 64.

39. Ibid., 90.

40. Brad Call, interview with the author, April 2017.

41. Ibid.

42. Monte Mitchell, "Moonshine Memories: Bootleggers and Revenuers Get Together on Wilkes County Farm to Recount Their Rivalry," *Winston-Salem Journal*, October 15, 2009, www.journalnow.com/news/local/moonshine-memories-bootleggers-and-revenuers-get-together-on-wilkes-county/article_6ceb29f1-9435-50fe-93c2-55baf1e2dc76.html.

43. Brian Call, family business interview with Cameron D. Lippard, May 10, 2017. Hereafter, all uncited personal quotes from Brian Call are sourced from this interview.

44. "Craft Certification," American Distilling Institute, accessed July 31, 2017, http://distilling.com/resources/craft-certification/.

45. "Beverage Industry Study finds more than 1,300 active craft spirits producers in US," Beverage Industry, October 18, 2016, accessed July 31, 2017, www.bevindustry.com/articles/89712-study-finds-more-than-1300-active-craft-spirits-producers-in-us.

46. Colin Spoelman and David Haskel, *Guide to Urban Moonshining: How to Make and Drink Whiskey* (Abrams, NY: Abrams Publishing, 2013), 90–95.

47. John F. Trump, *Still and Barrel: Craft Spirits in the Old North State* (Winston-Salem, NC: John F. Blair Publishing, 2017), 1–2.

48. Ibid.

49. Ibid.

50. See chapter 5 for more information on the laws. Trump, *Still and Barrel*, 1–2.

51. Spoelman and Haskel, *Guide to Urban Moonshining*, 90–95.

52. Trump, *Still and Barrel*, 6–14.

53. Brian Call, interview with the author, May 2017.

54. Brad Call, interview with the author, April 2017.

55. Trump, *Still and Barrel*, 23–28, 99–102.

56. Ibid., 97–98.

57. Brad Call, distillery interview with the author, April 2017. Hereafter, all uncited personal quotes from Brad Call are sourced from this interview.

58. Ole Smoky, "Born from Appalachian Mud and Mist," accessed July 31, 2017, http://olesmoky.com/about/history.

59. Trump, *Still and Barrel*, 103–8.

60. Emelie K. Peine and Kai A. Schafft, "Moonshine, Mountaineers, and Modernity: Distilling Cultural History in the Southern Appalachian Mountains," *Journal of Appalachian Studies* 18 (Spring/Fall 2012), 94.

PART III

Historic Preservation
and Tourism in the
Name of Moonshine

CHAPTER 9

Distilling Commercial Moonshine in East Tennessee: Mashing a New Type of Tourism

HELEN M. ROSKO

He had those East Tennessee moonshiner's blues
He had those Cocke County jail house blues
His name was Popcorn Sutton . . .
A true moonshiner from day one
His name was Popcorn Sutton
And he made moonshine 'til he's gone

—Hank Williams III (2010)

Whether you call it corn whiskey, corn liquor, mountain dew, white lightning, or moonshine, the rise of commercial distilling is undeniable. Supported by popular media such as country music star endorsements and the Discovery Channel's *Moonshiners*, the industry continues to grow in both capacity and exposure, reaching national and international markets. While the primary focus of this chapter is to understand the impacts of commercial moonshine in the making and remaking of tourism, it is connected to larger social, cultural, and economic issues. These issues are known throughout Appalachia in debates concerning the environment, existing stereotypes about mountain residents, and the region's lack of economically diversified jobs.[1] As introduced in the opening quote, the infamous case of renowned Tennessee moonshiner Popcorn Sutton serves as a proxy for understanding how moonshine connects to these larger issues. Committing suicide in 2009, days before he was "to serve an 18-month sentence for illegally brewing spirits and possessing a fire-arm as a felon," Sutton brought national attention to the illegal manufacture

Figure 9.1. Map of East Tennessee. Created by author.

of moonshine.[2] Months later, the legislature changed to allow the legal production of corn liquor in the state of Tennessee.[3] Before the enactment of this legislation, spirit production in Tennessee was limited to Moore, Coffee, and Lincoln counties, where Jack Daniel's Tennessee Whiskey, George Dickel Whiskey, and Prichard's Distillery respectively operate.[4] Sutton's story and the recent rise in the popularity of legal moonshine call our attention to broader social issues working in the region. These include but are not limited to access to new markets and industries, control of image and place construction, and tensions in both internal and external representations of Appalachia. While all these issues may be explored through the lens of commercial moonshine, this chapter examines the intersection between an emerging commercial moonshine industry and tourism. Specifically, this chapter asks: what is the role of commercial moonshine in (re)making a place of tourism in East Tennessee?

Studies in sociology, anthropology, and history provide important but differing entry points into the intersection of commercial moonshine and tourism in the region. However, understanding the transformations of a *place* of tourism in East Tennessee due to moonshine's now legal status is particularly suited for studies in human geography. This chapter explores the central research question through conceptions of neolocalism and authenticity as noted in the

Table 9.1. Profiles of Three East Tennessee Distilleries

	Employees (estimate)	Distribution	Marketing	Product types
Tennessee Hills Distillery	3–8	Regional, with plans for expansion	Local and regional, with plans for expansion	Moonshine, Rum, Whiskey (forthcoming)
Sugarlands Distilling Co.	55–75	26 states, with plans for expansion to all 48 continental states	Local, regional, national	Moonshine and Whiskey
Doc Collier Moonshine Distillery	12–15	Microdistillery, in-store only	Local only	Moonshine and Moonshine Brandy

Note: Estimate of each variable based on interviews by the author with distillery employees and a review of each distillery's website.

relevant place-making and tourism geographies literatures. A multimethod qualitative approach that combines discourse analysis, participant observation, semistructured interviews, and a comparative case study provides the selected methods for this research. The comparative case study, serving as the foundational method, focuses on three specific distilleries to evaluate moonshine's role in tourism of East Tennessee and greater Appalachia: Sugarlands Distilling Company and Doc Collier Moonshine, both in Gatlinburg, and Tennessee Hills Distillery in Jonesborough (see fig. 9.1).[5] With tourism revenues comprising a large portion of their overall economies, both Gatlinburg and Jonesborough are ideal towns for examining moonshine in a context of tourism.[6] In an attempt to provide a holistic understanding of how commercial moonshine is being produced in the region, these distilleries were also selected to accommodate varying capacities, scale, production, marketing, and distribution operations (see table 9.1). The remainder of this chapter explores how each of these distilleries (re)makes tourism in East Tennessee reflective of their own versions of authentic[7] and neolocal moonshine.[8]

This analysis highlights four themes that center on a place of East Tennessee, its historical connection to moonshine, and its continued importance in the region as contemporary producers of the now legal moonshine commodity. Critical to note, as each section highlights a different impact of tourism, each similarly serves a different role in (re)making a place of tourism in the region. For example, "Connecting to Existing Tourism in the Region" describes how existing tourism has ensured the continued success of the tourism industry (and moonshine) while also (re)making tourism with more sustainable, annual tourism draws. "Changing Tourist Demographics" depicts the changing demographics that contribute to different tourism opportunities and (re) make tourism to give moonshine a seat at the table. "Expanding Tourism Opportunities in East Tennessee" describes the transformation of tourism and the (re)making of a different and new place of East Tennessee tourism better aligned with commercial moonshine. Finally, "Countering Existing Narratives of Moonshine" elucidates the ways some distilleries (re)make moonshine tourism and its place in East Tennessee reflective of the tradition, craft, and resourcefulness of historical moonshine. In this way, all four elements build, contribute, and work together toward (re)making a place of tourism in East Tennessee.

Connecting to Existing Tourism in East Tennessee

The ability of the moonshine industry to recognize and connect to the pre-existing tourism economies in East Tennessee is paramount. Therefore, the goal of distilleries is to not only sell moonshine products but also to promote a sustainable tourist experience, drawing in new and repeat tourists to the region. Tourism literatures in geography understand that the making of place and its (re)making are deeply linked to tourism.[9] Ned Vickers, a former East Tennessee laywer and current CEO of Sugarlands Distilling Company, makes this connection: "Do you know how many people participated in the Kentucky Bourbon Trail last year? 550,000. Do you know how many people visited us last year? 750,000. We have bought the domain name www .mountainmoonshinetrail.com and that is something we intend to do."[10] Vickers connects his place of moonshine to a broader place of craft liquor tourism in the region. Modeling his idea for a moonshine trail on the successful

Kentucky Bourbon Trail, Vickers seizes an opportunity to promote moonshine and East Tennessee even further.[11] Given Gatlinburg's location near the entrance of the Great Smoky Mountain National Park (GSMNP), the most visited national park in the country, coupled with the region's historical connection to moonshine, opportunities for a moonshine trail seem endless. Sugarlands director of marketing and strategy, Brent Thompson, adds, "I can't imagine this being anywhere else. Having the foot traffic that we've got is really central to our ability to have an aggressive expansion strategy. It allows us to take it to market. If we were to just open up any ol' place and we saw few people walk through the door every day, I don't think we would have the resources to go out and introduce our product for more people. . . . It's pretty important for us to be here, and it fits, it makes sense, it's our story."[12] Acknowledging the importance of an already established tourism market for helping Sugarlands begin and expand its operations, Thompson touches on the significance of place in Gatlinburg. For Sugarlands being in Gatlinburg and at the entrance to the GSMNP "fits, it makes sense, it's our story." Thompson alludes to the notion that if the distillery were located anywhere else, it would somehow be rendered inauthentic.

Doc Collier Moonshine similarly recognizes the importance of tourism to a place of moonshine in Gatlinburg. Assistant manager Josh Stokes comments, "We are in the customer service buisness and if it wasn't for all these people coming from all over the world to my backyard, I wouldn't be able to pay my bills. . . . If we didn't have tourism, this would be nothing."[13] Gatlinburg, which hosts more tourists annually than Jonesborough, provides an invaluable partnership with Doc Collier and Sugarlands. While their moonshine may be perceived as authentic because of the locality embodied in their products, the success of both distilleries relies heavily on this tourist landscape.

As the state's oldest town and host to the International Storytelling Center, Jonesborough capitalizes on cultural and heritage tourism.[14] This allows Tennessee Hills Distillery to receive a fair number of visitors, but does not attract the same amount as distilleries in Gatlinburg. In order to succeed and beat out competition, the company's CEO, Stephen Callahan, looks beyond moonshine and regional markets in East Tennessee while maintaining his personal heritage to make the best possible products. Callahan comments, "Obviously you want to be a tourist attraction. The thing about this business is distribution. You can't solely count on foot traffic. If you want brand recognition and to leave a legacy, you need distribution. They can have what they have down there [in Gatlinburg]—it makes me nervous because if I was doing the bullshit sugar shine I could have stacks of bottles in here, but we want to make it our way."[15]

Callahan is not alone in his desire for increased distribution and name branding. Sugarlands, the largest distillery in the case study, distributes its liquor to twenty-six states with an aggressive expansion strategy to reach all forty-eight continental states and an international market as soon as possible.[16] The exception is Doc Collier Moonshine, which remains the only registered microdistillery in Tennesssee. As a microdistillery, it does not distribute outside of the tasting room and has no plans to begin distribution. Doc Collier's status as a microdistillery, however, ensures that tourists will visit the distillery while also encouraging loyal and repeat customers. The connection of moonshine to tourism is critical to the success of the overall moonshine industry in East Tennessee. Each distillery understands this important relationship and capitalizes on the preexisting tourism market, perpetuating it even further with the addition of commercial moonshine.

Changing Tourist Demographics

By creating demand for legalized moonshine products, tourists are vital to the success of commercial moonshine and its new role in the region's tourism industry. Not only are they customers and likely consumers, but all visitors come with different understandings of what East Tennessee means to them. In this way, moonshine tourists from across the country converge on a place of East Tennessee with one thing in common: a curiosity for commercial moonshine. As such, distilleries must be cognizant of not only the type of tourist they are selling to but also the place of moonshine they engage with each of their products.

Since the opening of commercial distilleries in East Tennessee, the high tourism economies of Gatlinburg and Jonesborough have witnessed changes in the demographics of visiting tourists. Traditionally, tourist demographics in both towns consisted of middle-aged families and older retirees.[17] However, in the recent years, there has been a shift in demographics to younger single people and younger couples without children.[18] Josh Stokes of Doc Collier speaks to this changing demographic:

> In the last four years, I can say from experience, I have seen a different caliber of people. . . . Now we have a lot more younger families come in. We had couples before, but it was mainly middle-aged families with kids in their early teens. Now we have younger families in their middle twenties with young babies—it's a completely different crowd. You can ask any business on the strip. I have a feeling it has a lot to do with moonshine. It didn't happen until about four years ago, and that is when Ole Smoky came in.[19]

Stokes ultimately credits shifting demographics in the region to the rising popularity and production of commercial moonshine. Whether this transformation is a direct response to the opening of moonshine distilleries or because of other factors, however, remains difficult to discern. Whatever the reasons, a place of tourism is (re)made through moonshine, and distilleries and tourists alike are reacting to this change. Authenticity comes to the forefront of this transformation as each distillery aims to sell its own authentic moonshine products as well as cater to tourists' desire in consuming authenticity. Situated within debates of authenticity, literatures discuss the idea that those in control of a place of tourism are often producers of this authenticity.[20]

Recognizing their role in this production, distilleries center their versions of authenticity on a historical place of East Tennessee. Scholarship on the craft beer industry notes that local breweries utilize place-based naming as a strategy for contributing to neolocalism and participating in place-making.[21] Similarly, in the commercial moonshine industry, distilleries employ place-based naming to construct their own individually catered version of authentic commercial moonshine for their customers. For example, Sugarlands Distilling Company obtains its name from the Sugarlands part of the GSMNP, historically known as a "moonshiner's paradise."[22] Meanwhile, Doc Collier Moonshine is named after the Collier family, who have been distilling moonshine in East Tennessee for several generations.[23] Finally, instead of naming his business Callahan Distilling Company, Stephen Callahan of Tennessee Hills Distillery ultimately decided to name his distillery after a common nickname that represents the region, "Tennessee Hills."[24] Engaging place-based naming allows each distillery to represent a different, individually constructed version of an authentic place of East Tennessee and, therefore, moonshine. As distilleries produce their individual versions of authenticity, customers ultimately must choose a moonshine product reflective of their own symbolic authenticity. Ned Vickers of Sugarlands Distilling Company explains, "We are getting people in Gatlinburg now that would have never thought to come here before the moonshine. We've had people from New York City come down here who never would have dreamed of coming to Gatlinburg, so we feel like we have the best product out there. You're in the wrong business if you don't. But we feel confident that if they come taste everyone's moonshine they will come and buy from us. Having a critical mass of distilleries, I think, draws a group of tourists who might not be here a lot."[25] Vickers highlights the connection of moonshine to tourism and the role of tourists.

Not only are the ages and the marital status of tourists changing but also the origins of tourists. Traditionally, both Gatlinburg and Jonesborough receive tourists that live relatively close to East Tennessee. However, Vickers credits tourists from New York and other distant states to the recent rise in popularity of legal moonshine in the region. Similarly, he asserts that by marketing his product as authentic, tourists will patronize Sugarlands. Finally, he recognizes the importance of the region's preexisting tourist market to the production and success of commercial moonshine. Like Sugarlands, Doc Collier also attempts to sell its products by promoting them as authentic and letting tourists decide which authentic moonshine works best for them. Josh Stokes adds, "We tell everybody to go everywhere. I boast Sugarlands Apple Pie, sometimes they boast our blackberry, but then you are an informed consumer and can make the decision. Real recognizes real, and that's all we are trying to do."[26] In the end, Doc Collier's authenticity relies on an idea of being open and transparent with not only their products but their competitors as well.

Recently, Tennessee Hills has begun to expand production beyond moonshine to capture an even more diverse group of tourists. Currently, Tennessee Hills offers only two moonshine products: Corn Liquor and Lemon Drop.[27] However, capitalizing on the success of the saturating moonshine market, the distillery engages other spirit markets through the production of craft spirits such as rum and brandy. Callahan explains:

That was totally the plan, to do moonshine from day one. Then when I got into this thing, I thought, well, how am I going to leave my mark? This moonshine business will decline eventually. What can I do that is really special? And put my foot down and say we are going to do it and do it right. We are in the moonshine categories, but at the same time corn liquor is an authentic product to this area. I didn't want to get into flavors—the only reason I am is because I have a huge demand for it. It is just good business. Eventually we will find those one or two products and that is all we do. It's like Jack Daniel's. How many products do they have? Not many.[28]

Referring to the success of Jack Daniel's Tennessee Whiskey in producing few staple products, Callahan aims to model his own spirit production in a similar fashion. Despite its status as the world's leading seller of whiskey, Jack Daniel's makes only five core whiskies on a regular basis.[29] Though the company produces several different specialty or reserve whiskies offered at limited times, Jack Daniel's Old No. 7 "Tennessee Sippin' Whiskey" is by far its most recognized brand.[30] Jack Daniel's has successfully created a niche in the whiskey world, and that is precisely what Callahan aims to do with his moonshine and other products. Trademarking the term "corn liquor" not only allows Callahan to differentiate his company from his competitors, all of whom call their products moonshine, but also secure his niche in the saturating moonshine market. By calling his product corn liquor, Callahan draws from an age-old term in Appalachian lexicon that is inherently tied to a place of East Tennessee and greater Appalachia, thereby asserting his authentic product for public consumption. Moreover, using the motto "Embracing Heritage," Tennessee Hills centers its branding efforts on the rich history and heritage of making craft spirits in East Tennessee.[31]

Another reason for a shift in demographics of tourists is the accessibility of the moonshine product through its different flavors and variety. All three distilleries offer not only classic, unflavored moonshine but also flavored types that tend to appeal to a more diverse customer base. It is clear even for the business-minded Callahan, who refuses to carry many flavors, that distilleries should make moonshine more accessible by improving its taste. However, though flavors increase moonshine's marketability, Callahan remains determined to produce an authentic moonshine that differs from competition. When asked specifically about flavored moonshine, Callahan responded:

> We've always planned to do a few flavored corn whiskies. The big thing that I will not do is saturate our shelves with thirty flavors year-round. I want to do more seasonal flavors using all-natural flavorings. I don't want to use grain neutral spirits that are at distilleries elsewhere and they add artificial flavorings and food colorings, which is what all the distilleries in Gatlinburg are doing. That would make us more of a bottling company instead of a distillery. Yes, there is a huge market demand for flavors, which is pretty much the only reason that I'm going to do a few.[32]

For Callahan, flavored moonshine provides a vehicle to access a broader group of consumers and tourists likely interested in his more niche and specialty products. Callahan creates an authentic product by using locally sourced natural flavorings to differentiate his corn liquor from competitors'. Contrary to Callahan's claims, both Doc Collier and Sugarlands also use locally sourced natural flavorings in their moonshine products. The use of these types of flavorings allows all three distilleries to participate in neolocal moonshine production and place-based authenticity. As these distilleries attempt to center their moonshine products around their own individually catered versions of authenticity, they similarly work to (re)make a place of tourism in East Tennessee and (re)make a type of tourist who is often young and single, or part of a childless couple, from myriad backgrounds and places within the United States.

Expanding Tourism Opportunities in East Tennessee

Thus far, it is evident through both the contributions of moonshine to existing tourism and the changes in demographics of these economies that moonshine also works to expand tourism in the region. For example, the possibility of a Tennessee moonshine trail not only connects to existing tourism opportunities but also builds upon and (re)makes a place of tourism in the region aligned with commercial moonshine. Similarly, the arrival of new tourists who visit the region because of moonshine also functions to (re)make a place of tourism geared toward spirit and moonshine enthusiasts. This theme explores the ways in which distilleries (re)make a traditional place of tourism and expand new tourism opportunities through the neolocal strategy of community engagement.[33]

In Jonesborough some community members have not fully embraced Tennessee Hills Distillery. "The thing about Jonesborough is they are so stuck in their ways," Callahan laments, pointing out that some residents want to continue to rely solely on storytelling, heritage, and other traditional forms of tourism. Nonetheless, Callahan remains confident that locals will become more accepting of his business in the future, attributing a changing direction in tourism attitudes to mayor Kelly Wolfe. In 2015 Wolfe endorsed a craft beer sampling ordinance that allows customers to sample draft craft beers before purchase at any convenience store or market in Jonesborough.[34] This legislation similarly permits distilleries to have tastings and give samples to customers before purchase, directly affecting Tennessee Hills's contribution to the tourist experience in Jonesborough.

For Tennessee Hills, contributing to neolocalism expands economic development in Jonesborough to engage both the local community and visiting tourists.[35] For Callahan, this is most accessible through events such as Wheels in the Hills.[36] Sponsored by Tennessee Hills Distillery and Dean Chesnut's General Store and Eatery, the first Wheels in the Hills, a free event that showcased motorcycles and vintage cars, brought in around four thousand tourists for the weekend. Since its inception in 2014, the event has grown with the support of Mayor Wolfe and local businesses. Community interaction and collaboration at Wheels in the Hills works for all parties involved. Callahan adds, "Jonesborough is home to me, and I feel like it deserves to have a good business that offers a lot to Jonesborough and have a lot to offer to us too."[37] Working with local residents and boosters, Tennessee Hills Distillery expands and (re)makes Jonesborough tourism in a way that aligns with the town's business goals. This (re)making further allows Tennessee Hills to brand its products around local heritage and culture for its continued success.

In a similar fashion, one way in which Sugarlands Distilling Company engages the local is by teaming with Smoky Mountain Guides. Brent Thompson explains, "We have a partnership with Smoky Mountain Guides, which is an outdoor expedition service. So, we get to take people from the distillery, head into the mountains and have a day hike, a backcountry trek and dine or just ride through the mountains and talk about the history of moonshining. We have different angles into our company because really at the end of the day, it's all about once you get here. The 'shine is just a vehicle for experiences."[38] For Thompson, Sugarlands products serve as "vehicles" for expanding tourism opportunities in Gatlinburg and surrounding communities. In the above quote, Thompson establishes that the Sugarlands version of an authentic place of moonshine extends beyond the tasting room and connects to the Sugarlands in the GSMNP for a more "experiential" moonshine. In addition, Sugarlands engages the local by hosting the only dedicated music venue in Gatlinburg, which draws in moonshine and music fans alike. Sugarlands also connects to and supports the local community through sponsoring charitable black tie events, the Symphony in the Park in Knoxville, and Floyd Fest, an arts and music festival in Floyd, Virginia.[39] Recently, Sugarlands has created a separate philanthropic division of the company called MoonShare, which provides monetary donations to several nonprofit organizations in the area and enables Sugarlands to move beyond being just a distillery to actively engaging and supporting local communities.

Meanwhile, as Sugarlands manufactures its own authentic place of moonshine tourism in the region, the distillery continues to draw on the idea of locality and tradition. Geographer Dydia DeLyser explains that perceptions of authenticity are "informed and influenced by" a place's natural aesthetic or important historical ties.[40] Thus, it is critical for Sugarlands to combine this tradition and locality not only in its production process but in its development and branding strategies as well. Daniel Fluitt, events coordinator at the distillery, adds, "A lot of the immigrants from Ireland and Scotland, where folk music kind of began, settled in this area and have been making moonshine in this area just as long as people have been making music. . . . We also work with WDVX radio in Knoxville. We are an underwriter with them and [collaborate] often. Everything is as local as possible . . . all the way from where we get our corn to sugar to t-shirts. That is one of the main things for us is to keep everything as local as possible."[41] Fluitt clearly sees a connection between authenticity, a historical place of moonshine, and engaging a contemporary place of East Tennessee through local collaborations.

While Tennessee Hills Distillery and Sugarlands Distilling Company engage with the local community to build and expand tourism opportunities, Doc Collier Moonshine does not. As the only registered microdistillery in the region, Doc Collier neither distributes nor markets its products outside of Gatlinburg. Consequently, tourists must go to the distillery, located at stoplight number 3 on the parkway in Gatlinburg, to purchase the company's liquor. Doc Collier ultimately relies on its status as a microdistillery and location near the parkway to attract new and repeat customers. As such, the distillery finds little need to actively participate in tourism collaborations or branding outside of Gatlinburg. However, the company does inadvertently attract tourists to visit Gatlinburg to taste the elusive Doc Collier 'shine. Keeping all aspects of production as local as possible is at the heart of authentic and neolocal place-making for Doc Collier. Regardless of the ways in which each distillery participates in its own (re)making, expanding the tourism market to moonshine is paramount for each distillery's vision and success.

Countering Existing Moonshine Narratives

Moonshine has long played a role in perpetuating two stereotypical images of Appalachian residents: the infamous hillbilly and the noble mountaineer. In contrast to dominant popular framings of modernity and progress, the hillbilly and mountaineer represent the mythical white, isolated, and forgotten mountain communities of American and Appalachian consciousness.[42] According to historian Anthony Harkins, the popularity of the hillbilly and mountaineer "stems from the dualistic nature of this cultural conception: it includes both positive and negative features of the American past and present, and incorporates both 'otherness' and self-identification."[43] As the hillbilly and mountaineer are continually created and recreated through popular American culture, the negative and positive features of each stereotype are simultaneously either reproduced or countered.

As each distillery in this case study demonstrates, authenticity is centered around its own ideas of a locality of East Tennessee and its historical and contemporary connection to a place of moonshine. These constructions of authenticity similarly work to combat what they perceive as negative stereotypes of the region, choosing instead to promote a narrative of moonshine that embodies tradition, craft, and resourcefulness. Countering the negative stereotypes embodied particularly in the hillbilly is a conscious effort for these three distilleries in branding and marketing their products. However, this is not the case for all distilleries in the region, many of which attempt to profit from existing popular narratives that portray moonshiners (and, by extension, mountain residents) as outlaws or ignorant hillbillies.

Because it is a microdistillery, Doc Collier Moonshine stays as local as possible by aligning its business goals locally and minimizing its branding and marketing efforts. This strategy is intentional and allows Doc Collier to maintain its authenticity as producers of East Tennessee moonshine. Buddy Keyes elaborates, "We don't want to market nationwide, it [is all] local marketing. We don't plan on going nationwide, we want to stay right here and keep it in the box instead of way outside the box."[44] Keyes's sentiments reveal the ways in which Doc Collier produces an authenticity embedded in the locality and place of East Tennessee while maintaining their vision of remaining a microdistillery. When asked about the branding strategies of competitors, such as the Sugarlands Legends Series campaign featuring moonshiners from the Discovery Channel's TV show *Moonshiners*, Keyes responds, "We see [ourselves] as the local good ol' boys. We don't want reality TV, we just want to do what we do, have fun and help people understand what we are and what we do. No slogan, just Doc Collier is who we are."[45] As Keyes explains above, mass marketing and national brand recognition produce a type of inauthenticity for their distillery. By keeping everything local, Doc Collier ensures its construction of authenticity through minimal branding and marketing. At the center of this locality, from Doc Collier's production processes to its marketing and selling strategies, lies a narrative of moonshine as traditional with its manufacture rooted in both science and hard work, a far cry from the unsophisticated hillbilly stereotype. Josh Stokes comments, "A lot of folks come in here thinking that moonshine is made from a hillbilly, but we work to change that understanding. I can see it click and the transformation happen, as we are talking."[46] Buddy Keyes adds, "It's just tradition, the stigma of moonshine is that you get it out of the mountains. We want to keep that, but we [also] want to open up to say hey, it is not what you think it is. There is a lot of science involved and hard work."[47]

Connecting moonshine to a narrative rooted in anything other than tradition and scientific craft promotes and represents an inauthentic version of commercial moonshine for Doc Collier. Unlike the other two distilleries under consideration, Doc Collier does not have a slogan, distribution plans, celebrity endorsements, or national or statewide marketing strategies. Keeping their products rooted in a locality of East Tennessee and talking with customers about the science and tradition of moonshine in the region ensures that Doc Collier's construction of authenticity fits its story and products.

Falling between Doc Collier and Sugarlands in branding and marketing efforts, Tennessee Hills Distillery attempts to showcase the traditional craft and heritage of moonshine through their production of a commercial product. Callahan comments on his reasoning for opening the distillery:

A lot of people from the outside looking in kind of see us for what we are. We are just small guys doing what we love. The good thing is we know a lot of people here in Jonesborough—I have a bottle of moonshine going to the governor of Tennessee this week. I am twenty-seven, but I am pretty renowned when it comes to making moonshine in these parts. I am trying to build a foundation for something that is bigger than myself. So . . . I am not really sure how it's going to go. A lot of people try to put us in the same category as Ole Smoky and Sugarlands. The thing about us is we are going to have to grow in an organic manner, and everything we do with our own hands. My whole idea is the art of making whiskey is being lost, and if I'm able to pass that down and showcase the art of making whiskey, that's important. Not a lot of people are doing that anymore, especially my age.[48]

Callahan is not just trying to cash in on an emerging industry. He is also passionate about the craft of making whiskey in East Tennessee, a place he calls home. By using the motto "Embracing Heritage," Tennessee Hills draws on Callahan's familiarity and connection to Jonesborough and the surrounding region to connect its authenticity to a similar narrative of moonshine. Like Doc Collier Callahan also refuses to employ the stereotype of the hillbilly to sell his liquor: "There are too many people from this area playing into the hillbilly stuff and everyone around here kind of portrays us as hillbillies and make it into their product. In all reality, I want to showcase what people have done to make a living and provide for their families for hundreds of years."[49] Callahan insists that his narrative of authentic commercial moonshine embodies the craft, heritage, tradition, and adaptability of East Tennesseans. Declaring that "there are too many people from this area playing into the hillbilly stuff," Callahan ultimately views his local competitors as capitalizing on an inauthentic narrative of moonshine and the region.

Of the three distilleries under consideration, Sugarlands Distilling Company has the most extensive branding, marketing, distribution, and production strategies. Their most recent and notable campaign is the Legends Series featuring select celebrities from the hit television show *Moonshiners*. The partnership between Sugarlands and the show's moonshine personalities is reflective of the overall transformation of moonshine to legality. Sugarlands provides legal entry for these moonshiners to manufacture and sell their product on the market.[50] As Brent Thompson explains, "the Legends Series is a product line that celebrates authentic moonshine craftsmen" and expands opportunities for tourists who are fans of *Moonshiners*. The company has and will continue to host events where fans can meet and talk to the show's legendary moonshiners. The Legends Series allows Sugarlands to promote a narrative centered on local moonshine craft and history through the proxy of these moonshine celebrities while also (re)making a new place of moonshine tourism in Gatlinburg.

Like Doc Collier and Tennessee Hills, Sugarlands refuses to brand and promote what it feels is an inauthentic narrative and stereotype of the hillbilly. Instead, the distillery chooses to construct its version of authenticity around the resourcefulness and adaptability of the early Sugarlanders in the East Tennessee Smoky Mountains. Brent Thompson expands on the role of Sugarlands in countering stereotypes about the region:

> That is actually one of the first things that I got pretty passionate about when I first came onto the project, was to really change the stereotype, because I am an East Tennessean . . . So when I think about the connotations of Appalachia, I do not think about people being uneducated. I think about people who had to find a way to survive . . . I feel the Sugarlands story is more about those sorts of things and less about the hillbilly, outlaw, and illegality side of history. Certainly, that is a part of moonshine history, but before that it was really distilling these spirits.[51]

Ned Vickers echoes Brent's comments, saying, "What we want to show is how resourceful the people were here, just because they aren't educated doesn't mean they aren't smart. There is a big difference between uneducated and unintelligent, and we want to show a sense of community. We are trying real hard to teach people about the heritage and history here [in the Sugarlands]."[52] Both Thompson and Vickers are cognizant of their role in shaping a narrative of new commercial moonshine. Symbolic of their constructions of authenticity, Sugarlands promotes a narrative of commercial moonshine that harkens back to the tradition, adaptation, and resourcefulness of the historical Sugarlanders of East Tennessee.

Though acknowledging that there are other narratives of moonshine such as that of the hillbilly, Sugarlands engages in a narrative that promotes a different, neolocal role of historical moonshine for people in the region.

While these distilleries construct their versions of authenticity around the tradition, craft, adaptation, and resourcefulness of historic moonshine, other distilleries in the area do not. The state's first and largest moonshine distillery, for instance, Ole Smoky Distillery in Gatlinburg relies heavily on hillbilly and outlaw stereotypes to market its liquor. Recently launching the "C'mon Live a Little" campaign, introduced by new spokesperson Gatlin T. Wolf, Ole Smoky captures consumers through a different narrative. The company's website details that the campaign "embodies everything Ole Smoky stands for: living in the now, taking chances and instigating mischievous behavior."[53] John Cochran, CEO of Ole Smoky, further explains, "Ole Smoky Moonshine is all about taking chances and having fun. Gatlin is going to encourage consumers to live a little on the wild side by firing them up to try our moonshine. Who wouldn't want to take a shot of moonshine to kick start the night?"[54] Ole Smoky currently aims to expand its operations and capture the millennial market outside the region by moving away from its local roots (and consumers).[55] To accomplish that goal, the distillery has begun to outsource its new campaign to non-local companies, most notably Standard Time out of Los Angeles and VaynerMedia out of New York City. This stands in contrast to the distilleries of this case study, all of which participate in neolocal place-making by incorporating local business in their versions of authentic moonshine. Ultimately, (re)making a narrative of moonshine aligned with the rich tradition, craft, and resourcefulness of historic moonshine is critical for these three distilleries as they engage in their own authentic (re)making of East Tennessee for commercial moonshine.

Conclusion

Opening the liquor market to commercial moonshine production is one way in which various actors seek to promote economic development in a historically depressed region.[56] Similarly, within the place-making and tourism literatures in geography, tourism is also a strategy for stimulating economic development.[57] For this reason, the commercial moonshine industry's connection to tourism in East Tennessee is critical for sustaining both aspects of the new economy: moonshine and tourism. As this case study demonstrates, it is evident that commercial moonshine works to (re)make a place of tourism in East Tennessee.

This (re)making is centered on each distillery's ability to construct their own versions of authentic moonshine products for likely tourists and consumers. As such, each distillery's construction of authentic moonshine is uniquely catered to its own business goals, background, and experience in the region. For all three distilleries, however, the construction of authenticity focuses on East Tennessee and its role as an already established place of tourism, its historical connection to moonshine, and its location in the mountains. Elucidated through the selected distilleries of this case study, producers of authenticity choose to focus on narratives and stereotypes of moonshine and the region rooted in tradition, craft, and resourcefulness. Similarly, by engaging neolocal strategies such as place-based naming and community engagement, each distillery further contributes to (re)making a place of tourism in East Tennessee.

While some impacts to the tourism industry may occur inherently through the addition of commercial moonshine, this chapter reveals that tourism is in fact changing in East Tennessee and that moonshine plays an important role in that transformation. First, the industry capitalizes on and connects to the region's preexisting tourism market. Both the availability and accessibility of commercial moonshine has also contributed to a shift in demographics of the types of tourists visiting the region. Moreover, the industry expands tourism opportunities in East Tennessee better suited for the success of moonshine. Finally, countering moonshine narratives of the hillbilly and outlaw, these distilleries (re)make a place of tourism around a narrative of moonshine that promotes the tradition, craft, adaptation, and resourcefulness of the region's historic moonshiners. All four themes of this intersection continue to center around a place of East Tennessee, its historical connection to moonshine, and its continued importance in the region as contemporary producers of the now legal commodity.

NOTES

1. For a sample of these debates, see Jeff Biggers, *The United States of Appalachia: How Southern Mountaineers Brought Independence, Culture, and Enlightenment to America* (Emeryville: Counterpoint Press, 2007); Timothy Ezzell, Dayton Lambert, and Eric Ogle, *Strategies for Economic Improvement in Appalachia's*

Distressed Counties: An Analysis of Ten Distressed and Formerly Distressed Appalachian Communities (Knoxville: University of Tennessee, 2010); and Mark A. Roberts, "The Performing Hillbilly: Redeeming Acts of a Regional Stereotype," *Appalachian Journal* 38 (2010): 78–90.

2. For more discussion on Popcorn Sutton, see chapter 2.

3. See Part II, "The Legalization of Modern Moonshine" for a more complete discussion. See also Tennessee Secretary of State, "Repeal of Prohibition," Tennessee State Library and Archives, last modified 2011, accessed October 7, 2014, www .tn.gov/tsla/exhibits/prohibition/repeal.htm.

4. See Cynthia Yeldell, "Ground Zero for Whiskey: Law Allows Production of Distilled Spirits in State," *Knoxville News Sentinel*, July 5, 2009, accessed September 8, 2014, http://archive.knoxnews.com/business/ground-zero-for-whiskey-law-allows-production-of-distilled-spirits-in-state-ep-409860713 -359327571.html.

5. For more information on the chosen methods and methodology for this research, see Pamela Baxter and Susan Jack, "Qualitative Case Study Methodology: Study Design and Implementation for Novice Researchers," *Qualitative Report* 13 (2008): 544–59; Hilary P. Winchester and Matthew W. Rofe, "Qualitative Research and Its Place in Human Geography," in *Qualitative Research Methods in Human Geography*, ed. Iain Hay (Oxford: Oxford University Press, 2010), 3–25; Jason Dittmer, "Textual and Discourse Analysis," in *The Sage Handbook of Qualitative Geography*, ed. Dydia DeLyser, Steve Herbert, Stuart Aiken, Mike Crang, and Linda McDowell (London: Sage Publications, 2010), 274–86; Rob Kitchin and Nick Tate, *Conducting Research in Human Geography: Theory, Methodology and Practice* (London: Person Education Limited, 2000).

6. For more information on tourism and the economy in East Tennessee, see Elizabeth Van Horn, "The Impacts of Tourism on Space and Place in Jonesborough Tennessee," (MA Thesis: University of Tennessee, 1998); Appalachian Regional Commission, "Tourism Development," accessed May 7, 2015, www.arc.gov/tourism; Sevier County Economic Development Council, "Gatlinburg Tourism," accessed September 15, 2015, www.scedc.com/gatlinburg -tourism.php; Jonesborough Tourism Office, "Business Summary," Jonesborough: Washington County Economic Development Council, accessed September 15, 2015, www.thewcedc.com/files/Business_Summary _Jonesborough_2015.pdf.

7. "Authenticity" here is defined as constructive authenticity, in which there is an ontological assumption that authenticity is a result of individual interpretations and construction (see Dean MacCannell, "Staged Authenticity: Arrangements of Social Space in Tourist Settings," *American Journal of Sociology* 79 (1973): 589–603; George Hughes, "Authenticity in Tourism," *Annals of Tourism Research* 22 (1995): 781–803; Ning Wang, "Rethinking Authenticity in Tourism Experience," *Annals of Tourism Research* 26 (1999): 349–70; Edward M. Bruner, "Abraham Lincoln as Authentic Reproduction: A Critique of Postmodernism," *American Anthropologist* 96 (1994): 397–415; and Dydia DeLyser, "Authenticity on the Ground: Engaging the Past in a California Ghost Town," *Annals of the Association of American Geographers* 89 (1999): 602–32).

8. "Neolocalism" is defined as a shift in American consumerism from mainstream, homogenized, global industries toward more localized, community-driven, niche industries. Neolocalism is the conscious attempt of people to engage local commodities, experiences, or traditions that connect them to a particular place. For more information on neolocalism in the craft-beer and food industries, see James R. Shortridge, "Keeping Tabs on Kansas: Reflections on Regionally Based Field Study," *Journal of Cultural Geography* 16 (1996): 5–16; Wes Flack, "American Microbreweries and Neolocalism: 'Ale-ing' for a Sense of Place," *Journal of Cultural Geography* 16 (1997): 37–53; Derrek Eberts, "Neolocalism and the Branding and Marketing of Place by Canadian Microbreweries," in *The Geography of Beer: Regions, Environment, and Societies*, ed. Mark W. Patterson and Nancy Hoalst Pullen (New York: Springer, 2014), 189–99; Steven M. Schnell and Joseph F. Reese, "Microbreweries as Tools of Local Identity," *Journal of Cultural Geography* 21 (2003): 45–69; Adam J. Matthews and Matthew T. Patton, "Exploring Place Marketing by American Microbreweries: Neolocal Expressions of Ethnicity and Race," *Journal of Cultural Geography* 33 (2016): 275–309; Jay Gatrell, Neil Reid, and Thomas L. Steiger, "Branding Spaces: Place, Region, Sustainability, and the American Craft Beer Industry," *Applied Geography* 90 (2018): 360–70.

9. See Gregory John Ashworth and Henk Voogd, *Selling the City: Marketing Approaches in Public Sector Urban Planning* (London: Belhaven Press, 1990); Edward L. Glaeser and Joshua D. Gottlieb, "The Economics of Place-Making Policies," *National Bureau of Economic Research*, no. w14373 (2008); Colin Michael Hall and Stephen Page, *The Geography of Tourism and Recreation: Environment, Place, and Space* (New York: Routledge, 2002).

10. Ned Vickers, CEO, interview by the author, Sugarlands Distilling Company, March 3, 2015.

11. Kentucky Bourbon Trail was formed in 1999 by the Kentucky Distillers' Association. For more information, see "History—KBTTM," Kentucky Bourbon Trail, accessed April 15, 2018, https://kybourbontrail.com/history.

12. Brent Thompson, director of marketing and strategy, interview by the author, Sugarlands Distilling Company, March 5, 2015.

13. Josh Stokes, assistant manager, interview by the author, Doc Collier Moonshine, March 17, 2015.

14. For more information about the International Storytelling Center and other tourism draws, see "About ISC," International Storytelling Center, accessed June 6, 2017, www.storytellingcenter.net/; "Tourism," Historic Jonesborough Tennessee, accessed June 6, 2017, www.jonesboroughtn.org/index.php/com ponent/k2/89-jonesborough-tourism; "Market Profile: Jonesborough," Washington County Economic Development Council, accessed September 16, 2015, www.thewcedc.com/files/Market_Profile_Jonesborough_2015.pdf.

15. Stephen Callahan, owner/CEO, interview by the author, Tennessee Hills Distillery, March 13, 2015.

16. Vickers interview. At the time, Sugarlands planned to be in all forty-eight continental states by the end of the year. As of 2017, per their website, this goal has not been reached. However, customers are able to order Sugarlands products online unless they live in one of the following states: Alabama, Alaska, Colorado, Connecticut, Delaware, Hawaii, Idaho, Illinois, Kentucky, Louisiana, Massachusetts, Minnesota, Mississippi, Montana, Nebraska, New Hampshire, New York, North Carolina, North Dakota, Pennsylvania, South Dakota, Tennessee, Texas, Utah, Washington, or Wisconsin.

17. Sevier County Economic Development Council, "Gatlinburg Tourism"; and Jonesborough Tourism Office, "Business Summary."

18. Buddy Keyes, interview by the author, Doc Collier, 2015; Vickers interview; and Callahan interview.

19. Stokes interview.

20. DeLyser, "Authenticity on the Ground"; Wang, "Rethinking Authenticity"; Stephen Gapps, "Mobile Monuments: A View of Historical Reenactment and Authenticity from Inside the Costume Cupboard of History," *Rethinking History* 13 (2009): 395–409.

21. For examples of this in the literature see Schnell and Reese, "Microbreweries

as Tools," 45–69; Ann M. Fletchall, "Place-Making through Beer-Drinking: A Case Studies of Montana's Craft Breweries," *Geographical Review* 106 (2016): 539–66; Adam J. Matthews and Matthew T. Patton, "Exploring Place Marketing," 275–309.

22. "Our Story," Sugarlands Distilling Company, last modified 2017, accessed May 10, 2015. www.sugarlandsdistilling.com/stories-in-every-jar/our-story/.

23. Stokes interview.

24. Callahan interview.

25. Vickers interview.

26. Stokes interview.

27. "Our Products," Tennessee Hills Distillery, last modified 2015, accessed June 9, 2017, www.tnhillsdistillery.com/.

28. Callahan interview.

29. "Our Products," Jack Daniel's Distillery, last modified 2017, accessed June 9, 2017, https://www.jackdaniels.com/en-us/our-products.

30. Ibid.

31. Callahan interview.

32. Ibid.

33. As the craft beer and local food industries note, community support and engagement are paramount in contributing to neolocalism. See the following for more: Schnell and Reese, "Microbreweries as Tools"; Schnell and Reese, "Microbreweries, Place, and Identity"; Fletchall, "Place-Making through Beer-Drinking"; Matthews and Patton, "Exploring Place Marketing"; Gatrell, Reid, and Steiger, "Branding Spaces."

34. Wolfe also approved the sale of alcohol at Wheels in the Hills Cruise In. See also Meghan McCoy, "BMA Moves Ahead to Allow Beer Sampling," *Meghan: The Words of a Journalist,* last modified February 18, 2015, accessed July 17, 2017, https://meghan80.wordpress.com/tag/tennessee-hills-distillery/.

35. Callahan interview.

36. Other events sponsored by Tennessee Hills include charitable Brody's Run and a blind corn-hole tournament at Jonesborough International Storytelling Center.

37. Callahan interview.

38. Brent Thompson, interview by the author, Sugarlands, 2015.

39. Daniel Fluitt, director and events coordinator, interview by the author, Sugarlands Distilling Company, March 3, 2015.

40. DeLyser, "Authenticity on the Ground."

41. Fluitt interview.

42. For more on the hillbilly, see Anthony Harkins, *Hillbilly: A Cultural History of an American Icon* (New York: Oxford University Press, 2004). For more discussion on stereotypes and identity in Appalachia, see Biggers, *United States of Appalachia*; Richard D. Starnes, "Tourism, Landscape, and History in the Great Smoky Mountains National Park," in *Destination Dixie: Tourism and Southern History*, ed. Karen L. Cox (Gainesville: University Press of Florida, 2012), 267–84; Emelie K. Peine and Kai A. Schafft, "Moonshine, Mountaineers, and Modernity: Distilling Cultural History in the Southern Appalachian Mountains," Journal of Appalachian Studies 18 (2012): 93–112.

43. Harkins, *Hillbilly*, 6.

44. Keyes interview.

45. Ibid.

46. Stokes interview.

47. Keyes interview.

48. Callahan interview.

49. Ibid.

50. For more information on the Sugarlands Legends Series, see various press releases from the company, such as "Legends," Sugarlands Distilling Company, last modified 2017, accessed August 8, 2017, www.sugarlandsdistilling.com/legends/.

51. Thompson interview.

52. Vickers interview.

53. Ole Smoky Distillery, "Ole Smoky Tennessee Moonshine Announces Phase Two of All-New 360 Marketing Campaign," last modified August 2, 2015, accessed May 25, 2017, http://olesmoky.com/news/ole-smoky-tennessee-moonshine-announces-phase-two-of-all-new-360-marketing-campaign.

54. John Cochran is quoted from the following article detailing the new campaign: "Ole Smoky Announces Newest Spokesperson, Gatlin T. Wolf III," *Chilled: Raise Your Spirits*, last modified 2015, accessed August 9, 2017. http://chilledmagazine.com/ole-smoky-announces-newest-spokesperson-gatlin-t-wolf-iii.

55. E. J. Schultz, "Ole Smoky Moonshine Sheds Its Hillbilly Roots," *Advertising Age*, last modified July 20, 2015, accessed May 25, 2017, http://adage.com/article/cmo-strategy/ole-smoky-moonshine-sheds-hillbilly-roots/299533/; Ole Smoky Distillery, "Ole Smoky Announces Newest Spokesperson."

56. William T. Cheek III, "Cooking up a New Law for 'Tennessee Moonshine,'" WillCheek.com, April 22, 2015; Cynthia Yeldell, "Ground Zero for Whiskey; Law

Allows Production of Distilled Spirits in State," *Knoxville News Sentinel,* July 5, 2009, accessed August 20, 2018, http://archive.knoxnews.com/business /ground-zero-for-whiskey-law-allows-production-of-distilled-spirits-in-state-ep-409860713-359327571.html.

57. For examples, see Ashworth and Voogd, *Selling the City;* Elin Berglund and Krister Olsson, "Rethinking Place Marketing: A Literature Review," *50th European Regional Science Association Congress* (2010): 19–23; Hall and Page, *Geography of Tourism.*

CHAPTER 10

Heritage Spirits in Heritage Spaces

KRISTEN BALDWIN DEATHRIDGE

Contemporary legal moonshine distillers advertise their links to the long history of 'shine running in and around the Appalachian Mountains. These connections help modern distilleries increase visitation and sales through cultural tourism. Several distilleries in the region take the further step of housing their operations in local historic buildings. Distillery owners make the intentional choice to use historic buildings in order to deepen their ties to the history of the region.

This chapter explores how three distilleries capitalize on "heritage" to promote their products: Old Forge Distillery in Pigeon Forge, Tennessee; Palmetto Distillery, with locations in both Anderson and Myrtle Beach, South Carolina; and Copper Barrel Distillery in North Wilkesboro, North Carolina. These sites were chosen both for their commonalities and their differences. All three states have roots in the historical Appalachian moonshine trade, and the distilleries are located in the mountains.[1] Both Pigeon Forge and Myrtle Beach host a bustling tourist trade. Anderson, a small mountain town, promotes itself as "South Carolina's Bright Spot," located halfway between Atlanta, Georgia, and Charlotte, North Carolina. North Wilkesboro, like Anderson, is a smaller town, with fewer tourists than Pigeon Forge or Myrtle Beach, but its roots in NASCAR ensure that those who visit there are aware of at least some of the history of moonshine.

This book as a whole explores the early-twenty-first-century phenomenon of unaged white whiskey and its craft distilleries. This particular whiskey, called by many colloquial names but most often called moonshine, has fascinated contemporary distillers and alcohol drinkers alike, not least for its historical associations. Though moonshine manufacturing has spread across the United States, many liquor operations in Appalachia use that region's long association with the product as a selling point. Folks come to try moonshine while on vacation to get a "taste" of Appalachia's heritage spirit. Of course, there are several moonshine distilleries that house their facilities in new construction, but those that choose to work in historical settings make that selection deliberately in part to connect with local history on another level. Moonshine distilleries capitalize on the advantages of linking their operations with historic preservation and heritage tourism.

Today, most distilleries include gift shops full of not only branded items, both wearable and for the kitchen, but also regional cookbooks, food, and beverage mixers. Each place carefully crafts its atmosphere to provide an experience for visitors that feels both local and unique. In moonshine distilleries, that atmosphere often include canning-style drinking jars for sale, shop workers (and often the master distillers themselves) wearing overalls, and an emphasis on southern accents. They do this in order to connect their spaces and their products with local heritage.

Heritage and Historic Preservation

In order to grasp the connections between historic preservation and distilleries, focusing on a few key concepts proves helpful. Among these are "heritage," "heritage tourism," and the National Register of Historic Places. What is "heritage"? UNESCO's World Heritage Convention defines "heritage" as "our legacy from the past, what we live with today, and what we pass on to future generations."[2] The World Heritage Convention discusses both natural heritage, meaning land- and sea-scapes like the Great Barrier Reef, and cultural heritage, including buildings like cathedrals and the Pyramids at Giza. The terms of the convention itself, adopted on November 16, 1972, further define cultural heritage as monuments, including single buildings, groups of buildings (or what the National Register of Historic Places would refer to as a historic district), or archaeological sites that "are of outstanding universal value from the point of view of history, art or science."[3] In sum, cultural heritage can be thought of as spaces of significant human impact.[4]

Sociologist Diane Barthel-Bouchier notes that in the wake of this convention and others like it, UNESCO had a simpler time designating World Heritage Sites than convincing governments to put the required funding into protecting and conserving those sites. She argues it was "easier to identify sites that should be 'saved' than to convince the public that it was their human right not simply to save the site, but to pay for the privilege."[5] Actually saving the sites is where commercial and local efforts to adaptively reuse heritage spaces prove helpful. "Adaptive reuse" is the most common phrase used to describe when people take a building that was constructed for one purpose and refit it to be utilized for something else. Any change in the primary purpose of a building constitutes an adaptive reuse, although most often it is accompanied by some changes in the fabric of a building, either interior or exterior.

Adaptive reuse need not follow any particular guidelines, but the secretary of the Interior offers standards for rehabilitation of a historic structure. These standards define "rehabilitation" as "the process of returning a property to a state of utility, through repair or alteration, which makes possible an efficient contemporary use while preserving those portions and features of the property which are significant to its historic, architectural, and cultural values."[6] A building may be rehabilitated to its former purpose or adapted to a new use; therefore, all adaptive reuse is rehabilitation, but not all rehabilitation is adaptive reuse.

The secretary's *Standards for Rehabilitation* are primarily used to evaluate construction on buildings listed on the National Register of Historic Places, to determine the appropriateness of construction that has been completed on buildings that owners wish to place on the register, and to decide if a building's owner has earned the rehabilitation federal tax credit. However, people who are undertaking a rehabilitation or adaptive reuse project often reference the *Standards* as they plan their work in order to earn tax credits as well as to maintain the character of a building. The *Standards* consist of ten statements aimed at preserving the historic characteristics and materials in a building. The secretary of the Interior's *Standards for Rehabilitation* does not comment on whether the former use of a building should be interpreted to the public after rehabilitation. In practice, particularly in the last forty years, preservationists and entrepreneurs have presented some sort of interpretation, typically ranging from a hidden plaque to a centrally located exhibit. Certainly, when distillery owners talk to the visitors and journalists about the history of their spaces, this is a form of interpretation.

None of the buildings discussed in this chapter are listed on the National Register, but it is possible that any of them could be determined eligible.[7] When historians and historic preservationists talk about historic spaces, they use these terms in a discipline-specific way, whether an old building is listed on the National Register or not. It is as important to understand the National Register as it is to understand concepts of heritage and heritage tourism.

In the United States one of the most common ways that heritage is defined in the built environment is through the National Register of Historic Places. Congress created the National Register of Historic Places in 1966 with the passage of the National Historic Preservation Act.[8] The National Register has two main purposes: to provide a record of historically significant properties and to provide historical information about those places. The record, essentially a list, is the function most often associated with the National Register, but the nomination forms themselves provide a wealth of publicly available information to researchers.

If a property is listed on the National Register, or if it is determined to be eligible for listing, then that status must be considered if any construction project involving federal funds is to take place on or near that property. Just because something is listed on the National Register does not mean that federally funded construction projects will be moved, although they may be. However, it could mean that the building (or archaeological site) would be recorded to the highest current standards and then destroyed anyway to make way for the construction. In the end, the only protection the register provides is that of awareness.

If heritage is the impact of human activity written on the landscape, and the National Register of Historic Places represents a significant segment of that heritage in the United States, what then is heritage tourism? There is, in fact, a federal definition. The Advisory Council for Historic Preservation is an executive-level group established by the National Historic Preservation Act of 1966. They manage the Preserve America program, and President George W. Bush formalized the program's relationship with the White House in 2003 through Executive Order 13287. Section 7 of that order defines heritage tourism as "the business and practice of attracting and accommodating visitors to a place or area based especially on the unique or special aspects of that locale's history, landscape (including trail systems), and culture." The National Trust for Historic Preservation began a Cultural Heritage Tourism Initiative in 1989, and its definition puts the action on the traveler, discussing heritage tourism as "travelling to experience the places, artifacts, and activities that authentically represent the stories and people of the past and present."[9] In 2002 81 percent of Americans included a stop at a cultural heritage site or event in their travel plans. Further, studies show that tourists who visit heritage sites spend more money on their travels.[10] With numbers like that, it is easy to understand why towns and businesses across the United States work to connect their history to tourist sites.

One issue that frequently comes up when discussing heritage tourism is that visitors crave authenticity. People have choices for where they visit, and they want "real" historical experiences. In addition, experience often matters much more than actual products. A 2002 study for the area around Saint Augustine, Florida, demonstrated that visitors found historic architecture highly authentic, and that one of the highest goals of a visit was to "experience the region's historic character."[11] While this was a relatively small study, it is reasonable to assume that these results would hold true for a majority of American travelers. Moonshine distillers intentionally tap into these trends in travel and promote the experiences that visitors can have on-site as authentic to the Appalachian region. In many cases, they augment this feeling of authenticity by operating in historic spaces. Turning to look at each site, the following pages discuss the history of the buildings as well as what stories each business tells about its heritage.

Copper Barrel

Due to its moniker as "the Moonshine Capital of the World," given by a journalist in 1950, North Wilkesboro, North Carolina, makes a fitting home for a contemporary moonshine distillery.[12] The town became home to Copper Barrel Distillery in 2015.[13] None of the articles on the company mention where its owner George Smith is from, but most note that he spent several years in Charlotte, North Carolina, after leaving "a Fortune 500 company."[14] While in Charlotte, Smith joined the Charlotte Bourbon Club, met many helpful people, and decided to open a distillery. Smith attended the North Carolina Main Street Conference, where he met Robert Johnson, the mayor of North Wilkesboro. According to Smith, several mayors were hopeful that he would choose their town for his distillery.[15] In the short film shown before distillery tours on-site, Smith noted that he wanted to be in a downtown area and to help revitalize communities. One of Smith's goals was to help North Wilkesboro "become the thriving community that it once was."[16]

Another reason why Smith chose North Wilkesboro was because of its moonshining history. Smith wanted to make bourbon but knew that 'shine would be profitable while waiting for the spirits to age.[17] Mayor Johnson proved an invaluable contact, suggesting to Smith that he team up with Roger Lee "Buck" Nance, a former moonshiner from Wilkes County.[18] Nance has made white whiskey his whole life, supposedly helping to craft some of the liquor that Junior Johnson ran in the area.[19] In October 2009 Nance was arrested and charged with possession of 926 gallons of "non tax-paid liquor."[20] Nance had learned how to distill alcohol from his father, Floyd Nance, and agreed to teach Smith his process and help him get set up. As they worked together, Buck Nance decided that he wanted to work for the distillery full time.[21] Nance is also a metal worker and built all of the equipment used by the distillery, and he based the main still on a design his father had used.[22]

As with other contemporary moonshine distillers, the folks at Copper Barrel emphasize their connection to the history of the spirit and the authenticity of the process. Nance creates the recipes, and Smith ensures they have access to the only well in town, so that even the water source is the same one used by local moonshiners during the twentieth century. The tagline on Copper Barrel's website reads, "Introducing A Taste of Genuine: Our spirits come from the deep rooted moonshining heritage of Wilkes County—the 'Moonshine Capital of America.' We make 100% true shine. And, each drop is distilled using grains and produce from North Carolina farms. It's time you got a taste of genuine."[23] For Smith in particular the building plays an important role in this marketing (see fig. 10.1). Copper Barrel is located in what was the Key City Furniture factory, which closed in 2013. When the distillery moved into the facility two years later, Smith kept as much of the original buildings as he could.[24] It appears that the shop and tasting room as well as a narrow building between what is now the distilling room and an antique mall are new construction. Copper Barrel continues to showcase the original building when possible. Copper Barrel does not use the entire facility; some of it is empty but will be used to store more of the distillery's stock or aged whiskey in the future, and one of the former factory buildings is currently leased to Key City Antiques.

The site takes up most of a North Wilkesboro city block and extends over a small alley to one of Key City Furniture's former warehouses. According to Wilkes County tax records, the furniture factory owned the entire block that

Figure 10.1. Copper Barrel's Facility. New construction to the left and right of the original Key City building (with the porch). Key City's storage tower and two other warehouses are also visible to the rear and right. Photo by author.

faces B Street (also known as Main Street). Key City was founded by James Caudill in 1926, and ownership stayed in the family. Key City moved from downtown North Wilkesboro (the current home of Copper Barrel) in 2003 and shuttered operations in 2013.[25] A review of North Wilkesboro's Sanborn Fire Insurance maps reveals that before Key City, the block was a mixture of dwellings and businesses.

Tours at Copper Barrel focus on the moonshine. Though the description of the process is accurate, it is quick in order to get folks to the tasting room. However, the tour guide does note historic features of the building, particularly those that were left in place. Removing several items from the factory era would have also required removing parts of the building. This is not only an expensive process; Smith also wanted to maintain the historic character of the space.

Palmetto Distillery

Palmetto Distillery is based in Anderson, a town in the foothills of South Carolina. The company also has a major outlet in Myrtle Beach, South Carolina, which is a more popular tourist destination. Palmetto lays claim to the title of South Carolina's first legal moonshine distillery, and owners Bryan and Trey Boggs had moonshiners in their family history. The Boggses secured their permit from South Carolina in early 2011 but did not establish their distillery until well into 2012. Palmetto Moonshine quickly became a success, and the Boggses began to sell two-year-old whiskey in mid-2015.[26] When they added the aged whiskey, the Boggs changed the official company name to Palmetto Distilling.

The Myrtle Beach location opened in 2014. It is a store and tasting room; there's no distilling on-site. The Boggses moved their original still to Myrtle Beach as a showpiece after they retired it from work in Anderson.[27] Trey Boggs said that because they began Palmetto as an homage to family history, a store in Myrtle Beach made a logical step, due to the many summers they spent there as adolescents. Bryan Boggs observed that the tourist town provided an excellent opportunity to reach a larger clientele and noted that moonshine is more than simply a southern product.[28] Indeed, Palmetto has a wider reach than either Copper Barrel or Old Forge; as of September 2015, consumers in twenty-five states and Canada could purchase the distillery's liquor.[29] Deals since then have expanded into other countries.

While they recognize their historic building (see fig. 10.2), the Boggses do not emphasize it the way that Copper Barrel and Old Forge do. Rather, they spend more time in interviews and on the distillery's website discussing the heritage of the spirits themselves. Trey Boggs notes that their recipe comes from an actual bootlegger, though the brothers do not reveal their source, and that they modeled the profile of their whiskey on that of the state-run liquor monopoly (1893–1907).[30] On the "About" page of Palmetto's website, the brothers describe how their relative Dock Boggs went from coal mining to manufacturing white whiskey in the early twentieth century.

Palmetto Distillery's distilling building, home to their first shop, is interesting precisely because of its commonplace nature. Google Maps indicates that the company's 200 West Benson mailing address directs people to the rear of the building, which makes sense for access to the loading dock, but the front,

Figure 10.2. Palmetto Moonshine Distillery Building, Christmas. Palmetto Distillery, https://www.palmettomoonshine.com/distillery.

with the parking lot, is where visitors want to go. Locating the front of the building required exploring Google's Street View; 211 West Whitner Street is roughly the front. The block that Palmetto Moonshine rests on sits just outside of the Anderson Downtown Historic District, which was listed on the National Register of Historic Places in 1979.

Exploring the Sanborn Fire Insurance Company maps for Anderson shows the evolution of the town and the block that Palmetto is now located on. The 1884 map shows only part of the block, and the entire town fits on a single sheet. The final Sanborn map for Anderson, drawn in February 1918, illustrates how the street name evolved from West Boundary to Towers Street. The buildings began as dwellings, but stables and carriage works grew to take over the majority of the block. Palmetto's website claims that the building is one hundred years old, but there is nothing that resembles the Palmetto building on the 1918 map.

The Boggses note that several businesses have used the warehouse over the decades, and that much is assured. According to them, the site was used by Anderson Armored Car and then by Wells Fargo after they purchased Anderson. Greyhound operated a bus depot out of this spot, as did an early taxi service.[31] This is the sort of early-twentieth-century brick warehouse that can be found in towns across the United States. The relative commonality of the building type provides Palmetto with a space that is both familiar to visitors and a historic space in which to sell their spirits.

Old Forge Distillery

Located in Pigeon Forge, Tennessee, Old Forge Distillery opened to the public in summer 2014 and offers three white spirits, each emphasizing a different grain: corn, wheat, or malted barley.[32] The all-corn grain build is their 1830 Original No. 001, and the other builds have different numbers.[33] Every article about Old Forge's opening emphasizes the history of the site, the history of the buildings, and the continuing use of local grains and herbs. Tellingly, none of the articles mention the owners of the site, though many mention the head distiller and some have quotes from the manager.[34]

Operating under the tagline "Distilling 200 years of tradition," Old Forge produces not only moonshine and flavored varieties of moonshine but also rum, vodka, and "Tennessee bourbon whiskey," which is aged for eight years. In each of their spirits, the crafters at Old Forge use grains that are milled on-site, and they emphasize this part of the process, explicitly linking it to the history of the place. However, it is unclear whether the bourbon whiskey comes from their site or is simply blended and bottled there. Whiskey takes several years to mature, and Old Forge has not been open long enough to accurately claim that its whiskey has been aged. Although the owners at Old Forge continue to underscore the deep traditions of moonshining in the Smoky Mountains, they plan to diversify their products in the future. Not only are they not solely dependent on moonshine varieties, they also use different bottle shapes for their liquor rather than sticking to canning-style jars only. Most commercial moonshine today is sold in jars to resemble the way folks sold untaxed liquor throughout Appalachia.[35] Even in several articles written to mark Old Forge's opening, when moonshine was the only spirit they had for sale, the authors noted that the owners intended to move beyond making and selling 'shine.[36]

There is quite a bit more information on Old Forge's website than on Copper Barrel's. The homepage includes a timeline that moves from the 1700s through the present. Clicking on any part of the timeline takes the visitor to a page that provides slightly more detail on the relevant history of the area.[37] According to the website, Isaac Love was mining and working iron in the area that today surrounds the Old Mill during the 1820s. There was not enough iron to sustain

Figure 10.3. Old Forge Distillery and the Old Mill Restaurant. Photo by Dollie Boyd.

Love's forge, and he and his sons built the Old Mill in 1830 over the original Old Forge. Love's forge, along the Little Pigeon River, provided the name for the town of Pigeon Forge.[38] In 1841, the same year that the new post office opened with the name "Pigeon Forge Post Office," the Loves sold the forge to Alexander Preston, who named the iron works the Sweden Furnace. In 1849 John Sevier Trotter purchased the property and continued working the mill and forge.[39] During the Civil War, weaving operations were set up in the mill to provide cloth for the military.[40] Trotter built much of the current mill building on the foundations of the earlier mill around 1870.[41] In 1883 the mill began sawing lumber, and in 1885 the forge was taken apart and sent to Kentucky.[42] The Trotters sold the site to John Marshall McMahan, who in turn sold part of the interest in the mill to A. T. Householder in 1890.[43] In the early twentieth century, Householder installed a power generator at the mill that provided electricity to the area through 1930.[44]

As seen in figure 10.3, Old Forge Distillery itself is located on the Old Mill property in a building that is more than one hundred years old. Old Forge proudly notes the history of the place in connection with its distilling operations. The distillery is part of an expansive heritage tourism property that includes not only the still running mill, but a general store, candy shop, ice cream parlor, pottery shop, a ladies' clothing and accessories store, and two restaurants.

Conclusion

Each of the distilleries, Copper Barrel, Palmetto, and Old Forge, make their liquor in the Appalachian Mountains, and each emphasizes connections to the long history of making untaxed white liquor in that area. Copper Barrel's main link to the historical moonshine trade is head distiller Buck Nance. On Palmetto's website, the Boggs brothers note their bootlegging ancestor. Keener Shanton, the head distiller at Old Forge, does not have the historical connections to moonshining that Buck Nance of Copper Barrel does or even the relative that the Boggses do. As such, when talking about Shanton, Old Forge focuses on his particular methods and experimentation. Shanton was a firefighter who moved through home brewing and into distilling. While this is not an obvious connection to historical moonshining in the region, and no information is given on Shanton's family on the website, Shanton's "self-taught" distilling methods are supposedly in keeping with mountain moonshining traditions.

Old Forge Distillery offers regular tastings, and tours are only "on request." This holds with the other distillers in the Pigeon Forge area, who cater to large parties of tourists looking to enjoy as many free tastings of moonshine as possible. Most visitors are not as interested in the operations as they are in the tasting. While Copper Barrel feels like a much smaller operation comparatively, because Wilkesboro has fewer tourists than Pigeon Forge, visiting Copper Barrel has a similar feel to the Pigeon Forge and Gatlinburg distilleries, including Old Forge. Copper Barrel does provide a tour, but it is short and gets to the tasting as quickly as possible. Call Family Distillers, also in Wilkesboro, provides a much deeper and more historically oriented tour, with fewer varieties of moonshine available to taste. Although Call is not in a historic space, the distillery has long roots in moonshining in western North Carolina, so their tours emphasize those connections (see chapter 8).

Regarding the buildings themselves, each distillery constructs a different narrative. The people at Copper Barrel proudly discuss their adaptive reuse of the historic Key City Furniture buildings, but they do not mention which parts of their operation are new construction. Smith and his partners made extensive modifications to the buildings, adding a new section for the tasting room and gift shop, as well as a new section that connects two of the original Key City buildings. The distilling itself is done in one of the historic buildings, and they have left the historic walls visible in the newly constructed spaces.

The Boggs brothers of Palmetto Distilling recognize the historic building where they distill spirits, but they do not emphasize it online or in interviews the way the people at Copper Barrel and Old Forge do. Old Forge emphasizes not only the historic building where the distillery is located but also discusses the history of several surrounding buildings. It helps that the adjacent mill building is listed on the National Register of Historic Places. On the whole, the distillers discussed in this chapter appear to use their historic buildings more as an added layer to the heritage stories they tell about their products rather than as part of a deeper philosophical commitment to historic preservation or to interpreting the spaces that they occupy. Smith of Copper Barrel is the only one who explicitly connects the use of an old building for the business to the current vogue that encourages revitalization of historic neighborhoods. It is unclear, considering all of the alterations that Smith has made, whether the Copper Barrel buildings would be eligible for listing on the National Register. It does not appear that the Boggses have made the type of modifications that would prevent their building from being listed, but it remains unclear why they have not pursued a listing.

Each building that these distillers have used is historic, but none of the spaces themselves have direct connections to moonshining. At the same time, Copper Barrel, Palmetto, and Old Forge have all made a specific effort to use historic buildings; they could have chosen to work with a space that could have been purpose-built or even something easier to modify, like a contemporary warehouse. How does using historic buildings add to the heritage image that these distilleries aim to project and sell to their customers? In some ways, using a permanent structure at all is antithetical to the outlaw roots of moonshine. But customers cannot purchase legal white whiskey directly from the back of someone's truck, nor can they meet them in the woods to observe the true heritage process. By using old buildings, then, these distillers borrow a sense of authenticity from their spaces. Historic buildings allow customers to feel connected to the history of an area, while they also enjoy a product that is regulated by the government and made on new, safer stills.

Is simply reusing a historic building an act of historic preservation? That question proves more difficult to answer than it appears. According to the National Trust for Historic Preservation, in 2011 at least 60 percent of breweries were located in adaptive reuse spaces.[45] While the National Trust piece discusses breweries, not distilleries, the industries are intimately related, and one can inform the other. Trent Margrif notes that many of these microbreweries do not follow the secretary of the Interior's *Standards for Rehabilitation of Historic Buildings*, but that "they do make use of larger, commonly brick, buildings that are otherwise underutilized or abandoned."[46] Both Copper Barrel and Palmetto fit this pattern, though the part of the historic building that Copper Barrel is currently using for distilling is a bit smaller. Old Forge is located in a wooden building, but it is larger and was underused before being converted into a distillery. Distilleries, like breweries, can encourage interest in semivacant downtown areas, an idea that Smith of Copper Barrel specifically tapped into with his location choice.

Making use of historic structures and encouraging business activity in downtowns is one way that distillers can endear themselves to local governments, earning their support for what can be a controversial business option in small towns. Towns also make use of brewing and distilling operations to connect to heritage tourism when they are located in historic buildings. Areas like Napa Valley in California and the whole of Kentucky encourage alcohol tourism (alcotourism), and other areas are looking to cash in on this phenomenon as well.[47] These are practical reasons that distillers would choose to invest in historic buildings. Businesses exist to make money, and adaptive reuse provides excellent financial incentives both for the individual business and for the towns they serve. For distilleries like Copper Barrel, Palmetto, and Old Forge, reusing historic buildings also allows them to add layers to their heritage stories. In some cases, these stories run deeper than others, but in the end historic buildings are still being saved.

In some ways, Old Forge Distillery remains an outlier in this discussion because Pigeon Forge is a true tourist town. The marketing in all of Pigeon Forge is over the top and an assault on the senses, often catering to customers who seek a caricature of mountain people. This form of "hillbilly" tourism has grown in Pigeon Forge since the opening of Great Smoky Mountains National Park in the 1930s, and many people love the area for its kitsch, not in spite of it.[48] Despite the factor of Pigeon Forge's larger draw, all three of these sites depend on tourists; the populations are simply not large enough to build a business of selling legal liquor to only locals in any of these towns. Old Forge, Palmetto, and Copper Barrel try to attract tourists by building upon the heritage and tradition of generations of moonshiners. The distillers in newer or purpose-built spaces are also marketing heritage tourism in a sense. However, Old Forge, Palmetto, Copper Barrel, and other distilleries that connect to the region's history by choosing to adaptively reuse buildings (even in some cases utilizing the same sources of water and grains for their operations that those who sold untaxed white whiskey did) are drawing on different Appalachian traditions through their use of heritage spaces.

NOTES

1. Palmetto's Myrtle Beach location is a shop only; the distilling takes place in Anderson, which is in the foothills of the Appalachian Mountains.
2. "About World Heritage," UNESCO World Heritage Convention, accessed July 2017, http://whc.unesco.org/en/about/.
3. UNESCO, "Convention Concerning the Protection of World Cultural and Natural Heritage," Article I, adopted November 16, 1972.
4. This does not address other aspects of cultural heritage, including heritage property (art, specimens, antiquities, etc.) and intangible cultural heritage (oral traditions, rituals, performance art, etc.), which are also considered significant human items and activities that should be preserved, according to UNESCO values and conventions. For more on these, see the UNESCO website and associated publications.
5. Diane Barthel-Bouchier, *Cultural Heritage and the Challenge of Sustainability* (Walnut Creek, CA: Left Coast Press, 2013), 7–8.
6. Anne Grimmer and Kay Weeks, *The Secretary of the Interior's Standards for Rehabilitation and Illustrated Guidelines for Applying the Standards*, National Park Service, 1992, www.nps.gov/hps/tps/tax/rhb/index.htm.
7. Official eligibility must be determined and approved by each state's historic preservation officer.
8. National Historic Preservation Act of 1966, as amended through December 16, 2016 54 USC 300101 et seq. (2016), accessed September 2016, www.achp.gov /nhpa.pdf.
9. Amy Jordan Webb, "A Decade of Heritage Tourism," *Forum Journal: The Journal of the National Trust for Historic Preservation* 13 (Summer 1999): 45–52; Jamisha Gibson, "Preservation Glossary: Today's Word: Heritage Tourism," National Trust for Historic Preservation, June 17, 2015, https://savingplaces.org/stories /preservation-glossary-todays-word-heritage-tourism#.WbwnEq3MyRs.

10. Cheryl Hargrove, "Authenticity in Cultural Heritage Tourism," *Forum Journal: The Journal of the National Trust for Historic Preservation* 18 (Fall 2003): 4–8.

11. Hargrove, "Authenticity in Cultural Heritage Tourism."

12. Jeremy Markovitch, "Ghosts of North Wilkesboro," *SBNation,* March 4, 2015, https://www.sbnation.com/longform/2015/3/4/8126311/north-wilkesboro -speedway-after-nascar.

13. Cooper Barrel appears to operate under the LLC Key City Spirits.

14. Ellen Gurley, "Copper Barrel Distillery," *My City Magazine,* October 13, 2015, www.mycitymagazine.net/index.php/component/content/article.html?id=544. However, a June 2015 *Watauga Democrat* article refers to Smith as a "Charlotte native." A book published earlier this year finally notes that Smith is from Vermont, but the delay and obscuring where Smith is from seems like a delib-erate attempt to keep the focus on local history and tradition. See John Francis Trump, "Copper Barrel Distillery," in John Francis Trump, *Still and Barrel: Craft Spirits in the Old North State* (Winston-Salem, NC: John. F. Blair, 2017), 99–102.

15. Gurley, "Copper Barrel Distillery."

16. Jared C. Shumate, dir., *The Foundation* (Wilkesboro, NC: White Manor Productions, 2016).

17. Erika Giovanetti, "Copper Barrel Distiller: (Legal) Moonshine Operation Starts Up in North Wilkesboro," *MountainTimes.com,* June 18, 2015, www.watauga democrat.com/mountaintimes/copper-barrel-distillery/article_905996d6-15c5 -11e5-a796-131824ac26ba.html.

18. Gurley, "Copper Barrel Distillery."

19. Glen Herbert, "Making Moonshine with Roger Lee 'Buck' Nance," *Patriarch,* June 8, 2015, https://patriarchmagazine.com/2015/06/08/making-moonshine -with-roger-lee-buck-nance/.

20. "926 Gallons of Moonshine Seized," *Watauga Democrat,* October 9, 2009, www .wataugademocrat.com/news/gallons-of-moonshine-seized/article_1504f 949-5772-56d4-b6df-901793bf7348.html.

21. Gurley, "Copper Barrel Distillery."

22. Giovanetti, "Copper Barrel Distiller."

23. Home page, Copper Barrel Distillery, accessed September 14, 2017, www .copperbarrel.com.

24. Trump, *Still and Barrel*, 99–102.

25. Jule Hubbard, "Key City Closes after 87 Years," *Wilkes Journal-Patriot,* August 5,

2013, www.journalpatriot.com/news/key-city-closes-after-years/article
_d873ecc4-fdf7-11e2-9673-0019bb30f31a.html.

26. Pam Windsor, "Moonshine Goes Mainstream," *The State*, September 5, 2015, thestate.com/news/state/south-carolina/article34220553.html.

27. "Palmetto Moonshine Opens Storefront in Myrtle Beach, S.C.," Palmetto Moonshine press release, *Bevnet*, June 5, 2014, bevnet.com/news/spirits/2014 /palmetto-moonshine-opens-storefront-in-myrtle-beach-s-c/.

28. "Palmetto Moonshine Opens Storefront."

29. Windsor, "Moonshine Goes Mainstream."

30. Ibid.

31. Palmetto Distillery, "The Distillery," accessed July 2017, www.palmetto moonshine.com/distillery. The author was unable to independently verify this information.

32. Tom Fischer, "Old Forge Opens, Releases 1830 Original Moonshine," *The Bourbon Blog*, July 10, 2014, https://www.bourbonblog.com/blog/2014/07/10 /old-forge-distillery-1830-original/.

33. Tom Sherlin, "New Distillery in Pigeon Forge to Offer More than Moonshine," *The Daily Times*, July 4, 2012, www.thedailytimes.com/community/new-distillery -in-pigeon-forge-to-offer-more-than-moonshine/article_0c693e9d-e360-5ab2 -843d-7bf095bfb1fd.html.

34. Old Forge Distillery is owned by the same company that owns the Old Mill Restaurant and the other businesses in Old Mill Square, Old Mill LLC.

35. It is worth noting that Copper Barrel uses glass bottles that resemble traditional milk jars rather than canning jars. Owner George Smith said that he wanted something that would stand out but would also continue to evoke a nostalgic feeling (interview with author, July 22, 2017). Palmetto uses canning-style jars.

36. In addition to the other articles noted, see Candace Fitzgibbons, "Old Forge Distillery Is More than a Moonshiner," *Sevier News Messenger*, July 3, 2014, www.seviernewsmessenger.com/2014/07/03/old-forge-distillery-is-more-than -a-moonshiner/.

37. Old Forge Distillery, "Distilling over 200 years of Tennessee Tradition," accessed July 2017, https://oldforgedistillery.com/history/.

38. National Register of Historic Places, Pigeon Forge Mill, Pigeon Forge, Sevier County, Tennessee, National Register no. 75001778.

39. Robbie Jones, *The History and Architecture of Sevier County, Tennessee* (Sevierville, TN: Smoky Mountain Historical Society, 1996), 24–25, 30.

40. The National Register nomination does not indicate whether Trotter was making Federal or Rebel uniforms, but Trotter's son, William, fought for the Union Army, and there were many Unionists in Sevier County (see Jones, *History and Architecture of Sevier County*). It is likely that Trotter was making uniforms for Federal soldiers.

41. Jones, *History and Architecture of Sevier County*, 45.

42. National Register of Historic Places, Pigeon Forge Mill, Pigeon Forge, Sevier County, Tennessee, National Register no. 75001778.

43. Veta W. King, "History of Pigeon Forge," *Pigeon Forge, Tennessee,* cityofpigeon-forge.com/history-of-pigeon-forge.aspx.

44. National Register of Historic Places, Pigeon Forge Mill, Pigeon Forge, Sevier County, Tennessee, National Register no. 75001778.

45. Trent Margrif, "Available in a Historic Building Near You: Local Beer!," *Forum Journal: The Journal of the National Trust for Historic Preservation* 25 (Winter 2011): 42.

46. Ibid., 43.

47. Ibid., 47.

48. For a discussion of the rise of tourism in Pigeon Forge, see C. Brenden Martin, "From Golden Cornfields to Golden Arches: The Economic and Cultural Evolution of Pigeon Forge, Tennessee," *Journal of the Appalachian Studies Association* 6 (1994): 163–72.

Chapter 11

Automotive Heritage and the Legacy of High-Octane Moonshiners: A Unique Cultural Intersection of Alcohol and Motor Vehicles

BARRY L. STIEFEL

In the quaint Appalachian town of Dawsonville, Georgia, there is an annual gathering in late October where moonshine connoisseurs come together to celebrate a unique aspect of the region's cultural heritage. In many respects, Dawsonville's Mountain Moonshine Festival is akin to many other moonshine-themed community events organized in towns and small cities across the American South, except for one significant element. The moonshine festival in Dawsonville, as well as a small number of other places that I explore here, also commemorates a distinct automotive heritage that is uniquely tied to the region's history of moonshine making—the Thunder Road bootlegger. Thus, many of the moonshine aficionados at Dawsonville's Mountain Moonshine Festival are also automobile enthusiasts, which changes the event programming and social atmosphere in profound ways. The sounds and smells of loud automobiles can be distinctively encountered as part of the event's ambiance. For example, the Mountain Moonshine Festival, which has taken place since 1967, begins with a "parade of moonshine and revenue cars" followed by a "Car Show, Cruise-In, and Swap Meet held at the Georgia Racing Hall of Fame." In addition, attendees have the opportunity to participate in a "Moonshine Run," meet with several "legendary race car drivers," and view "Vintage Race Cars and more Authentic Moonshine-Hauling cars than you'll ever see gathered in one place anywhere in the US!"[1] While the historical focus of the event centers on moonshine, the majority of activities not related to alcohol consumption are associated with the automobiles that helped define twentieth-century moonshine heritage.

This chapter investigates how the unique combination of moonshine and automobile heritage is being preserved, including via material culture and intangible traditions. These preservation activities have taken on an unconventional approach within American historic preservation practice due to the unique circumstances of moonshine smuggling being an illegal activity. The emphasis of public interest on high-octane moonshiners has been on documenting the oral history as well as identifying, preserving, and maintaining the small number of surviving automobiles from 1920 through the 1960s, when illicit distilling reached its zenith in the Appalachian South. Studying the preservation activities of automobiles and moonshine smuggling is significant because the participants and artifacts used were generally common people (the *volk*) and vernacular material culture, in contrast to high culture (*hochkultur*) that has more frequently received the attention of preservation studies.

The Rise of the Automobile

According to historian Daniel S. Pierce, whiskey making (including moonshine) in southern Appalachia dates back to the eighteenth century when the Scots Irish began to migrate into the region.[2] Yet the heritage personified at festivals in Dawsonville and other places celebrates the decades of national Prohibition and after. Today, the people of this heritage are often stereotyped as uneducated poor white farmers who snuck off into the woods to distill liquor under the cover of night and moonlight (sometimes dangerously using an automobile radiator as part of the distillation process!). From their clandestine distilleries, the bootleggers would speed out of the backwoods to deliver their white lightning in mason jars, strapped into hidden compartments of their souped-up jalopies, to waiting customers at speakeasies or other rendezvous points, all the while avoiding the revenuers in hot pursuit. It is this image of doing something technically illegal yet seemingly non-harmful to others that appeals to the public. The culprits are not the moonshiners but a big brother government that has gone too far in regulating the rights of poor country people to manufacture alcohol, especially following the repeal of national Prohibition in 1933. Therefore, how automobiles have played a role within the modern moonshine revival and within the marketing image related to consumer demand for legal "moonshine" in contemporary American culture is important.

Automobiles were easily built and modified to meet the specific needs of their drivers. According to historian David N. Lucsko, "the automobile itself was not a black-boxed technology. Ordinary users thus were free to shape and reshape their mass-produced cars to meet their own often quite specific needs: farmers used them to power washing machines and band saws, while the middle-class consumers often modified the bodies of their cars to make them more versatile and comfortable for long-range touring and camping."[3] With the commercial production of automobiles in the early twentieth century, it did not take long for alcohol to become involved. In 1907 Henry Ford developed the Model T, which included the first commercially sold automobile with a flex-fuel engine that could run on either gasoline or ethanol.[4] The significance of Ford's Model T—and many other early American-made automobiles—was that the engineering was simple and could thus be understood and adapted by mechanically inclined people. When national Prohibition began in 1920, the Census Bureau found that 30.7 percent of farmers in the United States already owned an automobile. The farmer ownership rate for automobiles further increased during the prosperous 1920s, making rural access to motor vehicles relatively common.[5] According to a survey conducted by B. F. Goodrich Rubber Co., in 1920 American automobile ownership was approximately 9.3 million vehicles, an average of 11.4 persons per car. Automobile ownership rates were highest in the Pacific Northwest and lowest in the Southeast. Within the Southeast, automobile ownership in Georgia was 157,000 (18.4 persons per car); North Carolina, 140,869 (18.2 persons per car); South Carolina, 93,843 (17.9 persons per car); and Tennessee, 101,852 (22.9 persons per car).[6]

Despite the stereotype that moonshiners and Thunder Road bootleggers were all white, some smugglers were African American. In 1925, for instance, Greenville County, South Carolina, officials apprehended a black man from Charlotte transporting illegal alcohol in a Cadillac touring car.[7] Sociologist Mieka Brand has conducted some research on African American participation in making and distributing moonshine in Union, Virginia, but without a name, the unidentified man from Charlotte is impossible to research further.[8] Nonetheless, evidence reveals that moonshine-related heritage in southern Appalachia was shared across racial lines. Therefore, a variety of Appalachian residents—struggling to make ends meet—began to use and modify these cars to transport moonshine and evade law enforcement.

Cars Modified for Moonshine Running

Mountain residents—mostly men—who modified and conducted maintenance and repairs on automobiles that hauled moonshine were often called shade-tree mechanics. Their nickname came about from them working in an irregular setting, either in a residential garage or a driveway (under the shade of a tree), though some managed to have formalized commercial workshops. Shade-tree mechanics often had limited supplies and resources to work with on automobiles and thus frequently had to improvise. The shade-tree mechanics often worked with smugglers, including both moonshiners and bootleggers. Moonshiners made and sometimes ran their own product. In contrast, bootleggers bought liquor made by others and then transported it to market.

While the modification of automobiles by shade-tree mechanics was not always consistent, there were some commonalities. For transporting contraband liquor, shade-tree mechanics often added wide tires and wheel rims to improve stability and traction and installed stronger springs to carry the additional weight of the cargo. The most important modifications were conducted to the engine to increase speed and performance.[9] During the Prohibition era, Model T Fords were the most common type of automobile used and modified by moonshiners to run liquor. In 1925, for instance, the Greenville County, South Carolina, sheriff's *Sales Books of Automobiles Seized while Transporting Contraband Liquors* reveals that of the seventeen vehicles that local officials confiscated and auctioned off that year, eleven were Model T Fords, including three coupes, two roadsters, and six touring cars. The remaining six automobiles included one Nash roadster, one Reo roadster, one Buick touring car, and three Cadillac touring cars.[10] While Cadillacs only accounted for about 18 percent of automobiles confiscated and auctioned off in 1925, the occurrence of these more expensive vehicles in Greenville County is an intriguing contrast to the more economical Model T Ford. The touring car type, designed with more room for passengers and luggage, became the most popular because they were larger than coupes and roadsters and could thus carry more cargo. Model T roadsters could be reconfigured to hold 90 gallons of liquor and touring cars even more (as much as 135 gallons, depending on the automobile). The late

1930s and 1940s souped-up Ford models could also carry more than 120 gallons of liquor and move at speeds of more than 100 miles per hour.[11]

Daniel Pierce comments on the variety of engines used in modified moonshine-running automobiles during the heyday of bootlegging in the mid-twentieth century, with the Ford V-8 being the most popular. Souping up these V-8 engines primarily entailed boring out the cylinders and installing bigger piston rings for greater power.[12] Sometimes larger engines from other high-powered cars and trucks would be swapped into a bootlegging automobile; for example, Mercury engines might be placed into Ford cars. Removable seats and hidden compartments were placed within the body and cabin space of automobiles to maximize their carrying capacity and conceal their illicit cargo. Bootleggers and moonshiners also regularly installed devices such as false rear bumpers, smoke screens, and contraptions that released tacks onto the road to foil law enforcement agents during a chase. Law enforcement tactics for pursuing Thunder Road bootleggers improved after 1934, when two-way radios became widely adopted by police and sheriff departments, allowing them to better coordinate and set up sophisticated road traps designed to capture moonshiners and avoid dangerous high-speed chases.[13] Consequently, Thunder Road bootleggers had to become more strategic in their smuggling routes to evade revenuers.

Modifying and maintaining an automobile for high speeds and moonshine smuggling was an expensive enterprise. Besides the upfront costs of the vehicle itself, gasoline, and oil, parts had to be repaired or replaced regularly through the wear-and-tear and damage incurred from speeding on poor roads with heavy liquid cargo. This is assuming that one's vehicle did not experience additional damage from run-ins with law enforcement officials. Statistics on the upfront expenses for modifying an automobile for moonshine smuggling could not be found, but following the legal establishment of post–World War II stock car racing and hot rodding, some inferences can be made from articles in *Popular Mechanics* that covered how to soup up vehicles. Depending on the work conducted, including parts and labor for "reboring, new cams, new ignition and the works," the price ranged between $500 and $1,475 per car circa 1950, resulting in a horsepower performance improvement of 65 to 85 percent in addition to other enhancements.[14] In 1950 the average new automobile cost about $1,500. Both new and used automobiles were modified for bootlegging, so we can assume between one-third to all of a car's unmodified net market value would be spent on these alterations, an expensive undertaking given that the average annual income for an American in 1950 was $3,200.[15] Thus, most small-time producers seeking to make extra money by manufacturing moonshine for local consumption were not as interested in the automotive aspect of the distribution. Large producers of moonshine and kingpins were more invested in modifying cars to transport their product. One such syndicate was based in Dawsonville, Georgia, where "Lightning" Lloyd Seay, Roy Hall, Raymond Parks, and Louis Jerome "Red" Vogt smuggled moonshine during the 1930s and 1940s. These men also helped to reconfigure the racing aspect of their profession into a lawful business through the establishment of the National Association for Stock Car Auto Racing, more popularly known by its acronym NASCAR.[16] In fact, many early NASCAR drivers were former bootleggers who had transferred their skills of outrunning law enforcement onto the racing tracks and became hometown heroes as media coverage of the sport increased during the 1970s and later.

Automobiles involved in moonshine smuggling still survive, some in better condition than others. For example, the website *Classic Cars for Sale* recently advertised the auction of a 1940 Ford Coupe "BARN FIND," in which the seller provides a detailed description of the modifications that previous owners had performed on the car. According to the seller, this vehicle may have been used to transport moonshine, but the specifics of the car's history and its provenance have not been adequately investigated.

> This car was originally stored in Alabama until it was sold in 1963 and brought to Georgia, where it was driven for approximately two years, by the new owner. Once again, in 1965, it was stored in a barn, and remained there, until I purchased the car in August 2015. (50 years later). I purchased the car "AS IS", because it is believed, that this car was used to transport illegal alcohol, also known as "MOONSHINE." I was told by people that were around these cars during that era, that the car has the suspension, common to cars driven by the MOONSHINE RUNNERS. There are heavy-duty rear shocks, with heavy-duty springs, to conceal the weight of the load of alcohol. Shocks were placed at offset angles for high-speed turns, front truck spring, and shocks with heavy-duty springs, with special brackets. It also has a larger radiator, with unique upper water hoses to clear a larger fan, to keep the engine water temperature cool. All consistent with a

MOONSHINE RUNNERS CAR. The engine is a 110HP Mercury Flathead with 15" Ford Wheels. The car remains slightly higher then a stock 1940 Ford Coupe. After 50 years of Barn dirt and dust, I washed the car, but did not detail it to retain the original patina. It has an older re-paint, a very solid straight body, and nice original interior. The 94 Carburetor and spark plugs were replaced with new ones. All the fluids have been changed in the engine and running gear. I did replace all the tires with new, and they are the exact size of the original tires. I have photos of the car with the original tires when I purchased it. Unfortunately, they were not holding air and I had to replace them. Hood, doors and trunk have excellent fit. The car drives and stops well. Many Early Fords, like this 40 Ford Coupe, were racing the back roads of Alabama, Tennessee, Mississippi, Georgia, and North Carolina, during the 40's and 50's. Unfortunately, many of these cars were confiscated by Federal Agents. It is a known fact of history, that quite a few NASCAR drivers started as MOONSHINE RUNNERS back in the day![17]

In the nondescriptive part of the advertisement, the seller provides the vehicle identification number (185594187), which could be used to trace the provenance of the car at a future time. The description of how a 1940 Ford Coupe was modified also provides a starting point for verifying the authenticity of vehicle changes, assuming the provenance is correctly associated with a "moonshine runner's car."

Preserving the Heritage Relationship between Moonshine and Automobiles

The preservation of moonshine heritage related to the automobile is comprised of both tangible and intangible elements. The most obvious tangible element, the physical container of corn-derived whiskey, is a topic that several essays in this book have addressed. The preservation and stewardship of automobiles with a history of moonshine smuggling, however, is less documented. The Historic Vehicle Association, which seeks "to promote the cultural and historical significance of the automobile and protect the future of our automotive past," is currently the largest old car organization in the United States, boasting a membership of more than 375,000.[18] In partnership with the National Park

Service—which manages the National Register of Historic Places—and the Library of Congress, the Historic Vehicle Association oversees the National Historic Vehicle Register, created in 2014. Although a vehicle associated with moonshine smuggling has not yet been listed on the National Historic Vehicle Register, other modified vehicles have, including the hot rod McGee Roadster, the custom-made Hirohata Merc, and the low-rider Gypsy Rose, all of Southern California origin.[19] Localized organizations, such as the Moonshine Museum and Garage in Baker County, Florida, and the City Garage Museums in Greeneville, Tennessee, have had cars that were used to run moonshine on display.[20] In some instances, replicas and forgeries have been made, depending on how the history of the vehicle is portrayed (a forgery differs from a replica in that forgers use deceit to create a false sense of history).

When evaluating modified automobiles for National Historic Vehicle Register consideration, the provenance, authenticity, and integrity must be established and verified. A car also has to meet the four stringent criteria related to historical significance for consideration—very similar to the National Register of Historic Places. Substantiating the historic origins of a building or vehicle that purposely does not have a documented history because the activities associated with it were at one time illegal, however, is incredibly challenging. The irony is that the mysterious draw of moonshine history and its lack of documentation is what attracts popular culture to it. The lack of historical records on moonshine smuggling by those who participated in these activities is precisely why preserving associated material cultural artifacts can be so difficult.

One successful tangible accomplishment of moonshine-related preservation is the Boyd and Sallie Gilleland House in Dawsonville, Georgia, which was listed on the National Register of Historic Places in 2009. One reason why the Gilleland House is significant is due to its "direct association with the production and sale of moonshine in Dawson County by Boyd Gilleland" during national Prohibition.[21] As part of the evidence that moonshine was clandestinely made within the house is the survival of a secret room accessible only through a closet. Within that room is a chimney connection for a stovepipe, which was also attached to the kitchen chimney. While moonshine was being distilled in the secret room, Boyd's wife, Sallie Gilleland, likely cooked in the kitchen to cover up the smell and steam from the whiskey still. Unfortunately, we do not know how many other places clandestinely produced moonshine.

Many were either found and destroyed by law enforcement or dissembled for a lack of need by the 1970s. The discovery of the secret room in the Gilleland House where a still had operated remains highly exceptional.

More pertinent to the topic of this chapter, the Gilleland family also managed an automobile service station and hardware store. Considering what the Gillelands could do with their businesses and the modifications made to their house, they may have also souped up automobiles for purposes of smuggling, especially given the lucrative bootlegger network that existed between Dawsonville and Atlanta. However, because the original automobiles owned by the Gillelands no longer exist, it is impossible to track down their fates. A VIN, engine number, or other unique mark recorded in association with a Gilleland-owned automobile theoretically could assist in locating a modified vehicle made or used by the Gillelands to transport moonshine. This is why the VIN for the 1940 Ford Coupe "BARN FIND" mentioned earlier is so potentially valuable. A unique means of identifying a specific automobile, such as a VIN, provides a way of investigating prior ownership and use to establish its moonshining provenance. Once a vehicle's origins have been substantiated, further research then can be conducted regarding who, what, where, when, and how it was used to discover its historical significance.

Moonshine Festivals: Preserving Intangible Traditions

In addition to stills, cars, and other artifacts used for bootlegging, there is also the need to preserve intangible traditions that provide both context and meaning to material culture related to moonshine heritage. In 1967—when illicit distilling and associated smuggling were in decline in Appalachia—Fred Goswick (1936–2012), a former bootlegger from Dawsonville, Georgia, "set up three tables out in front of the courthouse to sell souvenirs [on moonshining] to the leaf-lookers as they drove through Dawsonville to the mountains," establishing what would become the annual Mountain Moonshine Festival.[22] Thus began a preservation interest in the intangible aspects of southern Appalachian moonshining heritage.

Now in its fiftieth year, the Mountain Moonshine Festival is typically held in late October and spans three days. While the historical focus of the event centers on moonshine, the majority of activities not related to alcohol consumption are associated with the automobiles that were used to transport illicit liquor. In fact, many attendees drive their modified vehicles to the event to show them off to the public. After moonshine stills and mason jars, the souped-up automobiles displayed at the Mountain Moonshine Festival remain the next most relevant artifacts to the region's moonshine heritage.

In recent decades, other places in Appalachia have also begun to organize similar automobile-moonshine-themed festivals, most notably the Prohibition Hot Rod and Moonshine Festival in Wilkesboro, North Carolina; the Moonshine Cruiz-In in Hiawassee, Georgia; and the Moonshine Rod Run by the Hard Times Street Rod Run in Newport, Tennessee. Like the Mountain Moonshine Festival, these events enhance the economies of their host communities by boosting tourism and often use their proceeds to support charitable causes, such as helping impoverished children. They also serve as community gathering venues where elderly moonshiners and bootleggers pass on their stories to younger people. As such, these festivals are not just about drinking and racing. They play a vital role in preserving the region's moonshine heritage for future generations and community place-making.

By adding a special attraction to the festival, automobiles draw public interest to this unique heritage associated with moonshine and cars from a special time in American history. In 2016, for instance, the Prohibition Hot Rod and Moonshine Festival in Wilkesboro—boasting an attendance of two thousand people—displayed 173 hot rods and other modified vehicles built before 1976. Of the automobiles on exhibit were "two 1940 Fords from Georgia that actually were used in the illegal whiskey business."[23] Based on a visual survey of owners with vehicles on display at the event, most were middle-aged and elderly white men. Considering that maintaining a historic automobile can be an expensive undertaking, it is understandable that younger people with limited financial means do not own antique cars in great numbers.

Nonetheless, the festivals attract a broad spectrum of people. Among the attendees at the 2016 Prohibition Hot Rod and Moonshine Festival were African Americans, Latinos, women, young men, and children.[24] These visitors come not only to view moonshine cars but to also enjoy other aspects of Appalachian culture in a "family fun" environment.[25] The festivals are catered by venders who serve local food and beverages, with craft-made moonshine tastings for those of legal drinking age being the favorite culinary attraction. Performers who specialize in the region's popular music also provide live entertainment. In addition, attendees sometimes have the opportunity to meet former NASCAR drivers who began their careers as bootleggers and relive the early days of that sport. Ultimately, the festivities allow visitors to experience the senses through seeing the milieu of people and cars on the landscape, touching the historic automobiles, hearing the rumbling of car engines and local music, tasting the bite of white lightning, and breathing in mountain air mixed with the aroma of car exhaust.

In recent years, several distilleries have begun to capitalize on the popularity of these festivals, including Ole Smoky Distillery in Gatlinburg, Tennessee, which held a one-time event called the Fast Cars and Mason Jars Moonshine Festival in 2013.[26] Not surprisingly—given its close historical connection to moonshine and modified cars—NASCAR has also gotten in on the action. In 2013 it held the first annual Junior Johnson Midnight Moon Shine and Sign at the NASCAR Hall of Fame ceremony in Charlotte, North Carolina. Hosted by Johnson and sponsored by Piedmont Distillers—which makes Johnson's own Midnight Moon and other legal moonshine products—the members-only event often features former NASCAR drivers who talk about their experiences as bootleggers during the mid-twentieth century.[27]

Appalachia is not the only region that hosts moonshine festivals. Promoters have organized similar events in the states of Illinois and Texas as well as the country of Australia. The Moonshine Lunch Run in Moonshine, Illinois, is the smallest of all the festivals, spanning a single afternoon, and features motorcycles instead of modified cars. The two other automobile-moonshining events—the Hot Rod Bustle—Texas Moonshine Run in San Antonio, Texas, and the Annual Moonshine Run in Cottonvale, Queensland, Australia, which showcases American-made automobiles—are more recent and somewhat smaller in scale regarding their event programming when compared to those in Appalachia.[28] These festivals reveal that illicit distilling was not—contrary to popular belief—confined to the Mountain South and that efforts to preserve the tangible and intangible elements of moonshine heritage remain alive and well.

Issues of Moonshine Heritage Interpretation

History as perceived through the lens of popular culture has at times blurred the difference between two modified vehicle types: the Appalachian moon-shine-running car and the California hot rod. The confusion stems from the fact that both vehicles emerged at roughly the same time. However, each automobile had its own purpose. Modified primarily for recreation and sport, the Southern California hot rod's external physical appearance—flashy body, chrome work, and paint job—significantly sets it apart from the modified vehicles of mountain bootleggers. Indeed, part of the persona of a hot rod is its visual (and sometimes audible) flamboyance. The eye-catching, one-of-a-kind hot rod, however, is counterintuitive to evading law enforcement because of the attention it draws.[29] In contrast, the cars modified by bootleggers were mundane in appearance, and for good reason: stealth through looking like an average automobile was essential for bootlegging.

Despite these differences, moonshine festivals often portray both vehicles as the same. A case in point regarding the confusion between hot rods and modified automobiles used for bootlegging is the advertising for the Prohibition Hot Rod and Moonshine Festival in Wilkesboro, which celebrates the cultural milieu of automobiles and booze:

> Prohibition is a Hot Rod Show and Moonshine Festival celebrating the history of moonshine, hot rods, *and the history they have together. From running moonshine in hot rods*, to creating the largest racing sport in the US. Hot rods and moonshine have always gone together. Featuring a car show open to all types of vehicles 1976 and older. Featuring Live Music, Vendors, Food, as well as Moonshine, Beer and Wine tastings. This is a festival you do not want to miss![30]

In addition to the festival at Wilkesboro, the Moonshine Cruiz-In in Hiawassee, Georgia, also promotes a historically inaccurate representation of moonshine cars as hot rods. Depicted in the center of the event's 2017 poster, for instance, is a flashy, souped-up 1940 Ford Deluxe coupe hot rod with a flame paint job on the front hood (see fig. 11.1). Standing noticeably beside the hot rod is a stereo-typical poor white Appalachian inhabitant, wearing torn denim overalls and with a jug of moonshine laying by his feet. Opposite the mountain resident is a log cabin with a moonshine still next to it. The base of the poster is decorated with empty mason jars that formerly contained moonshine, and on the poster's top is depicted a setting sun on the horizon of a mountainous Appalachian landscape. However, while certainly false in a technical-historical sense, the moonshined-themed hot rod festivals have ultimately helped to preserve this heritage by cultivating broader public interest.

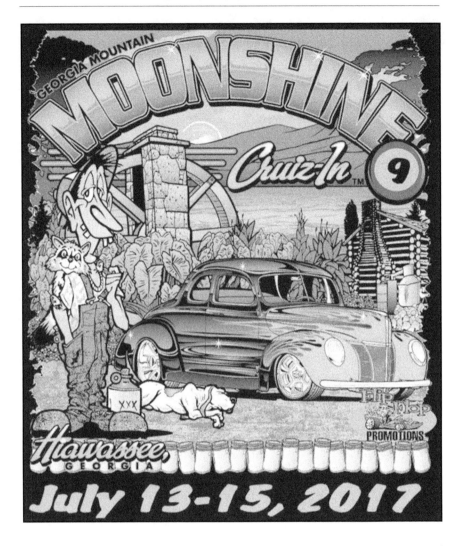

Figure 11.1. Annual Moonshine Cruiz-In in Hiawassee, Georgia, 2017 Poster. Courtesy of Robert Parrish at Flip Flop Promo.

Conclusion

In a manner of speaking, three iconic objects—the still, jar, and car—are inseparable representations of what we physically associate with the moonshiner mystique. Mostly located in southern Appalachia—particularly in eastern Tennessee, western North Carolina, and northeastern Georgia—the local moonshine festival events with automobiles draw thousands of people from around the region and beyond to celebrate this historic romanticized milieu. Attendees who own historic automobiles that actually ran moonshine are relatively rare, but those who bring their vintage cars to these festivals enjoy exhibiting them to the public and experiencing the thrill of driving them around through organized cruises (within legal limits). While the hot rods not associated with this moonshine history frequently comprise the bulk of the modified automobiles at the festival displays, the cars actually used for smuggling moonshine between 1920 and 1970 have a deeper level of respect and admiration, serving as the conduit for popular interest between moonshine and historic motor vehicles.

Maintaining the heritage automobile cruises as part of the festival event is an important preservation practice for the intangible aspects of experiencing a ride as well as encouraging owners to provide proper stewardship of their heirloom vehicles for future posterity. Owners take pride in showcasing their modified vehicles at these events, which is why those with hot rods that did not actually smuggle moonshine also like to come. Attendees without special automobiles also participate in the moonshine festivals to see and hear the historically maintained cars and partake in the moonshine camaraderie of the region's heritage. Driving while intoxicated is frowned upon, just as it was during the bootlegging heydays between 1920 and 1970. Nonetheless, moonshine and modified cars are an inseparable part of the heritage identity where these festivals take place.

NOTES

1. *Mountain Moonshine Festival*, 2016, accessed June 20, 2017, www.kareforkids .org/mountain-moonshine-festival.html.
2. Daniel S. Pierce, *Corn from a Jar: Moonshining in the Great Smoky Mountains* (Gatlinburg, TN: Great Smoky Mountains Association, 2013), 9.
3. David N. Lucsko, *The Business of Speed: The Hot Rod Industry in America, 1915–1990* (Baltimore: Johns Hopkins University Press, 2008), 9.
4. Technically, the Model T Ford engine could run on moonshine so long it was 150 proof or higher, though it is not known if or how many people actually

used it during the heyday of bootlegging because of the potential risk of engine damage from weak moonshine as well as its higher value sold as a contraband beverage (Aisha Harris, "Can You Really Run a Car on Moonshine?," *Slate*, August 31, 2012, accessed June 21, 2017, www.slate.com/blogs/browbeat/2012 /08/31/can_you_really_run_a_car_on_moonshine_fact_checking_the_new _movie_lawless_.html).

5. "30.7% of Nation's Farms Have Motor Cars: Growing Popularity Seen in Statistics," *Motor World*, August 31, 1921, 35.

6. B. F. Goodrich Rubber Co., "Shows Car Density Based on Population," *Automobile Topics*, 61, no. 10 (April 23, 1921): 922.

7. Greenville County (SC) Sheriff, *Sales Books for Automobiles Seized while Transporting Contraband Liquors, 1925–1927*, Series L 23196, Record Group 000023, South Carolina Department of Archives and History, Columbia.

8. Mieka Brand, "Making Moonshine: Thick Histories in a U.S. Historically Black Community," *Anthropology and Humanism* 32, no. 1 (2007): 52–61.

9. Jaime Joyce, *Moonshine: A Cultural History of America's Infamous Liquor* (Minneapolis, MN: Zenith Press, 2014), 100.

10. Greenville County (SC) Sheriff, *Sales Books for Automobiles*.

11. Joseph E. Dabney, *Mountain Spirits* (Lakemont, GA: Copple House Books, 1978), 151–53.

12. Daniel S. Pierce, *Real NASCAR: White Lightning, Red Clay, and Big Bill France* (Chapel Hill: University of North Carolina Press, 2013), 26.

13. Dabney, *Mountain Spirits*, 153, 164.

14. Lou Jacobs Jr., "Soup Up Your Car?," *Popular Mechanics* 98, no. 3 (September 1952): 120–22; "Detroit Never Satisfies Them," *Popular Mechanics* 89, no. 6 (June 1948): 114–20.

15. See Leslie H. Zemeckis, *Behind the Burly Q: The Story of Burlesque in America* (New York: Skyhorse Publishing, 2013).

16. This is a history that has been well investigated by Daniel S. Pierce in *Real NASCAR* and by Neal Thompson in *Driving with the Devil: Southern Moonshine, Detroit Wheels, and the Birth of NASCAR* (New York: Crown Publishers, 2007).

17. "1940 Ford Coupe 'BARN FIND,'" *Classic Cars for Sale*, 2017, accessed June 20, 2017, http://topclassiccarsforsale.com/ford/195206–1940-ford-coupe-barn-find .html.

18. "About the HVA," *Historic Vehicle Association*, 2017, accessed June 20, 2017, https://www.historicvehicle.org/.

19. "National Historic Vehicle Register," *Historic Vehicle Association*, 2017, accessed June 20, 2017, https://www.historicvehicle.org/national-historic -vehicle-register/.

20. Kevin R. Kosar, *Moonshine: A Global History* (London, UK: Reaktion Books, 2017), n.p.

21. Caroline Christie, *National Register of Historic Places Nomination Form: Boyd and Sallie Gilleland House* (Washington, D.C.: National Park Service, 2009), 7.

22. Michele Hester, "Festival Founder Dies: Goswick Hailed as a Visionary," *DawsonNews.com*, February 15, 2012, accessed December 20, 2016, www .dawsonnews.com/archives/8854/.

23. Chuck Hubbard, "Prohibition Show Brings Hot Rods to Downtown," *Wilkes Journal-Patriot*, November 7, 2016, August 29, 2017, www.journalpatriot.com /news/prohibition-show-brings-hot-rods-to-downtown/article_aa5c6fb6-a51d -11e6-b482-bb84932bd816.html.

24. Presently, the festival's image is of the stereotypical Appalachian of Scots Irish descent, despite the fact that African Americans and women from a broad age span were historically involved with moonshine smuggling in modified auto-mobiles. These demographics are an additional market for moonshine running that could be promoted better (Max de la Fuente, "*Prohibition Hot Rod and Moonshine Festival*," November 13, 2016, accessed August 29, 2017, https://www .youtube.com/watch?v=mTkgNzcNWfE.

25. ScottieDTV interview with Rakes Parrish, "Moonshine Cruize In 2013 Hiawassee GA," *ScottieDTV*, June 10, 2013, accessed August 29, 2017, https:// www.youtube.com/watch?v=FFs-i4xzc6Q.

26. "Check Out the Fast Cars and Mason Jars Moonshine Festival this Weekend," *PigeonForge.com*, September 24, 2013, accessed September 18, 2017, https:// www.pigeonforge.com/check-out-the-fast-cars-and-mason-jars-moonshine -festival-this-weekend/.

27. "NASCAR Hall of Fame Induction Week Activities and Media Opportunities," *NASCAR Hall of Fame,* January 23, 2015, accessed September 18, 2017, www .nascarhall.com/media/news/nascar-hall-of-fame-induction-week-activities -and-media-opportunities.

28. *The Hot Rod Bustle—Texas Moonshine Run*, 2017, June 20, 2017, www.carshow radar.com/shows/tx/the-hot-rod-bustle-texas-moonshine-run-2016/. This event actually categorizes historic vehicle events according to age and make: 1) pre-1940 class, 2) 1941–54 class, 3) 1955–66 class, and 4) vintage motorcycle class.

Hard Times Street Rod Run, *Moonshine Rod Run*, 2017, accessed June 20, 2017, www.hardtimesstreetrodclub.com/. This event is limited to cars made in 1958 or earlier, has taken place since 1981, and benefits Celebrate Life Cancer Support Group. *Moonshine Lunch Run*, 2017, June 20, 2017, http://moonshine-run.com /Moonshine/. This event also raises money for local charitable causes such as funds for a new community fire station. Jo Coddington, "0133: Jo Coddington Down Under and Bob Bennett's Hot Rod Party," *Wisconsin Hot Rod Radio*, February 18, 2017, accessed June 21, 2017, https://www.ottoradio.com/podcast /wisconsin-hot-rod-radio/0133—jo-coddington-down-under-and-bob-bennett-s -hot-rod-party-129. Australia also has its own unique history with illicit moon-shine making.

29. Tim Weadock, "Moonshine Cars," *Historic Vehicle Association*, December 10, 2013, accessed June 14, 2017, https://www.historicvehicle.org/moonshine-cars/.

30. Wilkesboro Crew Promotions LLC, Prohibition Hot Rod and Moonshine Festival, 2017, accessed June 14, 2017, https://www.prohibitionfestival.com/. Emphasis added.

CONTRIBUTORS

KAITLAND M. BYRD is an instructor in the Department of Sociology at Virginia Tech. Her research focuses on foodways, consumption, and underlying inequalities. She recently coedited a special issue of *Humanity and Society* that explores the intersection of food, inequality, and authenticity. Her current research focuses on food products as contested sites of authenticity with consequences for health and inequality.

NATHANIEL G. CHAPMAN is an assistant professor of sociology in the Department of Behavioral Sciences at Arkansas Tech University. His research focuses on craft beer and the production of culture in the United States. He recently coedited *Untapped: Exploring the Cultural Dimensions of Craft Beer* (2017), which focuses on the cultural dimensions of craft beer in the United States and western Europe. He is also coediting a special issue of the *Journal of Popular Music Studies* that will explore racial dynamics within electronic dance music. His research explores issues of whiteness, racial exclusion, and the creation of white spaces in the craft beer culture. He is also examining how gender is constructed in craft beer spaces and the craft beer industry.

KRISTEN BALDWIN DEATHRIDGE is an assistant professor of history at Appalachian State University. She earned her PhD in public history from Middle Tennessee State University and her MA in archaeology from the University of Reading. Within these disciplines, Deathridge focuses on public history, historic preservation, and twentieth-century American cultural and intellectual history. Her main research is on the adaptive reuse of religious buildings, and she is currently working on multiple National Register nominations with her graduate students.

EMILY D. EDWARDS is the author of *Bars, Blues, and Booze: Stories from the Drink House* (2016). Edwards was a journalist and media producer before she joined the faculty at University of North Carolina at Greensboro, where she is now a full professor in the Department of Media Studies. She received her PhD in journalism and mass communication from the University of Tennessee,

Knoxville. The writer, producer, and director of many films, Edwards has also published books and articles on popular media. She is currently working on a new book, *Graphic Violence: Illustrated Theories about Violence, Popular Media, and Our Social Lives,* under contract with Routledge.

JASON EZELL holds a PhD in American studies from the University of Maryland and is the instruction and research coordinator at the Loyola University New Orleans Monroe Library. His primary research interests are in LGBTQ history, critical rural and regional studies, and affect. His dissertation is an affective history of how gay liberationism persisted through its intersections with back-to-the-land movements in the 1970s Southeast.

J. SLADE LELLOCK is a PhD candidate in the Department of Sociology at Virginia Tech. His research interests include culture, digital sociology, consumption, taste, and qualitative methodologies. His work generally focuses social and symbolic boundaries, cultural status hierarchies and shifts, and inequality. His current research explores gender dynamics involved craft beer consumption. He is a coeditor of *Untapped: Exploring the Cultural Dimensions of Craft Beer* (2017).

CAMERON D. LIPPARD is a professor and interim chair of sociology at Appalachian State University. His research and teaching interests have focused on racism, immigration, war, and the sociology of culture. His research on Latino immigration to the American South has led to two books: *Building Inequality: Race, Ethnicity, and Immigration in the Atlanta Construction Industry* (2008) and *Being Brown in Dixie: Race, Ethnicity, and Latino Immigration to the New South* (2011). Recently, he has explored the cultural traditions of American foodways, leading to a coedited book on the cultural dimensions of craft beer in the United States and Western Europe titled *Untapped: Exploring the Cultural Dimensions of Craft Beer* (2017). Finally, with his teaching interests in war, he coauthored the book *War: Contemporary Perspectives on Armed Conflicts around the World* (2018).

DANIEL S. PIERCE is a professor of history at the University of North Carolina at Asheville, where he teaches courses in Appalachian, North Carolina, and environmental history. His books include *Hazel Creek: The Life and Death of* an *Iconic Mountain Community* (2017), *Corn from a Jar: Moonshining in the Great Smoky Mountains* (2013), *Real NASCAR: White Lightning, Red Clay, and Big Bill France* (2010), and *Great Smokies: From Natural Habitat to National Park* (2000). He is writing a book on moonshine in North Carolina.

ROBERT T. PERDUE is an assistant professor of sociology at Appalachian State University. His work focuses on the social, economic, and ecological impacts of resource extraction, the Appalachian region, and alternative development strategies.

HELEN M. ROSKO received her MS in the Department of Geography at the University of Tennessee, Knoxville, focusing her thesis on moonshine in East Tennessee. She works as a research assistant and PhD student in the Graduate School of Geography at Clark University in Worcester, Massachusetts. Her research interests include livelihoods approaches to development and climate change in sub-Saharan Africa and Appalachia.

KENNETH J. SANCHAGRIN is the research director for the Oregon Criminal Justice Commission. Sanchagrin's research interests are in criminology theory, social capital and social network analysis, and crime statistics. He has published articles in *Youth and Society*, the *American Sociological Review*, and the *Journal of Adolescent Health*.

BRUCE E. STEWART is an associate professor of history at Appalachian State University. He is the author of *Moonshiners and Prohibitionists: The Battle over Alcohol in Southern Appalachia* (2011) and the editor of *King of the Moonshiners: Lewis R. Redmond in Fact and Fiction* (2008) and *Blood in the Hills: A History of Violence in Appalachia* (2012). He has also published articles in the *Journal of Southern History*, *North Carolina Historical Review*, *Georgia Historical Quarterly*, *Appalachian Journal*, and *Environmental History*.

BARRY L. STIEFEL is an associate professor at the College of Charleston, where he is a member of the Department of Art and Architectural History, the historic preservation and community planning program, and the joint graduate program in historic preservation with Clemson University. Stiefel's research interests are in how the sum of local preservation efforts affects regional, national, and multinational policies within the field of cultural resource management and heritage conservation. He is the author and editor of several books, including *Sustainable Heritage: Merging Environmental Conservation and Historic Preservation*, coauthored with Amalia Leifeste (2018); *Community-Built: Art, Construction, Preservation, and Place*, coedited with Katherine Melcher and Kristin Faurest (2017); and *Human-Centered Built Environment Heritage Preservation: Theory and Evidence-Based Practice*, coedited with Jeremy C. Wells (2018).

Index

CPSIA information can be obtained
at www.ICGtesting.com
Printed in the USA
LVHW082059130219
607454LV00003B/4/P

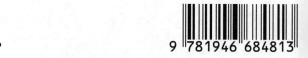